The Art of the Metaobject Protocol

The Art of the Metaobject Protocol

Gregor Kiczales, Jim des Rivières, and Daniel G. Bobrow

The MIT Press
Cambridge, Massachusetts
London, England

Fifth printing, 1999

©1991 Massachusetts Institute of Tecnnology

This book was set by Arthur Ogawa and Rachel Goldeen using the LaTeX typesetting system and was printed and bound in the United States of America.

Library of Congress Cataloging-in-Publication Data

Kiczales, Gregor.
   The art of the metaobject protocol / Gregor Kiczales, Jim des Rivières, and Daniel G. Bobrow.
       p.   cm.
   Includes bibliographical references and index.
   ISBN 0-262-11158-6 (hc). — ISBN 0-262-61074-4 (pbk.)
   1. COMMON LISP (Computer program language) 2. Object-oriented programming (Computer science) I. Des Rivières, Jim. II. Bobrow, Daniel Gureasko. III. Title.
QA76.73.C28K53 1991
005.13'3—dc20   91-16731
                                                                          CIP

Contents

Introduction   1

I   THE DESIGN AND IMPLEMENTATION OF METAOBJECT PROTOCOLS

1   How CLOS is Implemented   13

1.1   A Subset of CLOS   14

1.2   The Basic Backstage Structures   15

1.3   Representing Classes   17

1.4   Printing Objects   26

1.5   Representing the Structure of Instances   26

1.6   Representing Generic Functions   34

1.7   Representing Methods   36

1.8   Invoking Generic Functions   40

1.9   A Word About Performance   45

1.10   Summary   45

2   Introspection and Analysis   47

2.1   Introducing Class Metaobjects   48

2.2   Browsing Classes   52

2.3   Browsing Generic Functions   58

2.4   Programmatic Creation of New Classes   66

2.5   Summary   69

3   Extending the Language   71

3.1   Specialized Class Metaobjects   72

3.2   Terminology   74

3.3   Using Specialized Class Metaobject Classes   76

3.4   Class Precedence Lists   78

3.5   Slot Inheritance   83

3.6   Other Inheritance Protocols   90

3.7   Slot Access   96

3.8   Instance Allocation   99

3.9   Summary   105

4   Protocol Design   107

4.1   A Simple Generic Function Invocation Protocol   107

4.2   Functional and Procedural Protocols   110

4.3   Layered Protocols   119

4.4   Improving Performance   125

4.5   Protocol Design Summary   131

II   A METAOBJECT PROTOCOL FOR CLOS

5   Concepts   137

5.1   Introduction   137

5.2   Metaobjects   137

5.3   Inheritance Structure of Metaobject Classes   140

5.4   Processing of the User Interface Macros   145

5.5   Subprotocols   153

6   Generic Functions and Methods   163

A   Introduction to CLOS   243

B   Solutions to Selected Exercises   255

C   Living with Circularity   269

D   A Working Closette Implementation   277

E   Cross Reference to Full MOP   317

References   325

Index   327

Acknowledgments

The work described here is synthetic in nature, bringing together techniques and insights from several branches of computer science. It has also been essentially collaborative; we have had the pleasure to meet and work with people from a number of communities.

The largest of these communities has been the users of our prototype CLOS implementation, PCL. By using and experimenting with early metaobject protocols, these people provided a fertile ground for the ideas behind this work to grow. Their enthusiasm provided energy for this work and their successes provided the insight. Everyone who ever used the metaobject protocol facilities of PCL contributed to this work, but certain people deserve particular mention. Ken Anderson, Jim Kempf, Andreas Paepcke and Mike Thome were experts on different aspects of Metaobject Protocol use; their contributions to the CommonLoops mailing list helped many others learn to use the CLOS Metaobject Protocol. Richard Harris, Yasuhiko Kiuchi and Luis Rodriguez made significant contributions to the design and maintenance of PCL, a task that was also helped by each of the Common Lisp vendors who suggested implementation-specific ways to enhance PCL performance. The project also benefited from a number of users who had the courage and conviction to attempt large projects with early versions of the CLOS Metaobject Protocol: Ken Anderson, James Bennett, John Collins, Angela Dappert-Farquhar, Neil Goldman, Warren Harris, Reed Hastings, Chuck Irvine, Jim Kempf, Joshua Lubell, Yoshihiro Masuda, Phillip McBride, Steven Nicoud, Greg Nuyens, Andreas Paepcke, Peter Patel-Schneider, Dan Rabin, Doug Rand, George Robertson, Larry Rowe, Richard Shapiro and Arun Welch.

Electronic mail has been essential to the dialogue in this project. In particular, the CommonLoops mailing list has been the home of the PCL user community. Yasuhiko Kiuchi maintained this list for three years, overseeing its growth from less than one-hundred to almost eight-hundred readers. More recently, Arun Welch has taken this list over, maintaining both it and the gateway to the `comp.lang.clos` newsgroup.

Masayuki Ida has been the primary force for establishing and nurturing a PCL and CLOS Metaobject Protocol user community in Japan. His success at mediating the cross-cultural language and stylistic differences has enabled the community to include the Japanese users.

The CLOS design community has also been involved in this project. The people involved in that effort, or in the larger Common Lisp standardization effort, have participated in the development of both the fundamental principles of metaobject protocol design presented in Part I and in the full CLOS Metaobject Protocol presented in Part II. They are: Kim Barrett, Eric Benson, Scott Cyphers, Harley Davis, Linda DeMichiel, Gary Drescher, Patrick Dussud, John Foderaro, Richard P. Gabriel, David Gray, Ken Kahn, Sonya Keene, Jim Kempf, Larry Masinter, David A. Moon, Andreas Paepcke,

Chris Richardson, Alan Snyder, Guy Steele, Walter van Roggen, Dan Weinreb, Jon L White and Jan Zubkoff.

Work on reflection has been another source of inspiration guiding the design of the CLOS Metaobject Protocol and influencing its presentation. Smith's 3-Lisp had shown how the framework of a simple reflective interpreter can be used to clarify the relation between a language's reflective facilities and its implementation, by factoring out potentially distracting issues of circularity. Jim des Rivières, who joined the project at a relatively late stage, used his experience with reflection to develop the Closette implementation and pedagogical structure on which Part I of the book is based. We would especially like to thank the following members of the reflection community, who have made contributions to the development of this work: Giuseppe Attardi, Pierre Cointe, Roman Cunis, Mike Dixon, Brian Foote, Nicolas Graube, John Lamping, Pattie Maes, Satoshi Matsuoka, Ramana Rao and Takuo Watanabe.

The manuscript for this book has taken shape over a period of years. In addition to the members of the CLOS community previously mentioned, we would like to thank the following people for their extensive feedback on various drafts: Hal Abelson, Pierre Cointe, Doug Cutting, Mike Dixon, Brian Foote, Volker Haarslev, Masayuki Ida, Yasuhiko Kiuchi, Wilf LaLonde, John Lamping, Stan Lanning, Yoshihiro Masuda, Satoshi Matsuoka, Ramana Rao, Brian Smith, Deborah Tatar, Dave Thomas, Takuo Watanabe, Mark Weiser and Peter Wegner.

Finally, there are our friends and colleagues at Xerox PARC, who have helped and supported us through this long project. We thank them for the help they have given us, and for making PARC such a stimulating and enjoyable place to work. In particular, we want to thank: Bob Bauer, Alan Bawden, Nora Boettcher, John Seely Brown, Doug Cutting, Johan de Kleer, Mike Dixon, Mimi Gardner, David Goldstone, Volker Haarslev, Ken Kahn, Yashiko Kiuchi, John Lamping, Stan Lanning, Susi Lilly, Larry Masinter, Ramana Rao, Jonathan Rees, George Robertson, Luis Rodriguez, Brian Smith, Mark Stefik, Deborah Tatar and Mark Weiser.

The Art of the Metaobject Protocol

Introduction

Modern programming language design lives in tension between two apparently conflicting demands. On the one hand, high-level languages such as Scheme, Prolog, and ML incorporate significant advances in elegance and expressive power. On the other hand, many industrial programmers find these languages too "theoretical" or impractical for everyday use, and too inefficient. As a result, these languages are often used only in academic and research contexts, while the majority of the world's mainline programming is conducted in such languages as C and C++, distinguished instead for their efficiency and adaptability.

This book is about a new approach to programming language design, in which these two demands of elegance and efficiency are viewed as compatible, not conflicting. Our goal is the development of languages that are as clean as the purest theoretical designs, but that make no compromises on performance or control over implementation.

The way in which we have achieved elegance and efficiency jointly is to base language design on *metaobject protocols*. Metaobject protocols are interfaces to the language that give users the ability to incrementally modify the language's behavior and implementation, as well as the ability to write programs within the language.

Languages that incorporate metaobject protocols blur the distinction between language designer and language user. Traditionally, designers are expected to produce languages with well-defined, fixed behaviors (or "semantics"). Users are expected to treat these languages as immutable black-box abstractions, and to derive any needed flexibility or power from constructs built on top of them. This sharp division is thought to constitute an appropriate division of labor. Programming language design is viewed as a difficult, highly-specialized art, inappropriate for average users to engage in. It is also often assumed that a language design must be rigid in order to support portable implementations, efficient compilers, and the like.

The metaobject protocol approach, in contrast, is based on the idea that one can and should "open languages up," allowing users to adjust the design and implementation to suit their particular needs. In other words, users are encouraged to participate in the language design process. If handled properly, opening up the language design need not compromise program portability or implementation efficiency.

In a language based upon our metaobject protocols, the language implementation itself is structured as an object-oriented program. This allows us to exploit the power of object-oriented programming techniques to make the language implementation adjustable and flexible. In effect, the resulting implementation does not represent a single point in the overall space of language designs, but rather an entire *region* within that space.

The protocols followed by this object-oriented program serve two important functions. First, they are used by the designers to specify a distinguished point in that region, corresponding to the language's default behavior and implementation. Second, they allow users to create variant languages, using standard techniques of subclassing and specialization. In this way, users can select whatever point in the region of language designs best serves their needs.

Our development of the metaobject protocol approach has emerged hand-in-hand with our involvement, over the past several years, in the design of the Common Lisp Object System (CLOS) [CLtL, CLtLII, X3J13].[1] CLOS is a high-level object-oriented language designed as part of the forthcoming ANSI Common Lisp standard. That project brought us face to face with many of the classic problems of high-level languages, including the need for compatibility with existing languages, special extensions for particular projects, and efficiency. Our effort to deal with these problems led us to develop the approach to language design based on metaobject protocols and to implement a first practical instance, a metaobject protocol for CLOS.

The purpose of this book is twofold. First, in Part I, we present metaobject protocol design by gradually deriving a simplified metaobject protocol for CLOS.

Because we expect the notion of a metaobject protocol itself to evolve, we not only present the approach as we understand it today, but also point towards open issues and directions for further development.

In Part II we provide a detailed and complete description of a particular metaobject protocol we have designed for CLOS. This second CLOS metaobject protocol can be incorporated into production CLOS implementations and used for writing production-quality code.

The work reported in this book synthesizes a number of concerns and approaches from different parts of the computer science field. As a result we hope it will be of interest to a wide spectrum of the community:

- *Programming language designers* should benefit from our analysis of some of the problems users have with high-level languages. Some designers may be interested in adding a metaobject protocol to existing languages or designing a new language with a metaobject protocol.

  Augmenting a language with a metaobject protocol does not need to be a radical change. In many cases, problems with an existing language or implementation can be improved by gradually introducing metaobject protocol features. Also, compiler, debugger, and programming environment features can often be recast as metaobject protocols, with concomitant simplifications in their design, implementation, and documentation.

---

[1]Two of the authors (Bobrow and Kiczales) were members of the X3J13 subcommittee responsible for CLOS.

- *Programmers and software engineers* should be interested in our analysis of why high-level languages are often inadequate, and in our suggestions for how to improve them. Even if they are not working with a metaobject protocol, they may find that the analysis helps them conceptualize and address problems they are having with existing languages.

- People working with *object-oriented languages* will have two reasons to be interested in this work. First, since our approach relies extensively on object-oriented techniques, the book can simply be viewed as presenting a well-documented case-study within the object-oriented paradigm. Particular attention is given to issues of designing and documenting object-oriented protocols. Second, the book includes a discussion not only of the behavior of CLOS, but also of features that are characteristic of object-oriented programming languages in general. As well as examining how these features work, we focus on some of the issues involved in designing such languages.

- People interested in *reflection* will recognize that our approach also relies on the techniques of procedural reflection. We hope they will see what we have done as helping to bring reflection into wider practical use, by engineering reflective techniques to be robust, efficient, and easy to use.

- *The CLOS community*, being a cross-section of these other groups, will presumably share many of their interests. Furthermore, the book provides them with specific information on how to use, implement, and continue the development of the CLOS metaobject protocol.

The Problems We Faced

During the development of the CLOS standard, we realized that we were up against a number of fundamental problems. The prospective CLOS user community was already using a variety of object-oriented extensions to Lisp. They were committed to large bodies of existing code, which they needed to continue using and maintaining. Experience with these earlier extended languages had shown that various improvements would be desirable, but some of these involved incompatible changes. In fact the very notion of a single, standardized object-oriented extension to Common Lisp was an inherently incompatible change, since the set of earlier extensions were not compatible among themselves. We therefore faced a traditional dilemma: genuine needs of backward compatibility were fundamentally at odds with important goals of an improved design.

As is often the case, the situation was particularly aggravating because of an *essential compatibility* between the language being designed and each of the older ones—the fact that although they differed in surface details, they were all based, at a deeper level, on the same fundamental approach. Each, after all, was an object-oriented programming language with classes, instances, inheritance, methods, and generic functions[2] which, when called, automatically determine the appropriate method to run. From the broader perspective of the family of object-oriented programming languages, they differed only in how they interpreted various *aspects* of object-oriented behavior: the syntax for calling generic functions; the rules for handling multiple inheritance; the rules of method lookup; etc.

Along with this first challenge, of compatibility, we faced a second one, of extensibility. As well as using a small number of major existing languages, many of the prospective CLOS users had also developed custom languages of their own. In many ways these, too, were essentially compatible with the major languages, and with the new language we wanted to design. But each had its own distinguishing characteristics, supporting a number of additional features, or implementing variant interpretations of basic object-oriented behavior. For example, some of these languages provided special mechanisms for representing the structure of instances. Others employed various special inheritance and method lookup mechanisms.

Furthermore, it turned out on examination that these added functionalities and variations in the base object-oriented model were neither arbitrary nor superfluous. Because they satisfied various application-specific requirements, these incremental differences allowed programs to be clear, easy to write, and straightforward to maintain. Without them, the users would have lost the advantage of programming in a high-level language: expressive power well-matched to the problem at hand.

It was clear, furthermore, that some prospective CLOS users would always be in a similar situation. *No matter what design was agreed upon*, there would be times when a given user, for entirely appropriate reasons, would need this or that variant of it. For example, while CLOS was being designed, it emerged that some users were interested in the support of persistent objects, of the sort that would be provided by an object-oriented database. Our challenge was to find a way to enable such users, who wanted something close to CLOS, to adapt it to fit their needs.

The third problem we faced was that of ensuring that programs written in CLOS would run efficiently.[3] Unfortunately, the very expressiveness of high-level languages makes this

---

[2]In traditional object-oriented languages, the terminology used for a polymorphic operation is *message*. The terminology for invoking a such an operation is *sending* a message. In CLOS, the form taken by this functionality warrants the use of somewhat different terminology, which will be used throughout this book: the CLOS term for message is *generic function*, and the term for sending a message is *calling* or *invoking* a generic function. (Appendix A presents an introduction to CLOS.)

[3]We call this familiar problem the paradox of high-level programming languages. On the one hand, the primary rationale for high-level programming languages is that they are more expressive—i.e., that they allow better formulations of what our programs are doing. On the other hand, it is widely agreed that programs written in high-level languages are usually less efficient than programs written in lower-level ones. The paradox arises from the fact that there must be things about the high-level programs that aren't being expressed more clearly, since otherwise compilers would be able to notice and exploit them, making those programs more,

difficult. No single implementation strategy is likely to perform well on the full range of behaviors that user programs can be expected to exhibit.

Consider, for example, two different uses of CLOS classes. In the first, which might arise in a graphics application, instances represent screen positions, with two slots[4] for x and y coordinates. In such applications, it is safe to assume that slot access performance is critical—the faster the better. In the second, which might arise in a blackboard system, instances can potentially have a large number of slots, but in practice any given instance only uses a small number of them. If there can be a very large number of these instances, the space taken up by the instances would be of critical concern, making it important not to waste space on all the unused slots.

Even though the *behavior* of both of these classes is well captured by the CLOS language, they would clearly benefit from different implementation strategies. As a result, an implementation that used a single strategy would at best perform well on only one. The situation is further exacerbated by the fact that the information needed to choose the best implementation strategy might be difficult or impossible for a compiler to extract from the program text, since it depends on dynamic behavior, such as how many instances will be created, or how often their slots will be accessed. This is why efficiency is a challenge: somehow, within the context of a single language design, different users should be given the specific implementation and performance profiles they need.

While these goals of compatibility, extensibility and efficiency at first seemed different, we eventually came to see them as instances of the same underlying problem, and were therefore able to address them within a common structural framework.

The underlying problem is a lack of fit: in each case, the basic language design fails to meet some particular need. Compatibility is an obvious example: as soon as the language is changed to incorporate a new feature, it fails to match up with existing bodies of code. But the other cases have the same structure. The graphics program is well served by one implementation of instance representation, but the sparsely populated slots case requires another.

The unavoidable conclusion is that no single language will ever be universally appropriate, no matter how clever its design. So we adopted a different solution. Rather than supplying the user with a fixed, single point in the space of all language designs and implementations, we would instead support a region of possible designs within that overall space. This is the essence of the metaobject protocol approach. In the case of CLOS, for example, instead of providing a single fixed language, with a single implementation

---

rather than less, efficient than their low-level counterparts. In on-going work on metaobject protocols, not discussed in this book, we are focusing directly on this issue. Our goal is to make it easier to make a piece of code simultaneously clear and fast in a high-level language than to make it fast in a low-level language.

[4]In CLOS the fields of an instance, which in many languages are called *instance variables*, are called *slots*.

strategy, the metaobject protocol extends a basic or "default" CLOS by providing a surrounding region of alternatives. Users are free to move to whatever point in that region best matches their particular requirements.

This strategy has two tangible benefits. First, relying on the metaobject protocol to deal with a wide range of users' concerns allows the base case—CLOS itself—to be simpler and more elegant. The very existence of the metaobject protocol, in other words, takes some pressure off the design of the base language, to its benefit. Second, the strategy of supporting a CLOS region, rather than a single CLOS point, enables us to solve all three of our original problems.

The compatibility problem is solved by ensuring that the behavior of each of the earlier languages lay within the scope of the newly supplied region. As we have already said, those earlier languages were already incompatible with one other, and none was located at exactly the same point as basic CLOS. But, because of their essential similarity, we were able to delineate a coherent region of object-oriented languages that included them all. Users can select whichever language they prefer by adjusting default CLOS to the appropriate new point. Furthermore, they derive some additional benefits. Since the language behavior can be incrementally adjusted to any point in the region, not just to one or two pre-designated positions, users can gradually convert their programs from the old language to the new. And because different parts of a program can be assigned to different positions in the region, users can combine code written in different versions of the language within the same program.

The extensibility problem is solved in the same way. As long as the region includes the extended behavior the user wants, the default language can be simply adjusted to meet it. The efficiency problem can similarly be solved, so long as the user can readily alter the implementation strategy to suit each particular program or part thereof.

In sum, if a region can be identified that is comprehensible enough for the user to understand and large enough to include the user's needs, and if it is easy for the user to incrementally adjust the default language behavior and implementation within that region, then our three goals can be met, and the investment in the basic language implementation preserved. The question remains, though, of how this can be done.

Metaobject Protocol Based Language Design

While designing a language—or language region—in this way departs significantly from traditional practice, it can be done while preserving the important qualities of existing design approaches. There are two critical enabling technologies: reflective techniques make it possible to open up a language's implementation without revealing unnecessary implementation details or compromising portability; and object-oriented techniques allow the resulting model of the language's implementation and behavior to be locally and incrementally adjusted.

Reflective techniques [Smith 84, Maes&Nardi 88] allow the implementation to be exposed in a way that satisfies two important criteria. First, the access must be at an appropriately high level of abstraction, so that implementors retain enough freedom to exploit idiosyncrasies of their target platforms, and so that users aren't saddled with gratuitous (and non-portable) details. Second, that access must be effective, in the sense that adjustments must actually change the language behavior. These two properties are exactly what is provided by a reflective implementation model.[5]

What reflection on its own doesn't provide, however, is flexibility, incrementality, or ease of use. This is where object-oriented techniques come into their own. These techniques work by (i) defining a set of object types and operations on them, which can support not just a single behavior, but a space or region of behaviors—this is commonly called a protocol; (ii) defining a default behavior, a single point in the region, in terms of the protocol—this is the role of the default classes and methods; and (iii) making it possible to effect incremental adjustments from the default behavior to other points in the region—this is the role of inheritance and specialization.

These techniques, applied to the design and implementation of a programming language itself, are exactly what our strategy requires. First, the basic elements of the programming language—classes, methods and generic functions—are made accessible as objects. Because these objects represent fragments of a program, they are given the special name of *metaobjects*. Second, individual decisions about the behavior of the language are encoded in a protocol operating on these metaobjects—a *metaobject protocol*. Third, for each kind of metaobject, a default class is created, which lays down the behavior of the default language in the form of methods in the protocol. In this way, metaobject protocols, by supplementing the base language, provide control over the language's behavior, and therefore provide the user with the ability to select any point within the region of languages around the one specified by the default classes.

In the CLOS metaobject protocol, for example, the rules used to determine the implementation of instances are controlled by a small number of generic functions. This makes it possible to change those rules by defining a new kind of class, as a subclass of the

---

[5]Reflection also solves any problems of circularity that arise when the language used to implement the protocol is the same as the language implemented by the protocol. This merging of languages, which is often convenient, is adopted in CLOS, and the metaobject protocols presented in both Part I and Part II contain a number of such circularities. As in any reflective system, however, they can easily be discharged, as explained in Appendix C. It is important to note, however, that self-referentiality is not essential to the basic notion of a metaobject protocol. In on-going work that extends the ideas presented in this book, we are adding a metaobject protocol to Scheme, but we are using CLOS (not Scheme) as the language for expressing adjustments, so issues of self-reference don't arise. The two criteria discussed in the main text remain of central importance, and reflective techniques can still be used to support them.

default, and by giving it specialized methods on those generic functions. By doing this, the user is making an *incremental* adjustment in the language. Most aspects of both its behavior and implementation remain unchanged, with just the instance representation strategy being adjusted.

In this way, by combining these two techniques into an integrated protocol, we are able to meet a number of important design criteria:

- *Robustness*: moving the language around in the region to suit one program shouldn't have an adverse effect on other programs or on the system as a whole;
- *Abstraction*: in order to adjust the language, the user should not have to know the complete details of the language implementation;
- *Ease of use*: adjusting the language must be natural and straightforward, and the resulting languages must themselves be easy to use; and
- *Efficiency*: providing the flexibility of a surrounding region should not undermine the performance of the default language, nor curtail the implementor's ability to exploit idiosyncrasies of target architectures to improve performance of the entire region (in fact we retain our goal of having programs written in a language augmented with a metaobject protocol be more, not less efficient than programs written in a traditional language).

Our conclusion is that a synthetic combination of object-oriented and reflective techniques, applied under existing software engineering considerations, make possible a new approach to programming language design, one that meets a wider set of design criteria than have been met before. Doing so is the art of metaobject protocol design, the subject of this book.

Structure of the Book

The remainder of the book is divided in two parts. The first part presents metaobject protocol design. The second part gives a detailed specification of a metaobject protocol for CLOS.

In Part I, metaobject protocol design is presented as a narrated derivation of a metaobject protocol for CLOS. We begin with a (simplified) CLOS *sans* metaobject protocol, and gradually derive one for it. The derivation is driven by examples of the kinds of problems metaobject protocols can solve. This approach allows us to give attention not just to how metaobject protocols work and are implemented, but also to the process of analyzing user needs, and of incorporating those needs into the design of a protocol. In effect, metaobject protocol design requires determining the size, shape, and dimensions of the region to be provided. In the early stages of the derivation, the focus is on the basic motivation and approach of metaobject protocol design. In later stages, attention shifts to problems of ease of use and efficiency.

Throughout, we will work with actual code for a simplified implementation of CLOS, and as we develop it, its metaobject protocol. This will give the reader an opportunity to gain some practical experience with the evolving design. In the same vein, we have included a number of exercises, addressing important concerns and open issues—we encourage all readers at least to read them, if not actually to work them through. Solutions to those that can be answered with code are included in Appendix B; others require more discursive replies, from short essays to moderate sized term projects.

The presentation throughout this first part presumes a familiarity with Common Lisp and CLOS. Readers who are unfamiliar with CLOS, but familiar with other object-oriented languages, will find an introduction in Appendix A. Those who are not familiar with object-oriented programming can find an excellent introduction to both it and CLOS in [Keene 89].

Chapter 1 lays the groundwork by presenting a simplified subset of CLOS and a simple implementation of it. This CLOS subset and implementation will be the basis of all of Part I, so we encourage even those familiar with CLOS to read this chapter.

Chapter 2 begins the derivation of the metaobject protocol by looking at the needs of users writing browsers and other program analysis tools. We will develop a variety of *introspective* protocols, which make it possible to analyze the structure and definition of a program.

Chapter 3 continues the derivation of the metaobject protocol with examples of compatibility, extensibility and performance needs that require adjusting the default language behavior. This ability to "step in" or intercede in the behavior of the system will be provided by a set of *intercessory* protocols.

In Chapter 4, we continue to develop intercessory protocols. But, in this chapter, our focus is the problem of designing protocols that are efficient and easy to use. We discuss various protocol design considerations and techniques.

Part II presents a detailed specification of a metaobject protocol for CLOS. The specification is divided into two chapters, in a manner similar to the specification of CLOS itself [X3J13]. Chapter 5 presents basic terminology and concepts; Chapter 6 describes each function, generic function, and method in the protocol.

Readers interested in designing metaobject protocols for other languages will find that this part not only fills in specific technical details, but also conveys additional information about the overall nature of our design approach. For CLOS users and implementors, however, the primary interest of Part II will be as a specification of a complete metaobject protocol for CLOS. This protocol is not offered as a proposed standard, but as a basis for experimentation, which may subsequently lead to the development of a revised and standardized CLOS metaobject protocol. There is evidence that this is already underway; many Common Lisp vendors are already implementing metaobject protocols based on the one presented here.

I THE DESIGN AND IMPLEMENTATION OF METAOBJECT PROTOCOLS

1 How CLOS is Implemented

We will present metaobject protocol design in stages, by following the development of a simplified metaobject protocol for a subset of CLOS. Our technique will be to progressively design and implement a metaobject protocol for this language, motivating each step with an example of the kind of problem users have with CLOS. Each example will be resolved by showing how it is handled by the newly developed portion of the protocol.

Metaobject protocol design requires an understanding both of the language behavior (in this case CLOS), and of the common architecture of that language's implementations. The first task therefore, addressed in this chapter, is to present the architecture of CLOS implementations in the form of Closette, a simple CLOS interpreter.[1] Closette is the "everyman" of CLOS implementations—despite the simplifications, it is representative of the architecture of all CLOS implementations.[2]

Although understanding implementation architecture is important, it is vital to distinguish the implementation from the documented language. A useful metaphor for making this separation comes from the theatre. We can think of the documented language as being *on-stage*. Users, which we think of as the *audience*, only get to see this on-stage behavior. The internal parts of the implementation are *backstage*: they support what happens on-stage, but the audience doesn't get to see them. Finally, implementors are the *producers*: they get to see what happens both on and offstage, and they are the ones responsible for putting on the show.

In presenting Closette, we will be showing the essential structure of what can be found backstage in any CLOS implementation. We will see how this backstage structure supports the on-stage language behavior. This will be useful in later chapters as we design the metaobject protocol, because it will let us think about what information waiting in the wings might be useful to the user, and what possibilities there are for implementors to expose that information.

Throughout this part of the book, presentations are based on working code. This will allow readers to try the examples, work through the exercises, and try alternative approaches. In fact, we recommend this (see Appendix D for the complete code).

It will be assumed that the reader is familiar with Lisp and has some familiarity with CLOS programming. Those with a background in other object-oriented programming languages, such as Smalltalk or C++, can acquaint themselves with CLOS by reading

---

[1] To support the later addition of a metaobject protocol, we have structured Closette as an object-oriented program. In this case, the object-oriented language is CLOS itself. (We assume that the reader is comfortable enough with the idea of metacircular interpreters to trust that the manifest circularities can eventually be resolved; we defer discussion of these circularities until Appendix C.)

[2] The simplifications in Closette are for pedagogical purposes only. The most significant is that it is an interpreter rather than compiler-based implementation—that is, we have reduced complexity by neglecting performance. In addition, most error-checking code has been omitted.

Appendix A. Those who are not familiar with object-oriented programming can find an
excellent introduction to both it and CLOS in [Keene 89].

1.1   A Subset of CLOS

In the interests of pedagogy and (relative) brevity, we have chosen to work with a simplified subset of CLOS. All the essential features of full CLOS are included: *classes*, which
inherit structure and behavior from one or more other classes; *instances* of classes, which
are created, initialized, and manipulated; *generic functions*, whose behavior depends on
the classes of the arguments supplied to them; and *methods* which define the class-specific
behavior and operations of generic functions. The major restrictions of the simplified
dialect include:

No class redefinition. Full CLOS allows the definition of a class to be changed; the
changes are propagated to its subclasses and to extant instances. The subset does not
allow classes to be redefined.

No method redefinition. Full CLOS allows methods to be redefined, with the new
definition completely replacing the old one. The subset does not allow methods to be
redefined. (For convenience, the working code in Appendix D does support method
redefinition.)

No forward-referenced superclasses. Full CLOS allows classes to be referenced before they are defined. One class can be defined in terms of another before the second
has been defined. These forward references are not permitted in the subset.

Explicit generic function definitions. Full CLOS allows the definition of a generic
function to be inferred from the method definitions. The subset requires that a generic
function be explicitly introduced with a `defgeneric` form before any methods are
defined on it.

Standard method combination only. Full CLOS provides a powerful mechanism for
user control of method combination. The subset defines only simple "demon" combination (primary, before-, and after-methods).

No `eql` specializers. Full CLOS allows methods to be specialized not only to classes,
but also to individual objects. The subset restricts method specialization to classes.

No slots with `:class` allocation. Full CLOS supports slots allocated in each instance
of a class and slots which are shared across all of them. The subset defines only per-
instance slots.

Types and classes not fully integrated. Full CLOS closely integrates Common Lisp
types and CLOS classes. It is possible to define methods specialized to primitive classes

(e.g., `symbol`) and structure classes (defined with `defstruct`). The subset provides classes for the primitive Common Lisp types but not for structure classes.

Minimal syntactic sugar. A number of convenience macros and special forms are not included in the subset. These include: `with-slots`, `generic-function`, `generic-flet` and `generic-labels`.

1.2   The Basic Backstage Structures

In its simplest terms, a CLOS program consists of `defclass`, `defgeneric`, and `defmethod` forms mixed in with other more traditional Common Lisp forms. Executing these forms defines the program's classes, generic functions and methods.

Backstage, execution of these forms creates internal representations of the classes, generic functions, and methods, recording the information provided in their definitions. The implementation uses the information stored in the internal representation of a class to create instances of that class and to access their slots. Information stored in the internal representation of a generic function and its methods is used to invoke the generic function.

To make things concrete, consider the following example CLOS program:

```
(defclass rectangle ()
    ((height :initform 0.0 :initarg :height)
     (width  :initform 0.0 :initarg :width)))

(defclass color-mixin ()
    ((cyan    :initform 0 :initarg :cyan)
     (magenta :initform 0 :initarg :magenta)
     (yellow  :initform 0 :initarg :yellow)))

(defclass color-rectangle (color-mixin rectangle)
    ((clearp :initform (y-or-n-p "But is it transparent?")
             :initarg :clearp :accessor clearp)))

(defgeneric paint (x))

(defmethod paint ((x rectangle))              ;Method #1
  (vertical-stroke (slot-value x 'height)
                   (slot-value x 'width)))
```

```
(defmethod paint :before ((x color-mixin))          ;Method #2
  (set-brush-color (slot-value x 'cyan)
                   (slot-value x 'magenta)
                   (slot-value x 'yellow)))

(defmethod paint ((x color-rectangle))              ;Method #3
  (unless (clearp x) (call-next-method)))

(setq door
      (make-instance 'color-rectangle
        :width 38 :height 84 :cyan 60 :yellow 55 :clearp nil))
```

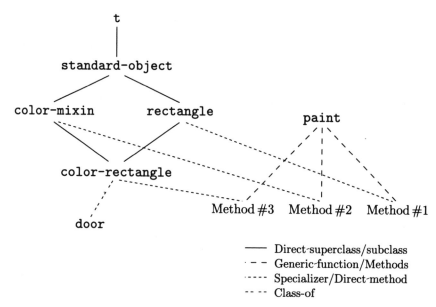

Figure 1.1 A First Glimpse Backstage.

These definitions cause several new internal objects to be created and connected as shown in Figure 1.1. They can be divided into two groups: classes and instances, and functions and methods. In the former group, each class object is connected to its direct (i.e., immediate) superclasses and subclasses. The instance **door** (which is the only on-stage object in the figure) is connected to its class, but not vice versa. In the latter group, the generic function **paint** is connected to its methods, and conversely the methods are connected to their generic function. Connecting the two groups are bidirectional links between methods and the classes they are specialized to.

Unlike instances of `color-rectangle`, such as the one `door` is bound to, which represent rectangles, the backstage objects, such as the one corresponding to the class `rectangle`, represent elements of the program. These backstage objects are called *metaobjects* because they represent the program rather than the program's domain. In fact, everything that goes on inside the implementation is considered to be at the "meta" level with respect to the program; i.e., *about* the program itself, rather than about whatever the program happens to be about. Of course, if you weren't peering into the insides of an implementation you might not even notice that there were such metaobjects; being backstage they are normally hidden from the user.

CLOS implementations divide the execution of defining forms (`defclass`, `defgeneric`, and `defmethod`) and the processing of metaobjects into a three layer structure—somewhat reminiscent of furniture construction:

- The macro-expansion layer that provides a thin veneer of syntactic sugar that the user gets to see; e.g., the `defclass` macro.
- The glue layer that maps names to the metaobjects; e.g., the function `find-class`, which looks up a class metaobject given its name.
- The lowest layer that provides all the support, and traffics directly in first-class metaobjects. This is where the behavior of classes, instances, generic-functions, and methods is implemented. (Our metaobject protocols will end up being concentrated in this layer.)

Given this overall picture, the remainder of the chapter will fill in the details by working through Closette, dealing in turn with the following issues:

- How classes are represented. (Section 1.3)
- How objects are printed. (Section 1.4)
- How instances are represented, initialized, and accessed. (Section 1.5)
- How generic functions are represented. (Section 1.6)
- How methods are represented. (Section 1.7)
- What happens when a generic function is called. (Section 1.8)

1.3   Representing Classes

The CLOS user defines classes with the `defclass` macro. It is natural, therefore, to start by examining how `defclass` is implemented. Although a lot of machinery will be introduced, remember that the definitions other than the `defclass` macro are internal to the implementation—they are hidden backstage.

Name:	color-rectangle
Direct superclasses:	(color-mixin rectangle)
Direct slots:	{clearp}
Class precedence list:	(color-rectangle color-mixin rectangle standard-object t)
Effective slots:	{clearp, cyan, height, magenta, width, yellow}
Direct subclasses:	none
Direct methods:	{paint method #3}

Figure 1.2 The metaobject for the class color-rectangle.

The term *class metaobject* is used for the backstage structure that represents the classes the user defines with **defclass**. For example, the class metaobject corresponding to the class named color-rectangle contains the information shown in Figure 1.2. In general, this information will include:

- Fields from the **defclass** form; e.g., the class's name (color-rectangle), direct superclasses (color-mixin and rectangle), and slot specifications ({clearp...}).
- Information that is derived or inherited; e.g., a list of all of the class's superclasses in order of precedence and the full set of slots including those inherited from superclasses.
- Backlinks to the class's direct subclasses and links to methods that include the class among the method's specializers.

As our first step in the construction of Closette, the class **standard-class** is defined to centralize the description of what class metaobjects look like. Instances of **standard-class** represent individual classes; or, to say it another way, class metaobjects are instances of **standard-class**. Here is the definition:

```
(defclass standard-class ()
    ((name :initarg :name
           :accessor class-name)
     (direct-superclasses :initarg :direct-superclasses
                          :accessor class-direct-superclasses)
     (direct-slots :accessor class-direct-slots)
     (class-precedence-list :accessor class-precedence-list)
     (effective-slots :accessor class-slots)
     (direct-subclasses :initform ()
                        :accessor class-direct-subclasses)
     (direct-methods :initform ()
                     :accessor class-direct-methods)))
```

Note that throughout this part of the book, all code that is part of the Closette implementation will be marked with a backstage door this way.

Each of the slots has been given accessor functions; these will be used consistently to access the slots of metaobjects (rather than employing `slot-value`).

1.3.1   The `defclass` Macro

In Closette's three layered implementation structure, the job of the `defclass` macro (macro-expansion layer) is to parse the class definition and convert it into a call to `ensure-class` (glue layer).

The implementation of `defclass` is organized so that the bulk of the macro-expansion work is carried out by `canonicalize-...` procedures:

```
(defmacro defclass (name direct-superclasses direct-slots &rest options)
  `(ensure-class ',name
      :direct-superclasses ,(canonicalize-direct-superclasses
                                   direct-superclasses)
      :direct-slots ,(canonicalize-direct-slots
                          direct-slots)
      ,@(canonicalize-defclass-options options)))
```

1.3.2   Direct Superclasses

The processing of the direct superclasses, which is performed by `canonicalize-direct-superclasses` *(286)*,[3] is responsible for ensuring that the class names are looked up in the global database. For example, the definition

```
(defclass color-rectangle (color-mixin rectangle) (...))
```

macro-expands into

```
(ensure-class 'color-rectangle
  :direct-superclasses (list (find-class 'color-mixin)
                             (find-class 'rectangle))
  :direct-slots (list ...))
```

The direct superclass names appearing in the `defclass` form expand into calls to `find-class` (glue layer) which retrieve the corresponding class metaobjects.

---

[3]The definitions of functions of lesser importance are not included in the running text. It can be found in Appendix D. Italicized numerals refer to the page on which the definition can be found. It should be noted that some functions are revised in later chapters as the metaobject protocol is developed; the code in the appendix reflects these revisions.

1.3.3   Direct Slots

The processing of a `defclass` form's direct slot specifications, which is carried out by `canonicalize-direct-slots` *(286)*, is more complex. It involves:

- Converting the slot's name into a `:name` property (each slot is encoded in the form of a property list).
- Converting the `:initform` option into an `:initfunction` property whose value is a zero-argument function[4] that gets called at instance creation time to execute the initialization form in the lexical environment of the `defclass`. The original `:initform` is retained for display purposes.
- Collecting multiple `:initarg` options into a single `:initargs` property.
- Separating `:accessor` options into `:reader` and `:writer` options, and collecting multiple `:reader` options into a single `:readers` property, and multiple `:writer` options into a single `:writers` property.

The result of this process is a list of property lists, each property list describing one slot. Our example class definition

```
(defclass color-rectangle (...)
    ((clearp :initform (y-or-n-p "But is it transparent?")
             :initarg :clearp :accessor clearp)))
```

macro-expands to

```
(ensure-class
  'color-rectangle
  :direct-superclasses (list ...)
  :direct-slots
    (list
      (list
        :name 'clearp
        :initform '(y-or-n-p "But is it transparent?")
        :initfunction #'(lambda ()
                          (y-or-n-p "But is it transparent?"))
        :initargs '(:clearp)
        :readers '(clearp)
        :writers '((setf clearp)))))
```

---

[4]Readers familiar with other dialects of Lisp may want to think of this as a *closure*. We have used the term function to be consistent with Common Lisp.

The property list describing the slot is later handed to `make-direct-slot-definition` *(289)* which creates a *direct slot definition metaobject*, supplying appropriate default values for any properties not mentioned explicitly. The details of the internal representation of direct slot definition metaobjects is not of concern to us; we need only know the various accessor functions that can be used with them:[5]

```
slot-definition-name
slot-definition-initargs
slot-definition-initform
slot-definition-initfunction
slot-definition-readers
slot-definition-writers
```

1.3.4   Class Options

Options included in the `defclass` form are processed by `canonicalize-defclass-options` *(287)*. We will ignore class options for now, but will return to them in Chapter 3.

1.3.5   ensure-class

The glue layer function `ensure-class` takes the name and description of a class as keyword arguments and defines a class with that name. `make-instance` is called to create and initialize the new class metaobject (i.e., a new instance of `standard-class`), and that class metaobject is then registered in the global database. (Because our CLOS subset does not allow class redefinition, we arrange for `ensure-class` to signal an error if there is already a class with the given name.)

```
(defun ensure-class (name &rest all-keys)
  (if (find-class name nil)
      (error "Can't redefine the class named ~S." name)
      (let ((class (apply #'make-instance
                          'standard-class :name name all-keys)))
        (setf (find-class name) class)
        class)))
```

The `all-keys` parameter receives all of the keyword arguments (`:direct-superclasses`, `:direct-slots`, and other class options) and passes them along to

---

[5]The implementation in Appendix D just uses the property lists themselves as the direct slot definition metaobjects. On the other hand, the full MOP specification in Part II defines a special class named `standard-direct-slot-definition` for this purpose.

`make-instance` where they are used to initialize the class metaobject. This general treatment means that neither `defclass` nor `ensure-class` needs to be aware of the options communicated from the `defclass` form through to the point of creation and initialization of the class metaobject. The only concern of `ensure-class` is class naming.

The glue-layer functions `find-class` and `(setf find-class)`, that maintain the global mapping from class names to class metaobjects, are defined as follows:

```
(let ((class-table (make-hash-table :test #'eq)))

  (defun find-class (symbol &optional (errorp t))
    (let ((class (gethash symbol class-table nil)))
      (if (and (null class) errorp)
          (error "No class named ~S." symbol)
          class)))

  (defun (setf find-class)⁶ (new-value symbol)
    (setf (gethash symbol class-table) new-value))
)
```

1.3.6   Initializing Class Metaobjects

`make-instance` is at the lowest layer, since it traffics in class metaobjects without concern for how they are named. When creating a class metaobject, there is additional initialization to be done, including:

- Providing a proper default value for the direct superclasses.
- Adding the direct subclass links to the new class's direct superclasses.
- Converting slot property lists into direct slot definition metaobjects.
- Defining any slot accessor methods (we come back to these in Section 1.7.2).
- Performing inheritance-related activities.

As is the convention in CLOS, these initialization operations are carried out by an after-method on `initialize-instance` specifically targeted for new instances of **standard-class**:

---

[6]In the new version of Common Lisp, (setf find-class) is the name of the function that is called by the expansion of (setf (find-class ⟨symbol⟩) ⟨new-value⟩). Notice that the ⟨new-value⟩ argument to setf ends up as the first argument to the function.

```
(defmethod initialize-instance :after
          ((class standard-class) &key direct-superclasses
                                       direct-slots)
  (let ((supers
          (or direct-superclasses
              (list (find-class 'standard-object)))))
    (setf (class-direct-superclasses class) supers)
    (dolist (superclass supers)
      (push class (class-direct-subclasses superclass))))
  (let ((slots
          (mapcar #'(lambda (slot-properties)
                      (apply #'make-direct-slot-definition
                             slot-properties))
                  direct-slots)))
    (setf (class-direct-slots class) slots)
    (dolist (direct-slot slots)
      (dolist (reader (slot-definition-readers direct-slot))
        (add-reader-method
          class reader (slot-definition-name direct-slot)))
      (dolist (writer (slot-definition-writers direct-slot))
        (add-writer-method
          class writer (slot-definition-name direct-slot)))))
  (finalize-inheritance class))
```

1.3.7   Inheritance

We have seen almost all of the steps involved in the creation of a class metaobject: from
defclass through ensure-class down to make-instance and initialize-instance.
The remaining steps are the inheritance-related activities:

- Computing and storing the class precedence list.
- Computing and storing the full set of slots defined directly in the class and inherited
  from superclasses.

finalize-inheritance, which is called from the preceding after-method on
initialize-instance, performs both of these activities:

```
☆. (defun finalize-inheritance (class)
      (setf (class-precedence-list class)
            (compute-class-precedence-list class))
      (setf (class-slots class)
            (compute-slots class))
      (values)⁷)
```

A class inherits structure and behavior from all its direct and indirect superclasses in
a specified order, from most specific to least specific. The class precedence list of a class
defines this order by including all of its superclasses in order of decreasing specificity.
Class precedence lists are stored in the class metaobject in the form of a list of class
metaobjects. For example, the class precedence list for `color-rectangle` consists of the
class metaobjects for `color-rectangle`, `color-mixin`, `rectangle`, `standard-object`,
and t, in that order. Notice that the class itself always appears first, and the classes
`standard-object` and t always appear at the end.

The algorithm used to compute class precedence lists is described in the section of
the CLOS Specification entitled "Determining the Class Precedence List". It involves
topologically sorting the list of direct and indirect superclasses of the given class, using
local precedence ordering as the constraint; a special rule is used to resolve ties. The full
details of this process are not important to this presentation; all that matters is that it
produce a predictable ordering of the set of a class's superclasses.

```
☆. (defun compute-class-precedence-list (class)
      (let ((classes-to-order (collect-superclasses* class)))
        (topological-sort classes-to-order
                          (remove-duplicates
                            (mapappend⁸ #'local-precedence-ordering
                                        classes-to-order))
                          #'std-tie-breaker-rule)))
```

`collect-superclasses*` collects the set consisting of a given class, all its direct superclasses, all their direct superclasses, and so on.

---

[7]We use this Common Lisp idiom to emphasize that the function returns no usable result.

[8]mapappend *(280)* is a non-standard, but immensely handy utility that applies a function to every element
of a sequence and appends the sequences that result. It could be defined as:
`(defun mapappend (fn seq) (apply #'append (mapcar fn seq)))`

```
(defun collect-superclasses* (class)
  (remove-duplicates
    (cons class
          (mapappend #'collect-superclasses*
                     (class-direct-superclasses class)))))
```

topological-sort *(291)* takes a set of elements to order, a set of ordering constraints between pairs of elements (the result of local-precedence-ordering *(292)*), and a function that can be called to arbitrate ties (the result of std-tie-breaker-rule *(292)*).

The full set of slots which a class inherits is computed by collecting all of the direct slot definition metaobjects from each class that appears on that class's precedence list. For the time being, we implement simpler slot inheritance rules than those used by full CLOS: when more than one class in the class precedence list has a slot with a given name, only the direct slot definition metaobject from the most specific class is retained— no merging of slot properties is supported.[9] The direct slot definition metaobjects are then converted into *effective slot definition metaobjects*, which are similar in structure to direct slot definition metaobjects but omit values that only make sense for direct slots (readers and writers).

The function compute-slots is responsible for slot inheritance:

```
(defun compute-slots (class)
  (mapcar #'(lambda (slot)
              (make-effective-slot-definition
                :name (slot-definition-name slot)
                :initform (slot-definition-initform slot)
                :initfunction (slot-definition-initfunction slot)
                :initargs (slot-definition-initargs slot)))
          (remove-duplicates
            (mapappend #'class-direct-slots
                       (class-precedence-list class))
            :key #'slot-definition-name
            :from-end t)))
```

make-effective-slot-definition *(289)* creates effective slot definition metaobjects, the details of which need not concern us. We need only know that, with the exception of slot-definition-readers and slot-definition-writers, all of the accessor functions

---

[9]In Chapter 3 we will discuss more elaborate forms of slot inheritance that are closer to what is provided in full CLOS.

which work on direct slot definition metaobjects also work on effective slot definition metaobjects.

This completes the presentation of class metaobjects and how **defclass** is implemented.

1.4   Printing Objects

In CLOS, printing of objects is controlled by the generic function **print-object**. All of the standard Common Lisp print functions (**print**, **pprint**, **format**, etc.) call **print-object** to actually print each object. Users can control the printing of objects by defining their own methods on **print-object**. We define **print-object** as follows:[10]

```
(defgeneric print-object (instance stream))
```

The default printed representation of objects should include the name of the object's class. For example, the object bound to the variable **door** should print as something like #<Color-Rectangle 324237>. We provide this default printed representation with a method specialized to the class **standard-object**. (Remember that all classes defined with **defclass** include the class **standard-object** in their class precedence lists; consequently methods defined on **standard-object** will, by default, be applicable to instances of these classes.)

```
(defmethod print-object ((instance standard-object) stream)
  (print-unreadable-object[11] (instance stream :identity t)
    (format stream "~:(~S~)" (class-name (class-of instance)))))
  instance)
```

1.5   Representing the Structure of Instances

CLOS provides a collection of user-visible functions for creating (**make-instance**), initializing (**initialize-instance**, **reinitialize-instance** and **shared-initialize**), interrogating (**slot-value**, (**setf slot-value**), **slot-boundp**, **slot-makunbound** and **slot-exists-p**), and changing the class of (**change-class** and **update-instance-for-different-class**) instances of user-defined classes. Implementing these functions places certain requirements on the low-level representation of instances:

---

[10]We simply assume that the printing functions have been modified to call **print-object** appropriately.

[11]In the new version of Common Lisp, **print-unreadable-object** can be used to automatically generate the leading "#<" and trailing ">". When used with a true value for the :**identity** argument, the object identification number is also included. Note that **print-unreadable-object** is a macro, not a function.

Object identity Different calls to `make-instance` must create distinct objects (i.e., non-`eq`).

Slot storage There must be a place to store the current bindings of each instance's slots.

Classification It must be possible to determine the class that a given object is an instance of.

Reclassification `change-class` must change the class of an instance without changing its identity.

For example, the `door` instance of `color-rectangle` is laid out along the lines of Figure 1.3. The actual implementation of the low-level instance representation is not important to this presentation. We simply assume the existence of an abstract data type called *standard instance* with the following functional interface:[12]

- (`allocate-std-instance` ⟨*class*⟩ ⟨*slot-storage*⟩) returns a brand new standard instance whose class is ⟨*class*⟩ and whose slot storage is ⟨*slot-storage*⟩.
- (`std-instance-p` ⟨*object*⟩) returns true only when ⟨*object*⟩ is a standard instance (i.e., the result of a call to `allocate-std-instance`, and not some other Common Lisp object, like a `cons` or a `symbol`).
- (`std-instance-class` ⟨*instance*⟩) provides access to the class of the standard instance ⟨*instance*⟩.
- (`std-instance-slots` ⟨*instance*⟩) provides access to the slot storage for the standard instance ⟨*instance*⟩.
- (`allocate-slot-storage` ⟨*size*⟩ ⟨*initial-value*⟩) returns a new chunk of storage big enough to hold the bindings of ⟨*size*⟩ number of slots; all are initialized to ⟨*initial-value*⟩.
- (`slot-contents` ⟨*slot-storage*⟩ ⟨*location*⟩) provides access to the binding of the slot at a given ⟨*location*⟩ in ⟨*slot-storage*⟩. Locations are numbered from zero.

```
Class:   color-rectangle
Slots:   clearp=nil, cyan=60, height=84, magenta=0, width=38, yellow=55
```

Figure 1.3 The structure of an instance of `color-rectangle`.

1.5.1   Determining the Class of an Instance

Every object in Common Lisp is an instance of a CLOS class. Internally, implementing generic function invocation and other operations requires that we be able to determine

---

[12]For the curious, see `std-instance` *(281)*.

the class of an instance. We define the function `class-of` to return a class metaobject given an instance. The class of a standard instance is stored with the instance. The class of other objects is determined in other highly implementation-dependent ways that we needn't go into; we simply assume that `built-in-class-of` returns the appropriate class metaobject. The definition of `class-of` is as follows:

```
(defun class-of (object)
  (if (std-instance-p object)
      (std-instance-class object)
      (built-in-class-of object)))
```

1.5.2   Allocating Storage for Slots

The slot storage of a standard instance holds the current values of all the slots associated with that instance. `allocate-instance` creates a new standard instance with slots initialized to a recognizable, but otherwise secret value. We will use the presence of this value in a slot to indicate that it is unbound.

```
(defparameter secret-unbound-value (list "slot unbound"))

(defun allocate-instance (class)
  (allocate-std-instance class
                         (allocate-slot-storage
                          (length (class-slots class))
                          secret-unbound-value)))
```

The complete list of slots associated with instances of a class is obtained from the class metaobject with `class-slots`. The length of this list tells us how much space is needed to store the instance's slots.

1.5.3   Accessing the Bindings of Slots

The standard CLOS slot accessing procedures (`slot-value` et al.) all use information about the slot's location in the slots to access the slot. Determination of a slot's location is centralized in the internal function `slot-location`:

```
(defun slot-location (class slot-name)
  (let ((pos (position slot-name
                       (class-slots class)
                       :key #'slot-definition-name)))
    (if (null pos)
        (error "The slot ~S is missing from the class ~S."
               slot-name class)
        pos)))
```

(slot-value ⟨*instance*⟩ ⟨*slot-name*⟩) returns the current binding of the slot named ⟨*slot-name*⟩ in the standard instance ⟨*instance*⟩, or reports an error if the slot is currently unbound:

```
(defun slot-value (instance slot-name)
  (let* ((location (slot-location (class-of instance) slot-name))
         (slots (std-instance-slots instance))
         (val (slot-contents slots location)))
    (if (eq secret-unbound-value val)
        (error "The slot ~S is unbound in the object ~S."
               slot-name instance)
        val)))
```

(setf (slot-value ⟨*instance*⟩ ⟨*slot-name*⟩) ⟨*new-value*⟩) changes the binding of the ⟨*slot-name*⟩ slot of the standard instance ⟨*instance*⟩ to ⟨*new-value*⟩:

```
(defun (setf slot-value) (new-value instance slot-name)
  (let ((location (slot-location (class-of instance) slot-name))
        (slots (std-instance-slots instance)))
    (setf (slot-contents slots location) new-value)))
```

(slot-boundp ⟨*instance*⟩ ⟨*slot-name*⟩) returns true if and only if the ⟨*slot-name*⟩ slot of the standard instance ⟨*instance*⟩ is currently bound:

```
(defun slot-boundp (instance slot-name)
  (let ((location (slot-location (class-of instance) slot-name))
        (slots (std-instance-slots instance)))
    (not (eq secret-unbound-value
             (slot-contents slots location)))))
```

(slot-makunbound ⟨*instance*⟩ ⟨*slot-name*⟩) unbinds the ⟨*slot-name*⟩ slot of the standard instance ⟨*instance*⟩:

```
(defun slot-makunbound (instance slot-name)
  (let ((location (slot-location (class-of instance) slot-name))
        (slots (std-instance-slots instance)))
    (setf (slot-contents slots location) secret-unbound-value))
  instance)
```

(slot-exists-p ⟨*instance*⟩ ⟨*slot-name*⟩) returns true if and only if the standard instance ⟨*instance*⟩ has a ⟨*slot-name*⟩ slot:

```
(defun slot-exists-p (instance slot-name)
  (not (null (find slot-name (class-slots (class-of instance))
                   :key #'slot-definition-name))))
```

1.5.4   Initializing Instances

Having seen how to allocate standard instances and access their slots, we next turn to the normal way in which the user would create standard instances, namely make-instance.

The principal method for the generic function make-instance looks up the class name supplied by the user and then calls make-instance again with the class metaobject.

```
(defgeneric make-instance (class &key))
(defmethod make-instance ((class symbol) &rest initargs)
  (apply #'make-instance (find-class class) initargs))
```

A secondary method allocates a new instance of the class using allocate-instance, and then calls initialize-instance to initialize it, passing along the keyword argument list that follows the class argument:

```
(defmethod make-instance ((class standard-class) &rest initargs)
  (let ((instance (allocate-instance class)))
    (apply #'initialize-instance instance initargs)
    instance))
```

For example, the call

```
(make-instance 'color-rectangle
               :width 38 :height 84 :cyan 60 :yellow 55 :clearp nil)
```

would invoke the former method, which would look up the class and call `make-instance` again. This time the latter method would be applicable; it would allocate a fresh standard instance, say `#<Color-Rectangle 542742>`, and call `initialize-instance` on that instance, passing along the original list of keyword arguments.

Both initialization and reinitialization of instances are funneled to the generic function `shared-initialize`.

```
(defgeneric initialize-instance (instance &key))
(defmethod initialize-instance ((instance standard-object)
                                &rest initargs)
  (apply #'shared-initialize instance t initargs))

(defgeneric reinitialize-instance (instance &key))
(defmethod reinitialize-instance ((instance standard-object)
                                  &rest initargs)
  (apply #'shared-initialize instance () initargs))

(defgeneric shared-initialize (instance slot-names &key))
(defmethod shared-initialize ((instance standard-object)
                              slot-names &rest all-keys)
  (dolist (slot (class-slots (class-of instance)))
    (let ((slot-name (slot-definition-name slot)))
      (multiple-value-bind (init-key init-value foundp)
            (get-properties¹³
              all-keys (slot-definition-initargs slot))
        (declare (ignore init-key))
        (if foundp
            (setf (slot-value instance slot-name) init-value)
            (when (and (not (slot-boundp instance slot-name))
                       (not (null (slot-definition-initfunction
                                    slot)))
                       (or (eq slot-names t)
                           (member slot-name slot-names)))
              (setf (slot-value instance slot-name)
                    (funcall (slot-definition-initfunction
                               slot)))))))))
  instance)
```

---

[13]The Common Lisp function `get-properties` searches a property list for any of a set of properties, returning the first property and value found (and a success flag indicating whether any of the properties were found).

shared-initialize binds values to an instance's slots in any of several ways. In order of decreasing precedence, they are:

1. From an explicit initialization argument whose keyword matches one of the slot's :initarg names.
2. From an existing binding of the slot.
3. From a slot's :initform if it has one, and provided that the name of the slot appears in the list of slot names passed in as the second argument to shared-initialize (t means all slots).
4. Do nothing whatsoever.

1.5.5 Changing the Class of an Instance

When the class of an existing instance is changed with change-class, the bindings of slots common to both the old and new classes must be carried over. After the class of the instance has been changed, the generic function update-instance-for-different-class is called to initialize the new slots and to provide the user an opportunity to salvage the slot bindings that are about to be dropped on the floor. For example, executing (change-class door 'rectangle) would change the class of door from color-rectangle to rectangle. Since rectangles don't have clearp, cyan, magenta, or yellow slots, the bindings of these slots are forgotten. In this case there are no new slots to initialize, but in general there might be (e.g., if we were to then change the class of door back to color-rectangle).

In order to engender this behavior, change-class allocates a new instance of the new class and initializes it from the old instance. Then the class and slot storage of these instances are simply swapped; this has the desired effect of preserving the instance's identity while changing its class and realigning its slots.

```
☆. (defgeneric change-class (instance new-class &key))
   (defmethod change-class ((old-instance standard-object)
                            (new-class standard-class)
                            &rest initargs)
     (let ((new-instance (allocate-instance new-class)))
       (dolist (slot-name (mapcar #'slot-definition-name
                                  (class-slots new-class)))
         (when (and (slot-exists-p old-instance slot-name)
                    (slot-boundp old-instance slot-name))
           (setf (slot-value new-instance slot-name)
                 (slot-value old-instance slot-name))))
       (rotatef¹⁴
         (std-instance-slots new-instance)
         (std-instance-slots old-instance))
       (rotatef
         (std-instance-class new-instance)
         (std-instance-class old-instance))
       (apply #'update-instance-for-different-class
              new-instance old-instance initargs)
       old-instance))
```

Just as with make-instance, a second method intercepts calls with a symbol in the second argument position, which it coerces into a class metaobject:

```
☆. (defmethod change-class ((instance standard-object)
                            (new-class symbol)
                            &rest initargs)
     (apply #'change-class instance (find-class new-class) initargs))
```

As mentioned above, the generic function update-instance-for-different-class serves a two-fold purpose. By default, it simply initializes all of the new slots that appeared because of the class change. But by defining other more specialized methods on it, the user gains (temporary) access to the old state of the instance (the old instance is now in its new state—remember the identity swap), making it possible to salvage any of the slot bindings that are disappearing

---

[14]The Common Lisp macro rotatef is similar to setf. It interchanges the value of its two arguments.

```
(defgeneric update-instance-for-different-class (old new &key))
(defmethod update-instance-for-different-class ((old standard-object)
                                                (new standard-object)
                                                &rest initargs)
    (let ((added-slots
            (remove-if #'(lambda (slot-name)
                            (slot-exists-p old slot-name))
                        (mapcar #'slot-definition-name
                                (class-slots (class-of new))))))
        (apply #'shared-initialize new added-slots initargs)))
```

This completes our presentation of standard instances.

1.6   Representing Generic Functions

The CLOS user defines generic functions with the **defgeneric** macro. In this section we see how **defgeneric** is implemented. All other definitions, such as the function **ensure-generic-function** and the class **standard-generic-function** are part of the supporting implementation and are not intended to be user-visible.

A *generic function metaobject*, which is created as the result of a call to **defgeneric**, captures the information supplied in the **defgeneric** definition, and stores the set of methods defined on the generic function. Figure 1.4 depicts the metaobject for the generic function **paint**. The class **standard-generic-function** has slots for the name and lambda list as obtained from the generic function definition, and one for the associated method metaobjects:[15]

```
(defclass standard-generic-function ()
    ((name :initarg :name :accessor generic-function-name)
     (lambda-list :initarg :lambda-list
                    :accessor generic-function-lambda-list)
     (methods :initform ()
                :accessor generic-function-methods)))
```

---

[15] In full CLOS, generic function metaobjects differ somewhat from ordinary instances. They are *funcallable instances*, that is, instances which both have slots and can be called as functions (passed to **funcall** or **apply**). In Part I, we have quietly assumed the existence of such funcallable instances; but the full Closette implementation in Appendix D provides a somewhat simpler approximation of this functionality.

Name:	paint
Lambda list:	(x)
Methods:	paint methods #1, #2, and #3

Figure 1.4 The metaobject for the generic function `paint`.

1.6.1   The `defgeneric` Macro

`defgeneric` is very much like `defclass`; it macro-expands into a call to the glue layer function `ensure-generic-function`. For example,

```
(defgeneric paint (x))
```

macro-expands into

```
(ensure-generic-function 'paint :lambda-list '(x))
```

The `defgeneric` macro is defined as follows:

```
(defmacro defgeneric (function-name lambda-list)
  `(ensure-generic-function ',function-name
     :lambda-list ',lambda-list))
```

`ensure-generic-function` creates the generic function metaobject (provided that there isn't one with that name already) and installs it as the global function definition for its name.

```
(defun ensure-generic-function (function-name)
  (if (fboundp function-name)
      (fdefinition¹⁶ function-name)
      (let ((gf (apply #'make-instance
                       'standard-generic-function
                       :name function-name all-keys)))
        (setf (fdefinition function-name) gf)
        gf)))
```

This completes our presentation of how `defgeneric` is implemented. The interesting behavior of generic functions (i.e., method lookup) will be presented after we introduce method metaobjects.

---

[16]This is the new Common Lisp replacement for `symbol-function` that can also be used with function names like `(setf foo)` which aren't symbols.

Lambda list:	(x)
Qualifiers:	(:before)
Specializers:	(color-mixin)
Body:	(set-brush-color ...)
Environment:	the top-level environment
Generic-function:	paint

Figure 1.5 The metaobject for `paint` method #2.

1.7   Representing Methods

The CLOS user defines methods with the **defmethod** form. In this section we see how **defmethod** is implemented. Again, all other definitions are part of the supporting implementation and are not user-visible.

Method metaobjects capture the information supplied in a **defmethod** definition and provide a direct link to the corresponding generic function metaobject. This information includes:

- The method's unspecialized lambda list.
- The list of method qualifiers (e.g., :**before**, :**after**).
- The list of class metaobjects that are the method's parameter specializers.
- The form that constitutes the body of the method.
- The lexically enclosing environment.
- The corresponding generic function metaobject.

Figure 1.5 shows the method metaobject for **paint** method #2.

We introduce a class **standard-method** whose instances are method metaobjects that store this information:

```
(defclass standard-method ()
    ((lambda-list :initarg :lambda-list
                   :accessor method-lambda-list)
     (qualifiers :initarg :qualifiers
                   :accessor method-qualifiers)
     (specializers :initarg :specializers
                   :accessor method-specializers)
     (body :initarg :body
            :accessor method-body)
     (environment :initarg :environment
                   :accessor method-environment)
     (generic-function :initform nil
                   :accessor method-generic-function)))
```

1.7.1   The defmethod Macro

The three-layered handling of defmethod is analogous to that of defclass and def-generic. For example,

```
(defmethod paint :before ((x color-mixin))      ;Method #2
  (set-brush-color (slot-value x 'cyan)
                   (slot-value x 'magenta)
                   (slot-value x 'yellow)))
```

macro-expands to

```
(ensure-method (fdefinition 'paint)
  :lambda-list '(x)
  :qualifiers '(:before)
  :specializers (list (find-class 'color-mixin))
  :body '(block paint
                (set-brush-color (slot-value x 'cyan)
                                 (slot-value x 'magenta)
                                 (slot-value x 'yellow)))
  :environment (top-level-environment) [17])
```

---

[17]Common Lisp only supports what could be called compile-time lexical environments, whereas what is needed here is the run-time lexical environment. In reality, the function top-level-environment doesn't exist in Common Lisp. Assume for the time being that it returns the top-level runtime lexical environment. This issue is discussed further in Section 1.8.3.

A critical concern at the macro expansion layer is to ensure that the lexical environment of the `defmethod` is captured so that it can be retrieved when the body of the method is executed. Unfortunately, Common Lisp makes this rather difficult to do. Rather than try to solve this problem, we will simply implement `defmethod` in a way that works only for the most common case of top-level definitions.

```
(defmacro defmethod (&rest args)
  (multiple-value-bind (function-name qualifiers
                         lambda-list specializers body)
      (parse-defmethod args)
    `(ensure-method (fdefinition ',function-name)
       :lambda-list ',lambda-list
       :qualifiers ',qualifiers
       :specializers ,(canonicalize-specializers specializers)
       :body ',body
       :environment (top-level-environment))))
```

The tedious job of parsing the form is given to the function `parse-defmethod` *(298)*; `canonicalize-specializers` *(298)* converts specializer names (class names) to actual specializers (class metaobjects).

`ensure-method` creates a new method metaobject and adds it to the generic function with `add-method`:

```
(defun ensure-method (gf &rest all-keys)
  (let ((new-method (apply #'make-instance 'standard-method all-keys)))
    (add-method gf new-method)
    new-method))
```

`add-method` adds the method to the generic function's list of methods and to each of the specializers' list of direct methods:

```
(defun add-method (gf method)
  (setf (method-generic-function method) gf)
  (push method (generic-function-methods gf))
  (dolist (specializer (method-specializers method))
    (pushnew method (class-direct-methods specializer)))
  method)
```

1.7.2 Accessor Methods

There is still one last "ı" to dot. In a class definition such as

```
(defclass color-rectangle (color-mixin rectangle)
    ((clearp :initform (y-or-n-p "But is it transparent?")
             :initarg :clearp :accessor clearp)))
```

the slot named clearp has automatically generated slot accessor methods associated
with it. These slot accessor methods are primary methods specialized to the containing
class; i.e., their written out equivalents would be:

```
(defmethod clearp ((object color-rectangle))
  (slot-value object 'clearp))
```

and

```
(defmethod (setf clearp) (new-value (object color-rectangle))
  (setf (slot-value object 'clearp) new-value))
```

The functions add-reader-method and add-writer-method, which are called when a
class is created, call ensure-method to create these methods directly:

```
(defun add-reader-method (class fn-name slot-name)
  (ensure-method
    (ensure-generic-function fn-name :lambda-list '(object))
    :lambda-list '(object)
    :qualifiers ()
    :specializers (list class)
    :body '(slot-value object ',slot-name)
    :environment (top-level-environment))
  (values))

(defun add-writer-method (class fn-name slot-name)
  (ensure-method
    (ensure-generic-function fn-name :lambda-list '(new-value object))
    :lambda-list '(new-value object)
    :qualifiers ()
    :specializers (list (find-class 't) class)
    :body '(setf (slot-value object ',slot-name) new-value)
    :environment (top-level-environment))
  (values))
```

This completes the presentation of how defmethod is implemented.

1.8   Invoking Generic Functions

Now that we have seen how the supporting metaobjects are constructed, we are finally
ready to see how generic function invocation is implemented. We will see that this brings
together all the pieces—instances, classes, generic functions, and methods.

Exactly which methods are run on any particular invocation of a generic function
depends, of course, on the arguments that are passed. More specifically, it depends on
the classes of the required (i.e., non-optional, non-keyword and non-rest) arguments.
Conceptually, CLOS divides generic function invocation into three pieces: determining
which methods are applicable (as dictated by the method specializers and the classes of
the required arguments); sorting the applicable methods into decreasing precedence order
(also dictated by the method specializers and the classes of the required arguments), and
sequencing the execution of the sorted list of applicable methods (as dictated by the
method qualifiers). This whole process is often lumped together under the title *method
lookup.*.

Our implementation follows this same conceptual breakdown. First, we arrange so that
whenever a generic function is called (by name or by `apply/funcall`), control is passed
to the function `apply-generic-function`, passing in the generic function metaobject
along with the generic-function's list of actual arguments;[18] e.g., the call (`paint door`)
is actually implemented by a call equivalent to:

```
(apply-generic-function #'paint (list door))
```

The function `apply-generic-function` calls `compute-applicable-methods-using-
classes` to both determine which of the generic function's methods are applicable to
arguments with these classes and to sort those methods into decreasing precedence order.
It then calls `apply-methods` to sequence the invocation of applicable methods.

```
(defun apply-generic-function (gf args)
  (let ((applicable-methods
          (compute-applicable-methods-using-classes
            gf (mapcar #'class-of (required-portion gf args)))))
    (if (null applicable-methods)
        (error "No matching method for the~@
                generic function ~S,~@
                when called with arguments ~:S." gf args)
        (apply-methods gf args applicable-methods))))
```

---

[18]There are several ways that this can be implemented, but all involve implementation details that are
irrelevant for our current purposes. We recommend reading Section 4.4.3 before trying to understand how the
code in Appendix D does it.

`required-portion` *(298)* simply returns that initial portion of the arguments that corresponds to the required arguments to the generic function.

1.8.1 Determining the Applicable Methods

`compute-applicable-methods-using-classes` returns a sorted list of the methods that are applicable to arguments of the given classes. First, method applicability is decided by looking at the method's specializers: a method is applicable if every required argument satisfies the corresponding parameter specializer. This will be the case if every required argument's class is equal to or a subclass of the parameter specializer. The list of method metaobjects is sorted in decreasing precedence order before being returned.

```
(defun compute-applicable-methods-using-classes (gf required-classes)
  (sort
    (copy-list¹⁹
      (remove-if-not #'(lambda (method)
                          (every #'subclassp
                                 required-classes
                                 (method-specializers method)))
                     (generic-function-methods gf)))
    #'(lambda (m1 m2)
        (method-more-specific-p m1 m2 required-classes))))
```

Class precedence lists are used to determine when one class is a (not necessarily proper) subclass of another: class C_1 is a subclass of C_2 if and only if C_2 is a superclass of C_1, and that holds if and only if C_2 occurs in the class precedence list of C_1. For example, `color-rectangle` is a subclass of `rectangle` because `rectangle` occurs on the class precedence list of `color-rectangle`. The function `subclassp` provides the lowest layer support for subclass determination:

```
(defun subclassp (c1 c2)
  (not (null (find c2 (class-precedence-list c1)))))
```

The function `method-more-specific-p` compares the precedence of two methods on the same generic function with respect to arguments of certain classes by examining the specialized parameters in left to right order. The first pair of parameter specializers that are not the same determines the precedence (false is returned if all parameter specializers are the same).

---

[19]Common Lisp's `sort` primitive destructively sorts its argument and we must avoid modifying the generic function's list of methods.

```
✿ (defun method-more-specific-p (method1 method2 required-classes)
    (mapc #'(lambda (spec1 spec2 arg-class)
              (unless (eq spec1 spec2)
                (return-from method-more-specific-p
                  (sub-specializer-p spec1 spec2 arg-class))))
          (method-specializers method1)
          (method-specializers method2)
          required-classes)
    nil)
```

For example, with respect to a single argument whose class is `color-rectangle`, the method that is specialized to `color-rectangle` (#3) is the most specific, followed by the method that is specialized to `color-mixin` (#2), and then the method specialized to `rectangle` (#1). Thus the list of applicable methods returned by `compute-applicable-methods-using-classes` is (method #3, method #2, method #1).

The subclass relationship can be used to order classes that are related as ancestor-descendent, but, because CLOS supports multiple inheritance, ordering applicable methods may involve comparing specializers that are not so related; e.g., neither `color-mixin` nor `rectangle` is a subclass of the other. The class of the actual argument in question provides the common yardstick for comparison: a class C_1 is a sub-specializer of another class C_2 with respect to a reference class C_{arg} (the class of the argument in question) if C_1 shows up earlier than C_2 on C_{arg}'s class precedence list.[20] So, for example, `color-mixin` is a sub-specializer of `rectangle` with respect to `color-rectangle` because `color-mixin` precedes `rectangle` in the class precedence list of `color-rectangle`. The function `sub-specializer-p` computes the strict sub-specializer relationship; i.e, a class is never a sub-specializer of itself.

```
✿ (defun sub-specializer-p (c1 c2 c-arg)
    (let ((cpl (class-precedence-list c-arg)))
      (not (null (find c2 (cdr (member c1 cpl)))))))
```

1.8.2 Sequencing the Applicable Methods

Having computed the sorted list of applicable methods, the task remains of orchestrating the invocation of the methods. The list of method qualifiers is used to categorize any method as a primary, before-, or after-method:

---

[20]Given a class C_x with direct superclasses $(C_1 C_2)$, and a class C_y with direct superclasses $(C_2 C_1)$, then C_1 will be a sub-specializer of C_2 with respect to C_x while at the same time C_2 will be a sub-specializer of C_1 with respect to C_y.

```
(defun primary-method-p (method)
  (null (method-qualifiers method)))

(defun before-method-p (method)
  (equal '(:before) (method-qualifiers method)))

(defun after-method-p (method)
  (equal '(:after) (method-qualifiers method)))
```

Under the rules of standard method combination, applicable before-methods are executed first, from most specific to least specific. The most specific applicable primary
method is executed next, followed by the applicable after-methods, from least specific to
most specific. The value(s) returned by the call to the generic function are the values(s)
returned by the primary method.

The function **apply-methods** does this sequencing, calling **apply-method** to invoke
individual methods on the arguments:

```
(defun apply-methods (gf args methods)
  (let ((primaries (remove-if-not #'primary-method-p methods))
        (befores (remove-if-not #'before-method-p methods))
        (afters (remove-if-not #'after-method-p methods)))
    (when (null primaries)
      (error "No primary methods for the~@
              generic function ~S." gf))
    (dolist (before befores)
      (apply-method before args ()))
    (multiple-value-prog1
      (apply-method (car primaries) args (cdr primaries))
      (dolist (after (reverse afters))
        (apply-method after args ())))))
```

1.8.3 Applying a Method

Applying a method is handled in basically the same way a Lisp interpreter handles a call
to a normal (non-primitive) function: evaluate the body form in the lexical environment
of the **defmethod** as extended with new variable binding resulting from matching the
lambda list against the list of actual arguments. Assuming that **add-variable-bindings**
does the matching and environment manipulations, this can be expressed as:

```
(eval²¹(method-body method)
      (add-variable-bindings (method-lambda-list method)
                             args
                             (method-environment method))))
```

This brings us to the mysterious third argument to `apply-method` that the reader may have noticed in the above definition of `apply-methods`. When there are multiple primary methods applicable to a set of arguments, the rules of standard method combination are that calls to the function `call-next-method` from within the body of one primary method should activate the next most specific applicable primary method (on either the original or an all-new set of arguments).²² This list of next methods is passed to `apply-methods`, which introduces lexical function binding (similar to `flet`) for `call-next-method` (and its companion, `next-method-p`) into the scope of the body of the method. The function bound to `call-next-method` simply passes the list of next methods back to `apply-methods`. Assuming that the function `add-function-bindings` adds function bindings to an existing environment, `apply-method` is defined as follows:

```
(defun apply-method (method args next-methods)
  (let ((call-next-method
          #'(lambda (&rest cnm-args)
              (if (null next-methods)
                  (error "No next method for the~@
                          generic-function ~S."
                         (method-generic-function method))
                  (apply-methods
                    (method-generic-function method)
                    (or cnm-args args)
                    next-methods))))
        (next-method-p
          #'(lambda ()
              (not (null next-methods)))))
```

---

²¹Not only are we assuming that run-time lexical environments exist, but also that `eval` takes an environment argument. While Common Lisp supports neither, the ideas are well-known to readers familiar with metacircular Lisp interpreters. Rather than complicate matters because of this shortcoming of Common Lisp, we opted to bend the rules. Later, when we introduce the notion of method functions in Section 4.4.2, a solution that does not involve calling the Lisp interpreter will become apparent. The working program in Appendix D does not use `eval` to invoke methods.

²²Arguments to `call-next-method`, when supplied, must have the same ordered list of applicable methods as the original arguments to the generic function.

```
(eval (method-body method)
      (add-function-bindings
        '(call-next-method next-method-p)
        (list call-next-method next-method-p)
        (add-variable-bindings
          (method-lambda-list method)
          args
          (method-environment method))))))))
```

This completes the presentation of generic function invocation.

1.9   A Word About Performance

Closette is simple, but it is woefully inefficient. At the very least, any real implementation of CLOS must handle generic function invocation and slot access more efficiently. We will discuss the interaction between metaobject protocols and optimization when we design the metaobject protocol for method lookup in Chapter 4. For the time being, a few comments about the basis for optimizing ordinary CLOS implementations are in order.

There are a wide range of approaches to optimizing CLOS implementations, but all stem from the same basic idea: improve performance by computing the results of critical internal computations once and then saving and reusing that result. This technique is known as *memoization*. For example, in Closette, determining a slot's location is a critical step in accessing the slot. Because our scheme for computing slot locations is such that the location of a given slot in a given class never changes, they can easily be memoized. This makes it possible to improve the performance of slot-value and other slot accessing functions. In real implementations, a number of similar values are memoized, often forming intricately linked structures of memoized values.

Exercise 1.1 The Closette implementation of generic function invocation offers numerous possibilities for memoizing meta-level computations. Modify apply-generic-function so that it memoizes previous results of compute-applicable-methods-using-classes. What are the conditions under which your memoized values remain valid?

1.10   Summary

We have now seen the backstage architecture common to all CLOS implementations. Metaobjects are used to represent components of CLOS programs: class metaobjects represent classes, generic function metaobjects represent generic functions, and method

metaobjects represent methods. The implementation uses information stored in the
metaobjects to run the program. For example, the information stored in class metaobjects is used to access the slots of the class's instances.

The processing of the source program to create the internal metaobject structure is organized into a three layer structure. The macro expansion layer (`defclass`, `defgeneric`
and `defmethod`) processes the syntax of the forms; the glue layer (`ensure-class`, etc.)
maps names to metaobjects; the lowest layer handles metaobjects directly and provides
the bulk of the language behavior.

2 Introspection and Analysis

In this chapter, we begin the process of designing a metaobject protocol for our subset of CLOS. We will do this by working through some examples illustrative of the problems users have in writing browsers and other program analysis tools. The metaobject protocols we will develop make it possible to write these tools easily and portably.

Having just worked through the code for a simple CLOS implementation, the reader has now seen the CLOS language from a curious "second" vantage point. The first vantage point (which was assumed at the outset) is the one that all users would know about CLOS—namely, the on-stage behavior of classes, instances, generic functions and methods. The second vantage point is the backstage one, which only a CLOS implementor would usually get to see. Given both viewpoints, the reader is now hovering omnisciently in the galleries watching what is happening on both sides of the curtain.

However, seeing things from a new angle should not be taken as a blurring of the distinction between on-stage and backstage, or between audience and producer. No such blurring has happened, nor will it. The implementation presented in the preceding chapter provides precisely the following on-stage CLOS functionality:

- Three user interface macros **defclass**, **defgeneric**, and **defmethod**, for defining classes, generic functions, and methods respectively.
- Several pre-defined classes named **standard-object**, **t**, **symbol**, etc., which can be used as specializers in **defmethod** forms.
- A set of functions for creating, initializing, displaying, interrogating, and otherwise manipulating instances of user-defined classes: **make-instance**, **initialize-instance**, **reinitialize-instance**, **shared-initialize**, **print-object**, **slot-value** et al., **change-class**, and **update-instance-for-different-class**.
- Two lexical functions, **call-next-method** and **next-method-p**, for invoking the next most applicable primary method from within the body of a user-defined method.
- **That's all.**

The class, generic function, and method metaobjects were not a part of the on-stage deal; nor were the metaobject classes **standard-class**, **standard-generic-function**, and **standard-method**, nor *any* of the other generic or regular functions. All are backstage fixtures.

But that is about to change. In this second chapter we begin the process of exposing some of the backstage fixtures—opening up the implementation to the user. We will show how this places useful functionality in the hands of the user. And very importantly, we will discuss how this can be done while honoring two important constraints: (i) staying within accepted parameters of good language design, and (ii) not hobbling the implementor.

The first step in this process of exposing backstage functionality is to let the user's program inspect its own classes, generic functions, and methods. Such introspective access is the basis for browsers and other program analysis tools.

The development of our metaobject protocol will supplement the original language, which will be expanded to include functions and objects not in the above list. On the other hand, in this chapter, the Closette implementation will require only trivial modifications. This is only possible because we "rigged" Closette so that the functions and objects that will be added to the language in this chapter would already be present. Don't be fooled by this: metaobject protocols are not designed or implemented by arbitrarily exporting the internal structure of existing implementations. As we go along, we will give explicit attention to the design principles underlying our evolving metaobject protocol. In later chapters, we will introduce metaobject protocols that will require portions of Closette to be rewritten.

2.1   Introducing Class Metaobjects

Browsers and other program analysis tools are an important part of any interactive programming environment. They allow the user to cope with large, complex programs by presenting answers to certain questions about the program in a specialized perspective. In some cases, it is even useful to have such tools tailored to a specific application. Unfortunately, browsers have traditionally been tightly coupled to internal aspects of the language implementation and, as a result, have not been portable. It has also been difficult for users to write program analysis tools of their own. We will see how, when properly exposed to the user, metaobjects and the information associated with them make it possible to write portable browsers and other program analysis tools.

Consider for a moment the very simple task of getting a list of the names of all classes defined in the user's application program. For last chapter's example program, that would be the list:

```
(rectangle color-mixin color-rectangle)
```

Larger programs would have commensurably longer lists. There are any number of ways that the user might procure this list for use by the application:

- Directly, as in:
  ```
  (defconstant my-classes '(rectangle color-mixin color-rectangle))
  ```
- By reading in the source file and locating all the defclass forms contained therein.
- By visiting all of the class metaobjects reachable via direct subclass links from the class standard-object.

The first way is simple and completely portable; however, the list has to be manually kept up to date whenever the application program's class structure changes. The other two ways automatically guarantee that the list accurately reflects the true class structure of the program, but have problems of their own. Reading the source file is not particularly straightforward;[1] tapping into the implementation's internal metaobject structure would seem to be much easier. But this last alternative can only be done portably if all implementations standardize on a way to provide access to this information. Although we (from our second vantage point) know exactly where this information is in Closette, access to it was not provided to users. So, if the user were to use their knowledge of Closette to gain access to the necessary information, the resulting program would be highly Closette-dependent, and would have little prospect of running in other implementations. It should be clear that access to this information must be a documented part of the language in order for users to be able to write portable programs that use it.

Since class metaobjects are not presently a part of the story the user sees, providing publicly accessible ways for the user to access them is going to be our first change to the language.

Conceptually, there are two ways to get access to class metaobjects. One is by name; any class defined with **defclass** has a name, so it makes sense to provide the user with a way to obtain a class metaobject given its name. The other is by asking a given object what its class is; since every object in the Lisp system has a class, this access is unproblematic. The functions **find-class** and **class-of** provide exactly the respective required functionalities *internal* to Closette. We can provide users with the desired functionality simply by adding these internal functions to the documented language:

(**find-class** ⟨*symbol*⟩ **&optional** ⟨*errorp*⟩) Returns the class metaobject corresponding to the class named by ⟨*symbol*⟩. If there is no class with this name and ⟨*errorp*⟩ is either missing or non-**nil**, an error is signaled.[2] If there is no class with this name and ⟨*errorp*⟩ is **nil**, then **nil** is returned.

(**class-of** ⟨*object*⟩) Returns the class metaobject corresponding to the class of ⟨*object*⟩.

Once again, even though these functions were already present in Closette, this is a real change to the language: we are requiring all implementations of the extended language to support class metaobjects and provide this functionality under these names.

As part of making class metaobjects available to the user, it is useful to improve their printed appearance to display the class's name. For example, the **color-rectangle** class metaobject should print something like **#<Standard-Class COLOR-RECTANGLE 323627>**.

---

[1] To properly handle macro-expansion, a complex code walker is required.

[2] In the parlance of the CLOS specification, saying that "an error is signaled" means that the programmer can rely on the implementation to detect and report the offending situation.

(Previously, the only reason to do this would have been for the convenience of the implementor since the user would never have seen a class metaobject displayed.) A simple change to Closette supports this.

```
(defmethod print-object ((class standard-class) stream)
  (print-unreadable-object (class stream :identity t)
    (format stream "Standard-Class ~S" (class-name class)))
  class)
```

We also document the identity conditions for class metaobjects: equality of class metaobjects can be tested with **eq**. To make meaningful use of class metaobjects, the user must also be given ways of extracting information from them. In Closette these services were provided internally by metaobject accessor functions (e.g., **class-name**). We continue to supplement the language by making these functions available to the user:

(class-name ⟨*class*⟩) Returns the name of the class metaobject ⟨*class*⟩ as given in the defining **defclass** form.[3]

(class-direct-superclasses ⟨*class*⟩) Returns a list of class metaobjects that are the direct superclasses of the class metaobject ⟨*class*⟩, in the order specified in the defining **defclass** form.

(class-direct-slots ⟨*class*⟩) Returns a set of direct slot definition metaobjects for the class metaobject ⟨*class*⟩, corresponding to the slot specifications in the class's **defclass** definition.

(class-precedence-list ⟨*class*⟩) Returns the class precedence list for the class metaobject ⟨*class*⟩.

(class-slots ⟨*class*⟩) Returns a set of effective slot definition metaobjects that correspond to all of the slots associated with the class metaobject ⟨*class*⟩.

(class-direct-subclasses ⟨*class*⟩) Returns a set of class metaobjects that are the direct subclasses of the class metaobject ⟨*class*⟩.

(class-direct-methods ⟨*class*⟩) Returns a set of method metaobjects, each of which has the class metaobject ⟨*class*⟩ among its list of specializers.

In order to make it easier for the implementor to provide these accessor functions, we include some general "fair use" rules that the user must respect. These rules are based on common software engineering practice for data abstractions.

---

[3]Assume that the built-in classes were pre-defined with **defclass** forms something like (**defclass** t () ()), (**defclass** standard-object (t) ()), (**defclass** symbol (t) ()), ...

1. The user should not make any assumptions about the order of elements in unordered collections. For example, `class-direct-subclasses`, which returns a *set* of class meta-objects, guarantees that there are no duplicates, but makes no promise about the order of the elements in the list it returns.

2. The user should not make any assumptions about whether the results are obtained by retrieval or by recomputation. For example, the lists returned by successive calls to `class-direct-superclasses` may not be `eq` even though they will be `equal`.

3. The user should not try to change the metaobject, either directly with something like `(setf (class-direct-subclasses ...) ...)`, or indirectly with some sort of destructive operation like `rplaca` applied to a list returned as a result. The results of smashing these structures are undefined.[4]

These rules do not overly inconvenience the user, but they do provide the implementor with some needed flexibility. For instance, the first two rules make it possible for an implementation to store the information in an alternate form, and only derive the documented form when an accessor is called. The last rule allows an implementation to compute and store a single list which can be used both internally and handed out to the user; without this provision an implementation wouldn't dare hand out anything but a copy of a list containing critical information.

The balance between user convenience and implementor freedom we have struck here—to provide the metaobjects and accessors but have rules about their use—is critical to metaobject protocol design. As with all other language design, we consider not only the advantage to users of our decisions, but also the potential effect on implementors.

Exercise 2.1 In Closette, the strategy used to implement `class-direct-subclasses` is to store the set of subclasses directly in the class metaobject. This is a simple strategy, but it's certainly not the only—or even the best—one. If most traversals of the class hierarchy go upwards (from subclasses to superclasses) rather than downwards, it may not be worth the added expense to store direct subclass links in each class metaobject. Show an alternate strategy for implementing `class-direct-subclasses` that doesn't use direct backlinks. Does your strategy depend on the freedom provided by the fair use rules? How?

---

[4]In the parlance of the CLOS specification, "the results of a given action are undefined" means that the results must be considered to be completely unpredictable. Programmers bear the responsibility of ensuring that their program avoids situations that are undefined.

2.2   Browsing Classes

With class metaobjects part of the extended language, we are now in a position to present user code that utilizes the information associated with them to build portable browsing tools. The functions introduced above provide a standard programmatic interface to the underlying class metaobjects. User code can call these functions to ascertain how the classes are related to one another, and what the structure of each class is.

2.2.1   Finding a Class's Subclasses

We can easily use the metaobjects to get information about the structure of the class hierarchy. The class precedence list, which we can obtain with **class-precedence-list**, gives us the set of a class and all its superclasses. We can also define the function **subclasses*** to return the set consisting of a given class, all its direct subclasses, all their direct subclasses, and so on:

```
(defun subclasses* (class)
  (remove-duplicates
    (cons class
          (mapappend #'subclasses*
                     (class-direct-subclasses class)))))
```

Just as we have been marking code that is part of the Closette implementation, we will also mark code that the user writes using the metaobject protocol with a mop. We will continue to leave both interactions with the lisp interpreter and example CLOS programs unmarked.

In some cases, we may find it more convenient just to get the subclasses without the class itself:

```
(defun subclasses (class) (remove class (subclasses* class)))
```

Returning to the running example of the last chapter, we can use this code to find the subclasses of the class **rectangle**:

```
⟹ (subclasses (find-class 'rectangle))
(#<Standard-Class COLOR-RECTANGLE 323627>)
```

Moreover, since all user-defined classes are subclasses of the class **standard-object**, the easy way for the user to automatically construct a list of the names of all user-defined classes is as follows:

```
(defvar my-classes
        (mapcar #'class-name
                (subclasses (find-class 'standard-object))))
⟹ my-classes
(COLOR-MIXIN RECTANGLE COLOR-RECTANGLE)
```

This solution is fully general, entirely automatic, reasonably efficient, and completely portable.[5]

2.2.2 Regenerating Class Definitions

In addition to information concerning the relationships among classes, class metaobjects also provide access to properties of the class itself. For example, suppose the user wanted to regenerate a `defclass` from a class metaobject. This requires extracting information stored with class metaobjects and displaying it in appropriate ways.

```
(defun display-defclass (class-name)
  (pprint (generate-defclass (find-class class-name)))
  (values))

(defun generate-defclass (class)
  `(defclass ,(class-name class)
     ,(mapcar #'class-name (class-direct-superclasses class))
     ,(mapcar #'generate-slot-specification (class-direct-slots class))))
```

However, in order to generate the slot specifications, the user needs to know something about slot definition metaobjects. This means that we must also document the relevant accessing functions as part of the language:

(slot-definition-name ⟨*slot*⟩) Returns the name of the slot.

(slot-definition-initargs ⟨*slot*⟩) Returns a set of :initarg keywords associated with the slot.

(slot-definition-initfunction ⟨*slot*⟩) Returns a function of no arguments that can be called to produce the value that is to be used to initialize the slot, or nil if the slot has no explicit :initform.

(slot-definition-initform ⟨*slot*⟩) Returns a rendition of the form that appeared as the slot's :initform, or nil if the slot has no explicit :initform.

---

[5]There is a catch, which we will discuss later: many system-defined classes will also appear among the subclasses of standard-object.

(slot-definition-readers ⟨*slot*⟩) Returns a set of function names, where each function named is a generic function with an automatically generated reader method that reads the slot. ⟨*slot*⟩ must be a direct slot definition metaobject.

(slot-definition-writers ⟨*slot*⟩) Returns a set of function names, where each function named is a generic function with an automatically generated writer method that stores into the slot. ⟨*slot*⟩ must be a direct slot definition metaobject.

The fair use rules mentioned on page 50 in the context of class metaobjects also govern the use of slot definition metaobjects.

With this knowledge, it is an easy matter for user code to regenerate an approximation of the original slot specification:

```
(defun generate-slot-specification (slot)
  `(,(slot-definition-name slot)
    ,@(when (slot-definition-initfunction slot)
        `(:initform ,(slot-definition-initform slot)))
    ,@(when (slot-definition-initargs slot)
        (mapappend #'(lambda (initarg) `(:initarg ,initarg))
                   (slot-definition-initargs slot)))
    ,@(when (slot-definition-readers slot)
        (mapappend #'(lambda (reader) `(:reader ,reader))
                   (slot-definition-readers slot)))
    ,@(when (slot-definition-writers slot)
        (mapappend #'(lambda (writer) `(:writer ,writer))
                   (slot-definition-writers slot)))))
```

We can now use display-defclass to display existing class metaobjects in a familiar format:

```
⟹ (display-defclass 'rectangle)
(DEFCLASS RECTANGLE (STANDARD-OBJECT)
    ((HEIGTH :INITFORM 0.0 :INITARG :HEIGTH)
     (WIDTH :INITFORM 0.0 :INITARG :WIDTH)))
```

Out of curiosity we can take a peek at the classes t and standard-object:

```
⟹ (display-defclass 't)
(DEFCLASS T () ())
⟹ (display-defclass 'standard-object)
(DEFCLASS STANDARD-OBJECT (T) ())
```

Everything is as expected.

2.2.3   Displaying Inherited Information

It is possible to display more than just the information that was explicitly supplied in the `defclass`; information about inheritance can be included as well. For instance, both the class precedence list and the complete list of slots are associated with the class metaobject; here we display them in a format resembling a `defclass`.

```
(defun display-defclass* (class-name)
  (pprint (generate-defclass* (find-class class-name)))
  (values))

(defun generate-defclass* (class)
  '(defclass* ,(class-name class)
     ,(mapcar #'class-name (cdr (class-precedence-list class)))
     ,(mapcar #'(lambda (slot)
                  (generate-inherited-slot-specification class slot))
              (class-slots class))))
```

The big difference between **generate-slot-specification** and **generate-inherited-slot-specification** is that the latter labels slots inherited from other classes with the name of the class that supplied it:

```
(defun generate-inherited-slot-specification (class slot)
  (let* ((source-class
           (find-if #'(lambda (superclass)
                        (find (slot-definition-name slot)
                              (class-direct-slots superclass)
                              :key #'slot-definition-name))
                    (class-precedence-list class)))
         (generated-slot-spec
           (generate-slot-specification slot)))
    (if (eq source-class class)
        generated-slot-spec
        (append generated-slot-spec
                '(:inherited-from ,(class-name source-class))))))
```

For example, the class `color-rectangle`, which inherits slots from both `rectangle` and `color-mixin` displays as:

```
⟹ (display-defclass* 'color-rectangle)
(DEFCLASS* COLOR-RECTANGLE (COLOR-MIXIN RECTANGLE STANDARD-OBJECT T)
    ((CLEARP  :INITFORM '(Y-OR-N-P "But is it transparent?")
              :INITARG :CLEARP)
     (CYAN    :INITFORM 0 :INITARG :CYAN
              :INHERITED-FROM COLOR-MIXIN)
     (MAGENTA :INITFORM 0 :INITARG :MAGENTA
              :INHERITED-FROM COLOR-MIXIN)
     (YELLOW  :INITFORM 0 :INITARG :YELLOW
              :INHERITED-FROM COLOR-MIXIN)
     (HEIGHT  :INITFORM 0.0 :INITARG :HEIGHT
              :INHERITED-FROM RECTANGLE)
     (WIDTH   :INITFORM 0.0 :INITARG :WIDTH
              :INHERITED-FROM RECTANGLE)))
```

2.2.4 Ordering of Classes in Multiple Inheritance

Multiple inheritance is a powerful tool for organizing large object-oriented programs, but there are cases where the very size of the program can cause the multiple inheritance behavior to be unclear. Given the metaobject accessors we have defined, the user can now write tools which enable them to analyze these sorts of issues. For example, suppose we were to add another class to our sample class hierarchy:

```
(defclass color-chart (rectangle color-mixin) ())
```

Recall that we have previously defined the class `color-rectangle` with the same superclasses, but in the opposite order. This means that in the class precedence lists of `color-chart` and `color-rectangle` the classes `rectangle` and `color-mixin` appear in different orders:

```
⟹ (mapcar #'class-name
          (class-precedence-list (find-class 'color-rectangle)))
(COLOR-RECTANGLE COLOR-MIXIN RECTANGLE STANDARD-OBJECT T)

⟹ (mapcar #'class-name
          (class-precedence-list (find-class 'color-chart)))
(COLOR-CHART RECTANGLE COLOR-MIXIN STANDARD-OBJECT T)
```

This lack of consistency in the order in which color-mixin and rectangle appear may be a problem for certain kinds of method definitions. For example, consider a generic function with exactly two primary methods, one specialized to the class color-mixin and the other to the class rectangle. When this generic function is invoked on an instance of color-rectangle, the method specialized to color-mixin will be run. On the other hand, when the generic function is called on an instance of color-chart, the method specialized to rectangle will be run. Depending on the methods, this may or may not be what is desired. In any case, it is useful to have a tool which can detect this case so that the programmer can be aware of it.

We say that a pair of classes C_1 and C_2 are *in order* provided that C_1 appears before C_2 in the class precedence list of all of their common subclasses.[6] If two classes are in order, we know that pairs of methods specialized to them will always be run in that order. The predicate in-order-p tests whether a pair of classes are in order:

```
(defun in-order-p (c1 c2)
   (flet ((in-order-at-subclass-p (sub)
           (let ((cpl (class-precedence-list sub)))
             (not (null (member c2 (cdr (member c1 cpl)))))))))
      (or (eq c1 c2)
          (every #'in-order-at-subclass-p
                 (intersection (subclasses* c1)
                               (subclasses* c2))))))
```

The classes color-mixin and rectangle are not in order because their common subclasses, color-chart and color-rectangle, are not in agreement:

```
⟹ (in-order-p (find-class 'color-mixin)
              (find-class 'rectangle))
NIL
```

On the other hand, the classes standard-object and t are in order. (It would be a sign of serious trouble if they weren't.)

```
⟹ (in-order-p (find-class 'standard-object)
              (find-class 't))
T
```

_____

[6]The rules of class precedence list computation are such that a class C is always in order with respect to each of its superclasses.

Exercise 2.2 Consider another scenario of multiple inheritance gone awry:

```
(defclass position ()
     (x y))
(defclass cad-element (position ...) ...)
(defclass display-element (position ...) ...)
```

The class `position` is supposed to be a general-purpose mixin with (x, y) coordinate positions. The class `cad-element` is supposed to model solid geometric objects, and includes `position` within its direct superclasses so as to model the position of that solid object in 2-space. Quite independently, the class `display-element` is used for data objects that can be displayed on the screen, and includes `position` within its direct superclasses to record the screen location of object. A class of data objects that both model solid objects and are displayable on the screen could then be defined as follows:

```
(defclass displayable-cad-element (display-element cad-element) ())
```

However, under the CLOS inheritance rules, the resulting class only has one pair of `x` and `y` coordinate slots, which is clearly wrong. (Under similar circumstances in C++ [Ellis&Stroustrup 90] there would be one pair for each different inheritance path.)

A *diamond* is a multiple inheritance situation where a class inherits from some other class along two different paths. In the above setting, there is a diamond with apex `position`. Write a function (`has-diamond-p` ⟨*class*⟩) that determines whether there are any diamonds with ⟨*class*⟩ at the apex.

2.2.5   Summary

By documenting a metaobject protocol for class metaobjects we have made it possible to write browsers and other program analysis tools portably. Our protocol gives the user a natural and convenient abstraction of their program's class structure. By following standard practice for data abstractions, we have been able to design the protocol so that it is useful but does not overly burden implementors.

The next section introduces similar metaobject protocols for dealing with generic function and method metaobjects, and shows how the one remaining piece of information about class metaobjects, namely the list of methods specialized to the class (the result of `class-direct-methods`), can be used to bridge the gap between the class and generic function halves of the metaobject world.

2.3   Browsing Generic Functions

Properly designed access to generic function and method metaobjects allows the user to browse the world of generic functions and methods as well as the one of classes and

instances. Just as with class metaobjects, we begin by documenting a way to get access
to generic function metaobjects. For generic functions defined with **defgeneric**, we
will say that the existing Common Lisp function **fdefinition** can be used to access
the generic function metaobject; for example, (**fdefinition** 'paint) can be used to
return the generic function metaobject for the generic function named **paint**. Method
metaobjects will usually be obtained via an accessor on the generic function metaobject
that owns them. Equality of generic function and method metaobjects can be tested
with **eq**.

We also revise Closette to improve the printed appearance of these metaobjects. Printing of generic function metaobjects should include the name of the generic function; so
the generic function **paint** prints something like #<Standard-Generic-Function PAINT
172341>. Printing of method metaobjects should include the name of the method's
generic function as well as the method's qualifiers and specializers; so that **paint** method
#2 would print like #<Standard-Method PAINT :BEFORE (COLOR-MIXIN) 787812>.

```
(defmethod print-object ((gf standard-generic-function) stream)
  (print-unreadable-object (gf stream :identity t)
    (format stream
            "Standard-Generic-Function ~S"
            (generic-function-name gf)))
  gf)

(defmethod print-object ((method standard-method) stream)
  (print-unreadable-object (method stream :identity t)
    (format stream
            "Standard-Method ~S~{ ~S~} ~S"
            (generic-function-name
              (method-generic-function method))
            (method-qualifiers method)
            (mapcar #'class-name
                    (method-specializers method)))))
  method)
```

The following additional metaobject protocols provide a functional interface to generic
function and method metaobjects similar to what we have already defined for class and
slot definition metaobjects:

(**generic-function-name** ⟨*gf*⟩) Returns the name of the generic function metaobject
⟨*gf*⟩, which is given in the defining **defgeneric** form.

(`generic-function-lambda-list` ⟨*gf*⟩) Returns the lambda list for the generic function metaobject ⟨*gf*⟩ from which it is possible to determine the number of required arguments and the presence of **&optional**, **&rest**, and **&key** arguments.

(`generic-function-methods` ⟨*gf*⟩) Returns a set of method metaobjects that are associated with the generic function metaobject ⟨*gf*⟩.

(`method-generic-function` ⟨*method*⟩) Returns the generic function metaobject with which the method metaobject ⟨*method*⟩ is associated; this method metaobject appears among that generic function's set of methods.

(`method-lambda-list` ⟨*method*⟩) Returns the unspecialized lambda list for the method metaobject ⟨*method*⟩ from which it is possible to determine the number of required arguments and the presence of **&optional**, **&rest**, and **&key** arguments for this method.

(`method-qualifiers` ⟨*method*⟩) Returns a list of atomic qualifiers for the method metaobject ⟨*method*⟩ which were given in the defining **defmethod** form.

(`method-specializers` ⟨*method*⟩) Returns a list of class metaobjects that are the specializers of the method metaobject ⟨*method*⟩, one per required argument position; each class metaobject has this method in its set of direct methods.

(`method-body` ⟨*method*⟩) Returns the form that is the body of the method metaobject ⟨*method*⟩.

(`method-environment` ⟨*method*⟩) Returns the lexical environment that enclosed the definition for the method metaobject ⟨*method*⟩.

Once again, the fair use rules mentioned for class metaobjects also apply to the handling of generic function and method metaobjects.

2.3.1   Regenerating Generic Function and Method Definitions

The task of regenerating **defgeneric** and **defmethod** forms from generic function and method metaobjects is straightforward:

```
(defun generate-defgeneric (gf)
  `(defgeneric ,(generic-function-name gf)
     ,(generic-function-lambda-list gf)))

(defun generate-defmethod (method &key show-body)
  `(defmethod ,(generic-function-name (method-generic-function method))
     ,@(method-qualifiers method)
     ,(generate-specialized-arglist method)
     ,@(when show-body (list (method-body method)))))
```

generate-specialized-arglist weaves the method's specializer names back into the method's lambda list:

```
(defun generate-specialized-arglist (method)
  (let* ((specializers (method-specializers method))
         (lambda-list (method-lambda-list method))
         (number-required (length specializers)))
    (append (mapcar #'(lambda (arg class)
                        (if (eq class (find-class 't))
                            arg
                            `(,arg ,(class-name class))))
                    (subseq lambda-list 0 number-required)
                    specializers)
            (subseq lambda-list number-required))))
```

The function `display-generic-function` pretty-prints a generic function along with its associated methods:

```
(defun display-generic-function (gf-name &key show-body)
  (display-defgeneric gf-name)
  (dolist (method (generic-function-methods (fdefinition gf-name)))
    (pprint (generate-defmethod method :show-body show-body)))
  (values))

(defun display-defgeneric (gf-name)
  (pprint (generate-defgeneric (fdefinition gf-name)))
  (values))
```

For example, we can have a look at the generic function `paint`:

```
⟹ (display-generic-function 'paint :show-body t)
(DEFGENERIC PAINT (X))
(DEFMETHOD PAINT ((X RECTANGLE))
  (BLOCK PAINT
    (VERTICAL-STROKE (SLOT-VALUE X 'HEIGHT)
                     (SLOT-VALUE X 'WIDTH))))
(DEFMETHOD PAINT :BEFORE ((X COLOR-MIXIN))
  (BLOCK PAINT
    (SET-BRUSH-COLOR (SLOT-VALUE X 'CYAN)
                     (SLOT-VALUE X 'MAGENTA)
                     (SLOT-VALUE X 'YELLOW))))
```

```
(DEFMETHOD PAINT ((X COLOR-RECTANGLE))
  (BLOCK PAINT
    (UNLESS (CLEARP X) (CALL-NEXT-METHOD)))))
```

Automatically generated slot reader and writer functions like `clearp` can also be displayed:

```
⟹ (display-generic-function 'clearp :show-body t)
(DEFGENERIC CLEARP (OBJECT))
(DEFMETHOD CLEARP ((OBJECT COLOR-RECTANGLE))
  (SLOT-VALUE OBJECT 'CLEARP))

⟹ (display-generic-function '(setf clearp) :show-body t)
(DEFGENERIC (SETF CLEARP) (NEW-VALUE OBJECT))
(DEFMETHOD (SETF CLEARP) (NEW-VALUE (OBJECT COLOR-RECTANGLE))
  (SETF (SLOT-VALUE OBJECT 'CLEARP) NEW-VALUE))
```

And so can standard generic functions like `shared-initialize`:

```
⟹ (display-generic-function 'shared-initialize)
(DEFGENERIC SHARED-INITIALIZE (INSTANCE SLOT-NAMES &KEY))
(DEFMETHOD SHARED-INITIALIZE ((INSTANCE STANDARD-OBJECT)
                             SLOT-NAMES
                             &REST ALL-KEYS))
```

2.3.2   Finding All Generic Functions

The user can find every generic function in the system by exploiting the links between the class hierarchy and the generic function and method world. Each method appears among the list of direct methods of the classes it is specialized to (even the class `t`). Since each useful generic function has at least one method, we are guaranteed that every useful generic function is reachable from some class in the class hierarchy.

The function `all-generic-functions` returns the set of all generic function metaobjects in the system:

```
(defun all-generic-functions ()
  (remove-duplicates
    (mapappend #'class-direct-generic-functions
               (subclasses* (find-class 't)))))
```

where `class-direct-generic-functions` is defined in terms of `class-direct-methods`:

```
(defun class-direct-generic-functions (class)
  (remove-duplicates
    (mapcar #'method-generic-function
            (class-direct-methods class))))
```

The (abridged) list of all generic functions in this system:

$\Longrightarrow$ (mapcar #'generic-function-name (all-generic-functions))
(CLEARP PAINT UPDATE-INSTANCE-FOR-DIFFERENT-CLASS
REINITIALIZE-INSTANCE INITIALIZE-INSTANCE CHANGE-CLASS
MAKE-INSTANCE (SETF CLEARP) SHARED-INITIALIZE
PRINT-OBJECT ...)

2.3.3 Finding Relevant Generic Functions

A somewhat more focused task is to find all generic functions which can be called on instances of a given class. These are just those generic functions with methods specialized to the class or one of its superclasses. Because there are a number of methods which are specialized to standard-object or t, it is useful to be able to set an upper limit on the search for methods.

```
(defun relevant-generic-functions (class ceiling)
  (remove-duplicates
    (mapcar #'method-generic-function
      (mapappend #'class-direct-methods
        (set-difference (class-precedence-list class)
                        (class-precedence-list ceiling))))))
```

For example, we can find all the generic functions that can be called with instances of the class color-rectangle:

$\Longrightarrow$ (relevant-generic-functions (find-class 'color-rectangle)
                                   (find-class 'standard-object))
(#<Standard-Generic-Function CLEARP 239548>
 #<Standard-Generic-Function PAINT 172341>
 #<Standard-Generic-Function (SETF CLEARP) 238721>)

Exercise 2.3 When there are several methods that may be applicable to particular arguments, it is sometimes helpful to be able to visualize exactly what will happen when a generic function is called; a Lisp form is one easy way to convey this information. For instance, using the stylized subform (`call-method` ⟨*method*⟩ ⟨*next-method-list*⟩) to indicate that a particular method is to be called with a particular list of next methods, the following form expresses what happens when the generic function `paint` is called with a `color-rectangle`:

```
(PROGN
  (CALL-METHOD
    (METHOD PAINT :BEFORE ((X COLOR-MIXIN))
      (BLOCK PAINT
        (SET-BRUSH-COLOR (SLOT-VALUE X 'CYAN)
                         (SLOT-VALUE X 'MAGENTA)
                         (SLOT-VALUE X 'YELLOW))))
    ())
  (CALL-METHOD
    (METHOD PAINT ((X COLOR-RECTANGLE))
      (BLOCK PAINT
        (UNLESS (CLEARP X) (CALL-NEXT-METHOD))))
    ((METHOD PAINT ((X RECTANGLE))
       (BLOCK PAINT
         (VERTICAL-STROKE (SLOT-VALUE X 'HEIGHT)
                          (SLOT-VALUE X 'WIDTH)))))))
```

Define a function (`display-effective-method` ⟨*gf*⟩ ⟨*args*⟩) that constructs and displays such a form showing how the applicable methods of the given generic function will actually be applied to the given set of arguments. Use Closette internal functions only if you are certain you could have defined them yourself using the documented accessors.

2.3.4   Finding All Slot Accessors

Typically, a number of the relevant generic functions will appear in the list only because of automatically generated accessor methods. It is useful to be able to filter such generic functions from the list. To do this, we need to be able to determine whether a given method is an automatically generated reader or writer.

We can determine whether a method is a reader method by checking the correspondence between the name of the method's generic function and the class the method is specialized to. If one of the class's slots defines a reader with the same generic function name, the method must be a reader. Writer methods can be recognized in an analogous way.

```
(defun reader-method-p (method)
  (let ((specializers (method-specializers method)))
    (and (= (length specializers) 1)
         (member (generic-function-name (method-generic-function method))
                 (mapappend #'slot-definition-readers
                            (class-direct-slots (car specializers)))
                 :test #'equal)))))

(defun writer-method-p (method)
  (let ((specializers (method-specializers method)))
    (and (= (length specializers) 2)
         (member (generic-function-name (method-generic-function method))
                 (mapappend #'slot-definition-writers
                            (class-direct-slots (cadr specializers)))
                 :test #'equal)))))
```

Given these two predicates, we can revise the definition of relevant-generic-functions as follows:

```
(defun relevant-generic-functions (class ceiling &key elide-accessors-p)
  (remove-duplicates
    (mapcar #'method-generic-function
      (remove-if #'(lambda (m)
                     (and elide-accessors-p
                          (or (reader-method-p m)
                              (writer-method-p m))))
        (mapappend #'class-direct-methods
          (set-difference (class-precedence-list class)
                          (class-precedence-list ceiling)))))))
```

The pruned list of generic functions is only a bit shorter in this example setting:

```
⟹ (relevant-generic-functions (find-class 'color-rectangle)
                               (find-class 'standard-object)
                               :elide-accessors-p t)
(#<Standard-Generic-Function PAINT 172341>)
```

Exercise 2.4 The definition we have given for `reader-method-p` (and `writer-method-p`) is somewhat indirect; it infers the result by checking class metaobjects to see what reader methods were created and what that says about the method in question. Predicates like these are common in object-oriented programming and there are two common techniques for implementing them more directly. The first is to mark each object as to whether it satisfies the predicate. I.e., a mark, perhaps using the value of a slot, on each method metaobject would indicate whether it was a reader. The second is to use a special subclass to indicate the special property. Modify Closette to implement `reader-method-p` (and `writer-method-p`) in each of these other ways and discuss the merits of each approach.

2.3.5 Summary

Documenting the information associated with class, generic function, and method metaobjects makes it possible for the user to write portable programs to do things such as locating all metaobjects of a given kind and determining salient properties of individual metaobjects (e.g., their subclasses) and important relationships among them (e.g., being in order at all common subclasses).

So far, we have augmented CLOS by adding mechanisms for accessing metaobjects and important information associated with them. In essence, this functionality makes it possible for a user to recover the definition of a program defined using `defclass`, `defgeneric` and `defmethod` forms. This is natural since the metaobjects provide a documented abstract representation of the user's program. In the next section we will see that there are situations in which using `defclass`, `defgeneric` and `defmethod` to define programs is inconvenient, and how documenting information required to create metaobjects allows the user to define programs more directly in these cases.

2.4 Programmatic Creation of New Classes

Consider a graphics application in which the program manipulates graphical objects of a number of geometric shapes which can be painted a variety of colors and labeled in one of several different ways. The classes defining these traits might look something like:

```
(defclass shape () ...)
(defclass circle   (shape) ...)
(defclass triangle (shape) ...)
(defclass pentagon (shape) ...)
...
```

```
(defclass color () ...)
(defclass fuchsia (color) ...)
(defclass orange  (color) ...)
(defclass magenta (color) ...)
...
(defclass label-type () ...)
(defclass top-labeled    (label-type) ...)
(defclass center-labeled (label-type) ...)
(defclass bottom-labeled (label-type) ...)
```

A orange circle with its label at the top would be an instance of the class with direct superclasses circle, orange, and top-labeled. Such a class could be defined with:

```
(defclass orange-top-labeled-circle (circle orange top-labeled)
     ())
```

Although it would be possible to write explicit class definitions for all valid combinations, it would be tedious to do so—and wasteful if only a few of the combinations are actually instantiated in any single execution of the graphics application. In such cases it would be desirable to hold off defining the combination classes and creating the corresponding class metaobjects until that combination is actually needed. So, for example, to create an instance of the class of orange circles labeled at the top, we would call some function make-programmatic-instance giving the names of the appropriate superclasses along with the initialization arguments for the instance:

```
(defun make-programmatic-instance (superclass-names &rest initargs)
   (apply #'make-instance
          (find-programmatic-class
            (mapcar #'find-class superclass-names))
          initargs))
```

An example programmatic instance creation:

```
⟹ (make-programmatic-instance '(circle orange top-labeled)
                               :title "Color Wheel"
                               :radius 10)
#<(CIRCLE ORANGE TOP-LABELED) 823456>
```

Assuming that there is only one class with a given list of direct superclasses, we can easily find out whether we have already encountered this combination of classes before:

```
(defun find-programmatic-class (superclasses)
  (let ((class (find-if
                #'(lambda (class)
                    (equal superclasses
                           (class-direct-superclasses class)))
                (class-direct-subclasses (car superclasses)))))
    (if class
        class
        (make-programmatic-class superclasses))))
```

As we saw in the last chapter, the Closette implementation is structured into three layers, the lowest of which deals exclusively with first-class metaobjects. The task of creating classes under program control is precisely the kind of task that is found at the lowest layer; what the user needs is enough information to be able to write (make-instance 'standard-class ...). Since make-instance is already a user-visible generic function, all we need to do is document the fact that class metaobjects are instances of the class standard-class, and disclose the relevant initialization arguments for creating them:

:name ⟨*object*⟩ Specifies the object ⟨*object*⟩ as the name of the new class. This value will be returned subsequently by calls to class-name on the new class metaobject. If this keyword argument is omitted, nil will be used.

:direct-superclasses ⟨*list*⟩ Specifies that the direct superclasses of the new class are to be the list of classes whose metaobjects appear on ⟨*list*⟩. This list is the value returned by class-direct-superclasses. If this keyword argument is omitted, or is (), it will default to a list containing just the class metaobject standard-object.

:direct-slots ⟨*list*⟩ Specifies that the direct slots of the new class are to be the set of slots whose property list-style specifications appear on ⟨*list*⟩.[7] The value returned by class-direct-slots will be the set of corresponding direct slot definition metaobjects. If omitted, this keyword argument defaults to the empty set.

We also define and document ground rules similar to the fair use rules for metaobject accessors. These rules prohibit the user from destructively modifying any of the list structures passed in as initialization arguments (so that the implementation needn't copy them) or invoking other operations that would change the class metaobject in uncontrolled ways (e.g., initialize-instance, and change-class).

---

[7]Assume that the format of the individual property list-style slot specifications has been documented in a similar manner.

Armed with this additional piece of metaobject protocol, it is now possible for the user to define `make-programmatic-class` directly in terms of `make-instance`. Because the veneer and glue layers are bypassed, there is no need to give the class a unique name for `find-class` to key on; here we name them using a list of the direct superclass names.[8]

```
(defun make-programmatic-class (superclasses)
  (make-instance 'standard-class
    :name (mapcar #'class-name superclasses)
    :direct-superclasses superclasses
    :direct-slots ())))
```

So, for example, issuing commands to create three instance of two different combinations results in the creation of just two new class metaobjects:

```
⟹ (class-direct-subclasses (find-class 'circle))
()
⟹ (setq i1 (make-programmatic-instance
             '(circle orange top-labeled))
        i2 (make-programmatic-instance
             '(circle magenta bottom-labeled))
        i3 (make-programmatic-instance
             '(circle orange top-labeled)))
⟹ (class-direct-subclasses (find-class 'circle))
(#<Standard-Class (CIRCLE MAGENTA BOTTOM-LABELED) 727553>
 #<Standard-Class (CIRCLE ORANGE TOP-LABELED) 200664>)
```

Programmatic creation of generic function and method metaobjects is supported by analogous metaobject protocols for invoking `make-instance`; the details of the protocols are not included here.

2.5 Summary

We have augmented the original language by documenting the existence of metaobjects, accessors for them, and an initialization protocol for creating them. This makes it possible for users to write portable browsers, program analysis tools and alternative interfaces to the programming language behavior.

---

[8]In CLOS, such a class is called *anonymous*. That is, given its name, it isn't possible to use `find-class` to get the class metaobject itself. A special case of anonymous classes are those for which `class-name` returns `nil`. These are called *unnamed* classes.

In designing these metaobject protocols, we have been careful to strike an appropriate balance between giving the user important functionality and allowing the implementor adequate flexibility. This balance stems from our use of common data abstraction techniques in the design of the protocols.

In closing, we return to the theatre metaphor to summarize our current situation. We haven't changed anything on-stage; what is there is still the basic CLOS behavior as defined in Chapter 1. Neither have we changed any of the backstage mechanisms; they are still in place and still serve to support the on-stage behavior.

We can see now that metaobject protocol design isn't simply a matter of removing the backdrop from traditional theatre to allow the audience to see backstage. Instead, it is a new kind of theatre in which we design a cleaned up portion of the backstage which the audience gets to see. The audience now sees the traditional on-stage and the new, stylized *on-backstage*. In the same way as we used to design the on-stage, we now design the on-stage and the on-backstage; the real backstage is still hidden and is a domain where only producers may go.

In the next chapter, we will develop metaobject protocols which go beyond allowing the audience to see the on-backstage. We will allow the audience to manipulate the on-backstage mechanisms to control what happens on-stage.

Exercise 2.5 Suppose one uses the simple criterion that anything that explicitly traffics in metaobjects is a metaobject protocol facility, and everything else is a part of the ordinary language. This would classify functions like `make-instance` as part of the metaobject protocol, even though there is a strong intuition that it is a piece of base level functionality. Do you think there should be a strong distinction between ordinary and metaobject protocol facilities? If so, what criteria would you use to tell them apart?

Exercise 2.6 Pick a programming language, or one particular implementation, and consider various facilities that are provided in the programming environment like browsers and debuggers. What support would you need if you wanted to write similar tools? How general, and how portable, would the resulting program be?

Exercise 2.7 We have been assuming that metaobjects are created in the process of loading a source file containing Lisp defining forms. In this chapter we saw that defining forms can be reconstructed from metaobjects (e.g., a `defclass` from a class metaobject), and how metaobjects may also be created directly, bypassing forms entirely. In residential programming environments the assumption is that internal objects are *the* principal permanent representation of the program, and that Lisp forms or text strings are simply familiar ways of presenting the information associated with these objects to the programmer. Adding a metaobject protocol to a language seems to provide a basis for residential environments. Discuss the relation between residential programming environments and metaobject protocols. (More information about residential environments can be found in [Barstow et al. 84] and [Bobrow et al. 87].)

3 Extending the Language

When working in real life situations, users of high-level programming languages encounter a number of common problems. Often, these can be expressed in the form of desires: for compatibility with other related languages; for customizations to support specific applications; for adjustments to the implementation in order to improve the performance of a given application program.

Lacking mechanisms to meet these goals, programmers are driven to employ workarounds, to give up on their desires, or to abandon the language completely. Sometimes, that is, they get by without a desired feature. Sometimes they learn to avoid inefficiently implemented constructs. Occasionally they are forced to change their approach, and to write their programs in an entirely new way (often at great cost to the clarity of the original conception). In extreme cases, they can even find themselves forced to switch to another vendor's implementation of the language, or to use a different language altogether (occasionally, some users will even develop their own languages from scratch).

Inherent in the notion of a metaobject protocol is an approach to this whole class of problems. As discussed in the introduction, the basic idea is to apply the general benefits of object-oriented programming (flexibility and incremental extensibility) to language implementation itself, thus endowing both language and implementation with enough "give" so that users can vary one or both, as needed. By adding a metaobject protocol, a single language with a single implementation can be transformed into a region of flexible, extensible implementations of flexible, extensible languages.

In order to achieve this goal, the metaobject protocol must be able to support changes to the default design. In contrast, the protocols developed in the previous chapter dealt only with "looking" at a program. By providing a documented interface to the internal representation of programs, we were able to give users the ability to build introspective facilities for analyzing the structure of their programs. In this chapter, however, we will extend these protocols to allow the user to "step in" and make adjustments, both to the language itself and to its implementation. The strategy will be to add a new set of protocols—which we call *intercessory*—to the introspective ones previously developed.

Intercessory facilities will be provided by placing certain key aspects of the language implementation under the control of documented generic functions—in essence, by developing an object-oriented protocol for the full language implementation. Given this protocol, the standard object-oriented techniques of subclassing and specialization can be used to create the desired specialized languages and specialized implementations.

3.1   Specialized Class Metaobjects

We begin by showing how familiar object-oriented techniques—particularly inheritance and subclass specialization—are used in intercessory metaobject protocols. The first example will be a simple one of defining a variant of standard-class that can be used to construct classes that count how many times they have been instantiated.

The expression

```
(defclass counted-class (standard-class)
    ((counter :initform 0)))
```

defines a specialized metaobject class, counted-class, as a subclass of the standard metaobject class standard-class. The new class has one additional slot named counter, but otherwise specifies the same behavior as its superclass. We can create instances of counted-class (which, of course, will themselves be class metaobjects) using make-instance. For example,

```
⟹ (setf (find-class 'counted-rectangle)
         (make-instance 'counted-class
           :name 'counted-rectangle
           :direct-superclasses (list (find-class 'rectangle))
           :direct-slots ())))
```

creates a new class metaobject named counted-rectangle. The class represented by this metaobject is a direct subclass of rectangle and has no slots. The only behavioral differences between this class metaobject, and the one for the class rectangle are their classes and the presence (in the case of counted-rectangle) of the extra counter slot:

```
⟹ (class-of (find-class 'rectangle))
#<Standard-Class STANDARD-CLASS 125054>
⟹ (class-of (find-class 'counted-rectangle))
#<Standard-Class COUNTED-CLASS 635478>
⟹ (slot-value (find-class 'rectangle) 'counter)
Error: The slot COUNTER is missing from the class
       #<Standard-Class STANDARD-CLASS 125054>.
⟹ (slot-value (find-class 'counted-rectangle) 'counter)
0
```

As we saw in Chapter 1, some parts of the CLOS implementation are controlled by generic functions operating on class metaobjects—generic functions for which the standard methods are specialized to standard-class. For these parts of the language behavior, counted-class simply inherits the behavior of standard-class. For example, we saw that the job of creating class metaobjects is handled by the following standard method on make-instance:

```
(defmethod make-instance ((class standard-class) &rest initargs)
  (let ((instance (allocate-instance class)))
    (apply #'initialize-instance instance initargs)
    instance))
```

Because of inheritance, this method is also applicable when make-instance is used to instantiate a counted class (e.g., with counted-rectangle as its first argument).

In order to make use of the counter slot, however, it makes sense to supplement the behavior of make-instance, in the case of counted classes, by defining a specialized method:

```
(defmethod make-instance :after ((class counted-class) &key)
  (incf (slot-value class 'counter)))
```

Now, when make-instance is used to create an instance of counted-rectangle, two methods will be applicable: the standard method, specialized to standard-class, and the supplemental after-method, just defined. The standard method will run and return a new instance; the after-method will run and increment the counter. In this way, counted classes such as counted-rectangle inherit all the standard behavior defined for make-instance, but can also add their own special behavior of counting how many instances have been created.

```
⟹ (slot-value (find-class 'counted-rectangle) 'counter)
0
⟹ (make-instance 'counted-rectangle)
#<COUNTED-RECTANGLE 236721>
⟹ (slot-value (find-class 'counted-rectangle) 'counter)
1
```

Finally, because the specialized method applies only to instances of counted-class, the behavior of the rest of the system—including all implementation- and user-defined classes—remains unaffected.

Although almost trivially simple, this example nonetheless illustrates the three steps of a process that underlies the use of all intercessory metaobject protocols: (i) defining a specialized metaobject class (`counted-class`); (ii) defining correspondingly specialized methods on the appropriate generic functions (the after-method on `make-instance`); and (iii) creating instances of the specialized metaobject class (`counted-rectangle`) which inherit most of their behavior from the standard metaobject class, but which, via the specialized methods, have some extended or different behavior as well.

Like standard metaobjects, specialized metaobjects can be viewed as representing fragments of the user's program. But, whereas standard metaobjects represent program fragments written in CLOS, specialized metaobjects are best understood as representing program fragments written in alternative (but usually only slightly different) languages. From this perspective, the class metaobject `counted-rectangle`, is not a CLOS class, but is instead a class in an extended language. The new language has all the behavior of CLOS, but has one additional property as well—classes count their instances. In other words, the first two steps of the three step process described above should be viewed as creating—using the object-oriented technique of subclass specialization—a derivative programming language. Similarly, the third step would be understood as the selection of that new language for a given piece of the user's program. Two aspects of this process, furthermore, are importantly incremental: the new language is incrementally defined in terms of the original one; and only a portion of the program is expressed in that new language.

As we develop our metaobject protocol, we will add to the set of generic functions that the user can specialize to control the language's behavior. This will increase the number of aspects of CLOS which can be adjusted, giving the user increased flexibility to produce variant languages based on standard CLOS.

3.2   Terminology

In working with these new protocols, it will be important to distinguish between system-supplied definitions and the standard language on the one hand, and user definitions and language extensions on the other. The following terminology makes this clear:[1]

- The classes `standard-class`, `standard-generic-function`, and `standard-method` are the *standard metaobject classes*. The user is free to define new metaobject classes as subclasses of the standard metaobject classes; these will be referred to as *specialized metaobject classes*. (See Figure 3.1.)

---

[1]The full MOP gives a more elaborate and precise definition of these distinctions (p. 142).

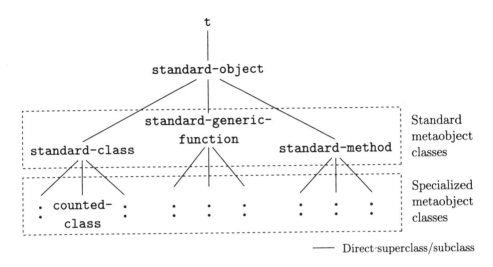

Figure 3.1 Metaobject Classes.

- Methods specialized to standard metaobject classes, (e.g., the method on **make-instance** specialized to **standard-class**) will be called *standard methods*. Methods specialized to specialized metaobject classes, (e.g., the after-method on **make-instance** specialized to **counted-class**) will be called *specialized methods*.

- Instances of metaobject classes will be called *metaobjects*. A *standard metaobject* is an instance of a standard metaobject class. A *specialized metaobject* is an instance of a specialized metaobject class.

  - A *class metaobject* is an instance of the metaobject class **standard-class** or one of its subclasses. (E.g., **rectangle** is a standard class metaobject, **counted-rectangle** is a specialized class metaobject.)
  - A *generic function metaobject* is an instance of the metaobject class **standard-generic-function** or one of its subclasses.
  - A *method metaobject* is an instance of the metaobject class **standard-method** or one of its subclasses.

- We refrain from using the term "metaclass" for classes like **standard-class**, choosing instead to use the more explicit phrase: class metaobject class. The sole exception is an option we will add to **defclass** called **:metaclass**, which has been retained for historical reasons.

3.3   Using Specialized Class Metaobject Classes

Before considering any substantial examples, we need to make it more convenient for
the user to use specialized metaobject classes. It is already simple to define specialized
class metaobject classes like `counted-class`, but no correspondingly convenient way
exists to create specialized class metaobjects. In the previous example, we resorted to
using `make-instance` to create the class `counted-rectangle`, but it would have been
more convenient to use the existing facility for creating class metaobjects—the `defclass`
macro.

Unfortunately, the version of `defclass` documented and implemented in the first chapter always creates instances of `standard-class`. We modify it, by adding a new option
named `:metaclass`, to control the class of the resulting class metaobject; when the
`:metaclass` option is not supplied, it defaults to `standard-class` as before. Given this
extension, the example class `counted-rectangle` from above could be defined (and given
a proper name) with:

```
(defclass counted-rectangle (rectangle)
    ()
  (:metaclass counted-class))
```

This change to `defclass` requires only modest changes to Closette. Recall that the
`defclass` macro expands to a call to `ensure-class`, which then calls `make-instance` to
create the class metaobject. When the `:metaclass` option is present, its value must be
communicated to `ensure-class`, which must then create an instance of that class. This
is handled in the same way as other parts of the `defclass` form; the expansion passes the
value to `ensure-class` using a keyword argument. The previously mentioned (but not
discussed) `canonicalize-defclass-options` *(287)* handles this. The above `defclass`
form expands to:

```
(ensure-class 'counted-rectangle
  :direct-superclasses (list (find-class 'rectangle))
  :direct-slots ()
  :metaclass (find-class 'counted-class))
```

The function `ensure-class` is similarly modified to accept the `:metaclass` keyword
argument, and to call `make-instance` with the value of that argument. If omitted,
`ensure-class` supplies `standard-class` as the default value. The revised definition is:

```
(defun ensure-class (name &rest all-keys
                          &key (metaclass (find-class 'standard-class))
                          &allow-other-keys)
  (if (find-class name nil)
      (error "Can't redefine the class named ~S." name)
      (let ((class (apply #'make-instance
                          metaclass :name name all-keys)))
        (setf (find-class name) class)
        class)))
```

With these changes, the entire functionality of defclass—including proper handling of :initforms, :accessors and all other features—is available when defining specialized as well as standard class metaobjects.

Having licensed the user to define subclasses of standard-class, it is also appropriate to allow specialized methods on initialize-instance and print-object. This gives the user the same control over initialization and printing in subclasses of metaobject classes as in subclasses of any other kind of class.

In the Closette implementation itself, we can alleviate some of the need for specializing print-object by modifying the standard method so that it displays the name of the class's class in addition to the name of the class itself.

```
(defmethod print-object ((class standard-class) stream)
  (print-unreadable-object (class stream :identity t)
    (format stream "~:(~S~) ~S"
            (class-name (class-of class))
            (class-name class)))
  class)
```

This ensures that instances of specialized metaobject classes will be automatically distinguished from standard class metaobjects even when there is no directly corresponding print-object method.

```
⟹ (find-class 'counted-rectangle)
#<Counted-Class COUNTED-RECTANGLE 737212>
⟹ (find-class 'rectangle)
#<Standard-Class RECTANGLE 125054>
```

We now resume development of our metaobject protocol with a series of examples demonstrating how a number of problems, common among users of object-oriented programming languages, can be solved by producing variants of CLOS with different kinds of inheritance behavior.

3.4   Class Precedence Lists

Many prospective CLOS programmers have extensive experience with programs written in other Lisp-based object-oriented programming languages such as Flavors [Cannon 82] or Loops [Bobrow&Stefik 83]. As is often the case when introduced to a new language, they would find the transition to CLOS more attractive if their existing code could be easily ported.

In most respects, Flavors, Loops, and CLOS are sufficiently similar that the task of mapping Flavors or Loops code into CLOS is (relatively) straightforward. Each language has classes, instances with slots (or instance variables), methods, generic functions (or messages), and all the other basics of object-oriented behavior.

On closer examination however, the languages differ in an important way: while they all support multiple inheritance, they use different rules to order the priority of superclasses. This means that a simple mapping of Flavors or Loops programs into CLOS can fail because of asymmetries in the inheritance of methods and slots. If it were possible to give the user control over the inheritance regimen so that, on a per-class basis, it was compatible with Flavors or Loops, a major stumbling block to compatibility would be removed.

In CLOS, as we saw in the model backstage architecture, the basis of all inheritance decisions is the class precedence list. Thus, a change to a class's class precedence list would affect both slot and method inheritance, making it possible to provide Flavors or Loops compatibility. What is the best way to give the user control over the class precedence list?

The most obvious approach might be to allow the user to modify the class precedence list of a class metaobject explicitly using `setf` with `class-precedence-list`. With this kind of flexibility, arranging for a given class to use alternative inheritance rules would be straightforward. Unfortunately, however, while simple and powerful, this proposal opens up the language more than is desirable. Consider two example scenarios.

First, suppose that a user, using this scheme, were to define a variant of CLOS in which the class precedence lists changed frequently throughout the program's execution. This might be powerful—and the resulting programming language would certainly be exciting to program in—but such behavior would affect too many other parts of the language. What, for example, should happen to extant instances if the change to the class precedence list causes the set of slots defined in a class to change? What should happen if, while a method is running, a class precedence list changes in a way that affects the sequence of next methods?[2]

Second, suppose the user were to change a class's class precedence list so that it no longer included the classes `standard-object` and `t`. Again, this might be useful, but it presents a serious inconvenience to the implementor. Note, for example, that an instance of such a class might have no applicable method on `print-object` (since the previously defined system-supplied method, specialized to `standard-object`, would no longer be applicable). While the user could repair this problem by defining their own method on `print-object`, other internal generic functions, critical to the implementation, could not be so easily repaired. For example, the garbage collector might be written using generic functions, and the implementor might like to assume that a method specialized to `t` is, in fact, applicable to *all* objects.

In essence, these problems stem from giving the user the power to alter the language so radically that very few of its original characteristics remain. This is outside the goals of metaobject protocol design, which are simply to make the language flexible enough so that it can be extended to a range of relatively similar languages. We wanted to open the language from a single point in design space to the surrounding region. Instead, we have opened it almost to the entire space of programming language design. Deciding how much flexibility to support in a protocol (i.e., how large to make the region) is a balancing act. The more flexible the protocol, the more the user will potentially be able to do; the less flexible the protocol, the more basic properties of the language the user and implementor both will be able to rely on in all extensions.

In the case at hand, we strike this balance by requiring: (i) that a class's class precedence list be a fixed property of the class; (ii) that it include all of the class's superclasses; and (iii) that those superclasses include the classes `standard-object` and `t`. This gives the user the power to adjust the inheritance behavior over a wide range—including that of all the major object-oriented programming languages—while still providing useful basic guarantees on the inheritance behavior of any language extension.

If a class's class precedence list cannot change, we might as well make this explicit in the protocol. In our model backstage architecture, `compute-class-precedence-list` was the function that did the real work of computing class precedence lists, and `class-precedence-list` was the function that fetched the previously computed value. We will put both of these in our metaobject protocol, allowing the user to define methods on the former, but only to call the latter. The user will not be permitted to use `setf` with `class-precedence-list`.

---

[2] These problems are similar to those associated with `change-class` in full CLOS.

We are now ready to document the new piece of protocol:

(`compute-class-precedence-list` ⟨*class*⟩) This generic function is called to compute
the class precedence list for the class metaobject ⟨*class*⟩. The result must be a list of
class metaobjects; the first element of the list must be ⟨*class*⟩ itself, the last two elements must be `standard-object` and t, in that order, and the intermediate elements
must be a permutation of the other superclasses of ⟨*class*⟩. The class precedence list
of a class may not change once it is computed; the implementation will call `compute-`
`class-precedence-list` once and then store its value. The value can then be accessed
by calling the function `class-precedence-list`. The results of destructively modifying the value are undefined.

Note that this restriction of power has efficiency advantages as well. In Chapter 1
we mentioned that the basis of slot access optimization is memoization of slot locations.
Under the original, unrestricted suggestion of allowing arbitrary changes to the class
precedence list, it is difficult to imagine how the implementor could retain this optimization technique. Slot locations could not be memoized because the implementor would
have no idea as to what might cause them to change. The new protocol, while it allows a
wide range of inheritance and therefore slot inheritance behavior, has enough restrictions
that slot locations can still easily be memoized. Once the class precedence list has been
computed, the set of slots for a class can be fixed, and the slot locations can be computed
once and for all.

Implementing the new protocol in Closette requires only that we convert `compute-`
`class-precedence-list` to a generic function, and that we provide a standard method
to implement the normal CLOS rules. The code in the body of this method is unchanged
from its original definition as a function (p. 24).

```
(defgeneric compute-class-precedence-list (class))
(defmethod compute-class-precedence-list ((class standard-class))
  (let ((classes-to-order (collect-superclasses* class)))
    (topological-sort classes-to-order
                      (remove-duplicates
                        (mapappend #'local-precedence-ordering
                                   classes-to-order))
                      #'std-tie-breaker-rule)))
```

3.4.1   Alternative Class Precedence Lists

Given this new protocol, the user can write code to implement variants of CLOS that
provide the Flavors and Loops inheritance rules. Those rules can be summarized as:

"depth-first, left-to-right, up to joins," with the root class being treated specially. They differ from each other only in whether a class that is encountered more than once—a join class—gets traversed on its first or last visit. The behavior of each language's rules, as well as the difference between them, can be seen in the following example:

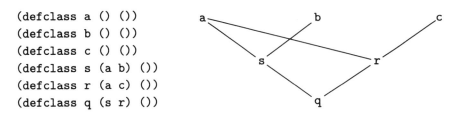

```
(defclass a () ())
(defclass b () ())
(defclass c () ())
(defclass s (a b) ())
(defclass r (a c) ())
(defclass q (s r) ())
```

The class precedence lists for the class q in each of the languages are as follows:

Flavors	(q s a b r c standard-object t)
Loops	(q s b r a c standard-object t)
CLOS	(q s r a c b standard-object t)

The Flavors ordering can be implemented using a depth-first, preorder traversal of the class's superclass graph, removing all but the first occurrence of any class that appears more than once. The root classes, standard-object and t, are not included in the traversal; they must be added to the end of the precedence list explicitly. In the example, the class a appears twice in the the the depth-first, preorder traversal (q s a b r a c), only the first occurrence would be retained. The precedence ordering used by Loops retains the last rather than the first occurrence of any duplicate class.

We can define these alternative precedence rules with two specialized class metaobject classes, flavors-class and loops-class. Methods on compute-class-precedence-list, specialized to each of the classes, actually implement the different rules.

```
(defclass flavors-class (standard-class) ())

(defclass loops-class (standard-class) ())

(defmethod compute-class-precedence-list ((class flavors-class))
  (append (remove-duplicates
            (depth-first-preorder-superclasses* class)
            :from-end t)
          (list (find-class 'standard-object)
                (find-class 't))))
```

```
(defmethod compute-class-precedence-list ((class loops-class))
  (append (remove-duplicates
            (depth-first-preorder-superclasses* class)
            :from-end nil)
          (list (find-class 'standard-object)
                (find-class 't))))

(defun depth-first-preorder-superclasses* (class)
  (if (eq class (find-class 'standard-object))
      ()
      (cons class (mapappend #'depth-first-preorder-superclasses*
                             (class-direct-superclasses class)))))
```

The user could then go on to define a Flavors class as follows:

```
(defclass q-flavors (s r) ()
  (:metaclass flavors-class))
```

Instances of this class can be created in the usual way, with `make-instance`; their slots can be accessed with `slot-value`; and they can be passed to both user and system-defined generic functions. That is, despite the difference in inheritance behavior, this class and its instances interoperate with standard CLOS (and with other language extensions as well).

3.4.2   Summary

We have now presented the framework common to all intercessory metaobject protocols. We critically relied on the main power of object-oriented programming techniques: the ability to organize both the behavior and the implementation of a system in such a way as to enable users to modify and extend it in incremental ways.

In the case of metaobject protocols, the system in question is a programming language. Implementing it using object-oriented techniques allows users to use subclass specialization to create alternative programming languages that better suit their needs. In the case of class precedence lists, for example, we were able, as users of the metaobject protocol, to create two variant languages, one modeled on Flavors, one modeled on Loops. Each retains most of the original CLOS behavior, but provides slightly different multiple inheritance behavior. The effort required to create the new languages was modest, consisting of only a few specialized class and method definitions. The change affects all aspects of the new language's inheritance behavior in predictable and appropriate ways: slot inheritance and method applicability alike.

How can we understand what we have done in terms of our original theatre metaphor? The new kind of metaobject protocol is, like the old, a cleaned up on-backstage. The difference now is that the audience can not only *see* this on-backstage; they can also manipulate it thereby affecting what happens on-stage. Manipulating the on-backstage to change what happens on-stage—producing a variant language—is like making minor changes in the script, the lighting, or the sets.

As before, we have subtly shifted the kind of theatre being produced. It can now be viewed as a participatory theatre in which a few members of the audience are allowed to "go on-backstage," where they can influence the play's outcome. We say a *few* members to reflect the fact that metaobject protocol users typically write only a small amount of code to create a variant language and then write much larger amounts of code in that new language. It is important to stress that the on-backstage is still not the real backstage—members of the audience who get to work with it can only affect the play's outcome within the framework established by the real producers.

Exercise 3.1 In CLOS, all instances of `standard-class` have `standard-object` as a superclass. In this way, `standard-class` and `standard-object` operate in tandem: instances of `standard-class` represent user-defined classes and the class `standard-object` provides default behavior for user-defined classes. In Closette this default superclass is provided during the initialization of the class metaobject—when a class is created with no superclasses, a list consisting of just the class `standard-object` is used.

Often, when defining a specialized class metaobject class, it is convenient to similarly define a specialized default superclass as well. For example, in Flavors, there is a default superclass called `vanilla-flavor`. Our definition of the specialized metaobject class `flavors-class` would be more complete if we also arranged for `vanilla-flavor` to be a default superclass for all instances of `flavors-class`. Show how this extended defaulting behavior can be supported in the same way as the standard defaulting behavior—with a specialized method on `initialize-instance`. (You are free to use an around-method in your solution.)

3.5   Slot Inheritance

Our next example addresses the need some users have for programming language features that are specialized to their particular application domain. Even when most of a user's needs could be met by an existing language, if they are not *all* met, the traditional approach has required building a complete, customized language from scratch. In contrast, providing an appropriate metaobject protocol can make it possible for users to extend an existing language to provide for their special needs.

Knowledge-representation languages such as Strobe [Smith,Barth&Young 87] are an excellent example. They tend to be heavily object-oriented in nature, and in many ways could easily be mapped onto CLOS. But these languages also include certain special features not found in CLOS (or any other common object-oriented programming language). One such feature is the notion of *slot attributes*. Slot attributes (or sub-slots, as they are sometimes called) are named locations, attached to slots, which can be used to store information about the value in the slot.

Given an appropriate metaobject protocol, this feature could easily be implemented as an extension to CLOS. The following class definition is intended to indicate that each instance of the class `credit-rating` is to have a slot named `level` with two independently settable attributes named `date-set` and `time-set`.

```
(defclass credit-rating ()
    ((level :attributes (date-set time-set)))
  (:metaclass attributes-class))
```

Just as (slot-value $\langle x \rangle$ $\langle s \rangle$) accesses the value of the slot named $\langle s \rangle$ of the instance $\langle x \rangle$, (slot-attribute $\langle x \rangle$ $\langle s \rangle$ $\langle a \rangle$) should access the value of the attribute named $\langle a \rangle$ of the slot named $\langle s \rangle$ of the instance $\langle x \rangle$. Unlike slots, attributes will always be bound to some value, initially `nil`.

A sample use of this extension would produce the following behavior:

```
⟹ (setq cr (make-instance 'credit-rating))
⟹ (slot-attribute cr 'level 'date-set)
NIL
⟹ (setf (slot-attribute cr 'level 'date-set) "12/15/90")
⟹ (slot-attribute cr 'level 'date-set)
"12/15/90"
```

Attributes should be inherited in the natural way; in a given class, the set of attributes associated with a slot should be the union of the attributes defined for slots of the same name in the class's superclasses. For example, in the following subclass of `credit-rating`, the slot named `level` would end up with attributes named `date-set`, `time-set`, `last-checked` and `interval`:

```
(defclass monitored-credit-rating (credit-rating)
    ((level :attributes (last-checked interval)))
  (:metaclass attributes-class))
```

The desired extension to CLOS can be divided into three parts. Together with a rough description of the metaobject protocol support required by each, they are:

- Adding the :attributes slot option to defclass. As with other such slot options (e.g., :initform), its value should be stored in the corresponding direct slot definition metaobject so that it can later be accessed. To support this, the metaobject protocol must give the user control over the way in which options from the defclass form are stored, and how those stored values can later be accessed.
- Computing the inheritance of slot attributes. For a given slot in a given class, the full set of attribute names should be stored in the corresponding effective slot definition metaobject. To support this, the metaobject protocol must give the user control over the way same-named direct slot definition metaobjects are coalesced to produce an effective slot definition metaobject.
- Implementing slot-attribute. Extra storage will be needed in each instance to store the values of the slot attributes. To support this, the metaobject protocol must give the user control over the process that decides how much storage to allocate per instance of a class.

3.5.1 Slot Inheritance Protocol

Generally speaking, the second and third parts of this extension require a metaobject protocol that provides the user with control over the way a class determines the set of slots accessible in its instances. The second part requires control over how the same-named slots from the class and its superclasses are combined—the user must be able to add the inheritance of attributes to the normal inheritance behavior. The third part requires control over how the full set of slots that will be accessible are determined—the user can request extra storage simply by adding extra slots.

In our model backstage architecture, these kinds of decisions are made by the function compute-slots (p. 25). Using the class precedence list and the direct slots of each class in it, this function computes the set of effective slot definitions for a class. Because of our previous simplification to the rules of slot inheritance, this function uses a trivial mechanism for combining same-named direct slot definition metaobjects—only the most specific direct slot definition is used. The need for more sophisticated control over this aspect of the slot inheritance process suggests a two-part protocol in which gathering the full set of slots from which to inherit and combining same-named slots are handled separately.

(compute-slots ⟨class⟩) This generic function is called to compute the full set of slots that will be accessible in instances of ⟨class⟩. The result is a set of effective slot definition metaobjects, each with a distinct name. This set is stored and can subsequently be retrieved with the function class-slots. Class slot computations are based solely on the class's class precedence list and the direct slots of each class in that list. At the time `compute-slots` is called, the class precedence list will already have been computed and stored. Methods on `compute-slots` gather together lists of same-named direct slot definition metaobjects from the class and its superclasses, and then call `compute-effective-slot-definition` to coalesce these into a single effective slot definition metaobject.

(`compute-effective-slot-definition` ⟨*class*⟩ ⟨*slots*⟩) This generic function is called to coalesce ⟨*slots*⟩, a non-empty list of direct slot definition metaobjects, each with the same name. The result must be a single effective slot definition metaobject, which will be used for the class metaobject ⟨*class*⟩. The ⟨*class*⟩ argument is typically not consulted in the body of the methods; it is supplied only so that specialized methods can be defined. The direct slot definition metaobjects in the list ⟨*slots*⟩ are arranged with the highest priority slot appearing first—that is, in the same order as their classes of origin appear in the class precedence list.

In addition, we allow the user to call `make-direct-slot-definition` and `make-effective-slot-definition` to create direct and effective slot definition metaobjects.

Closette requires only minor modifications to support this new protocol. The function `compute-slots` is replaced with a generic function. The standard method on the generic function provides the specified behavior, calling `compute-effective-slot-definition`, as required, to combine same-named slots:

```
(defgeneric compute-slots (class))
(defmethod compute-slots ((class standard-class))
  (let* ((all-slots (mapappend #'class-direct-slots
                               (class-precedence-list class)))
         (all-names (remove-duplicates
                      (mapcar #'slot-definition-name all-slots))))
    (mapcar #'(lambda (name)
                (compute-effective-slot-definition
                  class
                  (remove name all-slots
                          :key #'slot-definition-name
                          :test-not #'eq)))
            all-names)))
```

The standard method on `compute-effective-slot-definition` implements the default rules for combining same-named slot definitions. Since the new protocol provides convenient control over the combination of same-named direct slot definitions, we take advantage of this opportunity to introduce the proper inheritance behavior that was left

out in Chapter 1. The initialization form is inherited from the most specific slot that
provides one, and initialization arguments are computed by taking the union over all
slots to be coalesced.

```
(defgeneric compute-effective-slot-definition (class direct-slots))
(defmethod compute-effective-slot-definition ((class standard-class)
                                               direct-slots)
  (let ((initer (find-if-not #'null direct-slots
                             :key #'slot-definition-initfunction)))
    (make-effective-slot-definition
      :name (slot-definition-name (car direct-slots))
      :initform (if initer
                    (slot-definition-initform initer)
                    nil)
      :initfunction (if initer
                        (slot-definition-initfunction initer)
                        nil)
      :initargs (remove-duplicates
                  (mapappend #'slot-definition-initargs
                             direct-slots)))))
```

3.5.2 User Code for the Slot Attributes Extension

We can now present the user code required to implement the slot attributes extension.
For the time being, we are setting aside issues surrounding the extension of defclass.
We simply assume that the :attributes slot option is properly handled, and that its
value is incorporated into the direct slot definition metaobject where it can be accessed
with the function slot-definition-attributes.[3] (We will return to defclass as the
subject of Exercise 3.3.)

As usual, we begin by defining the new class metaobject class:

```
(defclass attributes-class (standard-class) ())
```

The proper inheritance of slot attributes, and the storing of the value in each effective
slot definition metaobject, is provided by a specialized method on compute-effective-
slot-definition.

---

[3]This function can be defined in a manner similar to the other slot definition metaobject accessors (e.g.,
slot-definition-initform *(290)*).

```
(defmethod compute-effective-slot-definition ((class attributes-class)
                                              direct-slots)
  (let ((normal-slot (call-next-method)))
    (setf (slot-definition-attributes normal-slot)
          (remove-duplicates
            (mapappend #'slot-definition-attributes direct-slots)))
    normal-slot))
```

To hold the values of attributes, storage is required in each instance, over and above the storage needed to hold the values of the slots themselves. We do this simply by inventing a single extra slot, which will store attribute values for all the slots. (A doubly-nested alist is used, keyed on the slot and attribute name.) We add the extra slot, named `all-attributes`,[4] and arrange for it to be initialized appropriately with a specialized method on `compute-slots`.

```
(defmethod compute-slots ((class attributes-class))
  (let* ((normal-slots (call-next-method))
         (alist
          (mapcar
            #'(lambda (slot)
                (cons (slot-definition-name slot)
                      (mapcar #'(lambda (attr) (cons attr nil))
                              (slot-definition-attributes slot))))
            normal-slots)))
    (cons (make-effective-slot-definition
            :name 'all-attributes
            :initform '',alist
            :initfunction #'(lambda () alist))
          normal-slots)))))
```

The effect of this method is that every instance of the class `credit-rating` or `monitored-credit-rating` (indeed, every instance of every class whose class is `attributes-class` or a subclass thereof) is created with the extra slot. All that remains to be implemented are the functions that access the attributes:

```
(defun slot-attribute (instance slot-name attribute)
  (cdr (slot-attribute-bucket instance slot-name attribute)))
```

---

[4]We are blithely assuming that this name does not conflict with the names of any real slots. A better approach would be to use the Common Lisp package system to ensure that the name of the slot would be a symbol the user could never use. As a humanitarian gesture, we have spared our readers this confrontation with the package system.

```
(defun (setf slot-attribute) (new-value instance slot-name attribute)
  (setf (cdr (slot-attribute-bucket instance slot-name attribute))
        new-value))
```

The helping function `slot-attribute-bucket` does all the work of finding the appropriate bucket:

```
(defun slot-attribute-bucket (instance slot-name attribute)
  (let* ((all-buckets (slot-value instance 'all-attributes))
         (slot-bucket (assoc slot-name all-buckets)))
    (unless slot-bucket
      (error "The slot named ~S of ~S has no attributes."
             slot-name instance))
    (let ((attr-bucket (assoc attribute (cdr slot-bucket))))
      (unless attr-bucket
        (error "The slot named ~S of ~S has no attribute~@
               named ~S." slot-name instance attribute))
      attr-bucket)))
```

With the user code complete, we can run the example code from page 84. After doing so, examining the extra slot shows the attribute buckets and values.

```
⟹ (slot-value cr 'all-attributes)
((LEVEL . ((DATE-SET . "12/15/90") (TIME-SET . NIL))))
⟹ (slot-value (make-instance 'monitored-credit-rating) 'all-attributes)
((LEVEL . ((LAST-CHECKED . NIL) (INTERVAL . NIL)
           (DATE-SET . NIL) (TIME-SET . NIL))))
```

Exercise 3.2 In the object-oriented languages C++ and Common Objects [Snyder 86], the rules of slot inheritance are markedly different from the ones used in CLOS. These languages are designed to provide strong support for data hiding or *encapsulation*, so they hide a class's slots not only from outside code, but also from its subclasses. A slot defined in a given class can only be accessed *directly* (the analog of calling `slot-value`) from within the body of methods specialized to that class. Methods specialized to subclasses must send a message (the analog of calling a generic function) to access the value of the slot.

The focus of this exercise is an extension to CLOS which supports this behavior. Consider the class definitions:

```
(defclass c1 ()
    ((foo :initform 100))
  (:metaclass encapsulated-class))
(defclass c2 (c1)
    ((foo :initform 200))
  (:metaclass encapsulated-class))
```

The intent is that instances of c2 have two slots named foo. One is private to the class c1 and one is private to the class c2. The function (private-slot-value ⟨instance⟩ ⟨slot-name⟩ ⟨class⟩) is like slot-value except that the ⟨class⟩ argument indicates which class's private slot should be accessed. (To be more true to these kinds of languages, a special mechanism should be provided to make direct access to slots from within the body of a method more convenient. We will return to provide this additional behavior in Section 4.2.3.)

```
(defmethod mumble ((o c1))
  (private-slot-value o 'foo (find-class 'c1)))
(defmethod mumble ((o c2))
  (+ (private-slot-value o 'foo (find-class 'c2))
     (call-next-method)))

⟹ (mumble (make-instance 'c1))
100
⟹ (mumble (make-instance 'c2))
300
```

Implement this extension to CLOS, including the function private-slot-value.

3.6   Other Inheritance Protocols

As another example of the kind of language extension that metaobject protocols can support, consider default initialization arguments, a feature of full CLOS omitted from our initial subset. Default initialization arguments are specified with the :default-initargs option in the defclass form; they provide default arguments to make-instance whenever instances of the class are created.

For example, consider the definition:

```
(defclass frame (rectangle)
    ()
  (:metaclass default-initargs-class)
  (:default-initargs :width 10))
```

If `make-instance` is now called to create an instance of **frame**, and the `:width` initialization is not explicitly provided in the call, the effect should be as if it had been provided, with a value of 10. That is,

```
(make-instance 'frame :height 20)
```

has the same effect as

```
(make-instance 'frame :height 20 :width 10)
```

Default initialization arguments are also inherited in the predictable way; a subclass of **frame** would have its own default initialization arguments as well as those provided by **frame**.

This extension can easily be implemented using the existing metaobject protocol. First, we assume that `defclass` canonicalizes the `:default-initargs` option into the `:direct-default-initargs` option to `ensure-class`. The `defclass` form above expands to:[5]

```
(ensure-class 'frame
  :direct-superclasses (list (find-class 'rectangle))
  :direct-slots ()
  :metaclass (find-class 'default-initargs-class)
  :direct-default-initargs (list ':width '10))
```

The new class metaobject class is defined with a slot, `direct-default-initargs`, which will be used to store the set of default initialization arguments appearing in the `defclass` form; e.g., in the class **frame** the slot has the value (`:width` 10).

```
(defclass default-initargs-class (standard-class)
    ((direct-default-initargs
        :initarg :direct-default-initargs
        :initform ()
        :accessor class-direct-default-initargs)))
```

Computing the full set of default initialization arguments for a class is accomplished by appending together the direct default initialization arguments for each class in the class

---

[5]As implemented here, default initialization argument forms are not evaluated. In full CLOS, they are—in the dynamic environment of the call to `make-instance`, and the lexical environment of the `defclass` form. Implementing the full CLOS behavior can be done in a manner similar to what is shown here, using the same metaobject protocol in essentially the same way. The differences are simply ones of complexity in the user code. The same is true of the refinement discussed in the next section that improves the efficiency of the default initialization arguments extension.

precedence list. Because not all of the classes in the class precedence list will be instances
of `default-initargs-class` (e.g., `standard-object` and `t`) we define an extra method
on `class-direct-default-initargs` to return the empty list for other classes.

```
(defun compute-class-default-initargs (class)
  (mapappend #'class-direct-default-initargs
             (class-precedence-list class)))6

(defmethod class-direct-default-initargs ((class standard-class))
  ())
```

Finally, `make-instance` must be extended so that it supplements the explicitly supplied initialization arguments with the default ones.

```
(defmethod make-instance ((class default-initargs-class) &rest initargs)
  (apply #'call-next-method
         class
         (append initargs
                 (compute-class-default-initargs class))))
```

Testing confirms the correct behavior.

```
⟹ (setq f (make-instance 'frame :height 20))
⟹ (slot-value f 'height)
20
⟹ (slot-value f 'width)
10
```

3.6.1   Precomputing Default Initialization Arguments

This user extension to support default initialization arguments has the desired behavior,
but is relatively inefficient. The source of the inefficiency is the needless duplication,
on each call to `make-instance`, of the computation of default initialization arguments.
Since classes and their default initialization arguments cannot be redefined, the default
initialization arguments could be computed just once and then stored with the class
metaobject for subsequent use by `make-instance`.

The precomputation of default initialization arguments is an inheritance-related activity similar to the class precedence list and slot computations. It is sufficiently different,

---

[6]In Common Lisp, it is permissible for initialization arguments to be duplicated. The first, or leftmost,
occurrence takes precedence over all the others. Together, this definition, and the following specialized method
on `make-instance`, rely on this property.

however, that neither of those existing protocols is particularly appropriate. For one thing, the class precedence list needs to be computed and stored before the default initialization arguments can be computed.

This suggests that we need to provide the user with a more general purpose protocol for handling inheritance activities. The clear suggestion from Closette is to make **finalize-inheritance** a generic function that is the focus for all inheritance-related computations for the class.

This requires another simple modification to Closette, the conversion of **finalize-inheritance** from a function to a generic function. The body of the standard method is the same as in the original function definition (p. 23).

```
(defgeneric finalize-inheritance (class))
(defmethod finalize-inheritance ((class standard-class))
  (setf (class-precedence-list class)
        (compute-class-precedence-list class))
  (setf (class-slots class)
        (compute-slots class))
  (values))
```

Notice that the role of the standard method is to modify the class metaobject in important ways. This means that we must be sure that specialized methods do not prevent the standard method from running. For example, if a specialized primary method failed to call **call-next-method**, the class precedence list and the full list of slots would not be computed and stored. (We will return to this issue in greater detail in Chapter 4.) The appropriate specification for this generic function is then:

(finalize-inheritance ⟨*class*⟩) This generic function is called to compute and record all inheritance-related information associated with the class metaobject ⟨*class*⟩. The value returned is unspecified. It is guaranteed that after the standard method runs the class's class precedence list and set of slots will be available. The standard method, which is specialized to **standard-class**, *cannot* be overridden.

With this new protocol in place, the user implementation of default initialization arguments can be made more efficient. First, we replace the earlier definition of **default-initargs-class** (p. 91) with one that defines an additional slot to hold the precomputed default initialization arguments:

```
(defclass default-initargs-class (standard-class)
    ((direct-default-initargs
        :initarg :direct-default-initargs
        :initform ()
        :accessor class-direct-default-initargs)
     (effective-default-initargs
        :accessor class-default-initargs)))
```

This new slot is filled in after the class metaobject has been otherwise finalized.

```
(defmethod finalize-inheritance :after ((class default-initargs-class))
    (setf (class-default-initargs class)
          (compute-class-default-initargs class)))
```

Finally, the specialized `make-instance` method (p. 92) is replaced with one that calls `class-default-initargs` to retrieve the precomputed list instead of calling `compute-class-default-initargs` to compute them.

```
(defmethod make-instance ((class default-initargs-class) &rest initargs)
    (apply #'call-next-method
           class
           (append initargs (class-default-initargs class))))
```

Exercise 3.3 We have now seen two examples (slot attributes and default initialization arguments) in which we have had to assume the existence of an appropriate extension to the behavior of `defclass`. This suggests that our metaobject protocol should include a mechanism for extending the behavior of `defclass`.

One approach to this problem is to put the expansion of `defclass` under the control of generic functions operating on class metaobjects. The framework of such a protocol can be seen in the following revised definition of `defclass`:

```
(defmacro defclass (name direct-superclasses direct-slots &rest options)
  (let* ((metaclass-option
           (find ':metaclass options :key #'car))
         (metaclass-name (if metaclass-option
                             (cadr metaclass-option)
                             'standard-class))
         (sample-class-metaobject
           (allocate-instance (find-class metaclass-name)))
         (canonical-supers
           (canonicalize-direct-superclasses direct-superclasses))
         (canonical-slots
           (canonicalize-direct-slots direct-slots))
         (canonical-options
           (canonicalize-defclass-options
             sample-class-metaobject
             (remove metaclass-option options))))
    '(ensure-class ',name
       :direct-superclasses ,canonical-supers
       :direct-slots ,canonical-slots
       :metaclass (find-class ',metaclass-name)
       ,@canonical-options)))

(defun canonicalize-defclass-options (sample-class options)
  (mapappend #'(lambda (option)
                 (canonicalize-defclass-option sample-class option))
             options))

(defgeneric canonicalize-defclass-option (sample-class option))
(defmethod canonicalize-defclass-option
           ((sample-class standard-class) option)
  (error "Unrecognized defclass option ~S." (car option)))
```

The generic function `canonicalize-defclass-option` is called to canonicalize each individual option. Because it receives a sample instance of the class metaobject class as its first argument, specialized methods can be defined to handle extended options. Since the `:metaclass` option is now handled specially, the standard method supports no options.

Show the specialized method the user would write, as part of the default initialization arguments extension, to support the `:default-initargs` option. Note that in order to experiment with this exercise in Closette, you will want to give the new macro an alternate name (e.g., `defclass*`).

3.7   Slot Access

In an object-oriented language like CLOS, some kinds of user extensions will require protocols that control low-level slot access. For example, such a protocol is required to write an extension that records all accesses to the slots of an instance. In this section, we develop metaobject protocols for controlling slot access.

The lowest level slot access operations are the functions `slot-value`, `(setf slot-value)`, `slot-boundp` and `slot-makunbound`. To design an appropriate protocol for controlling these operations, we first consult Closette to understand the relevant underlying architecture. The implementation of each operation is similar, and involves the class metaobject, the instance itself, and the slot name. (The definition of `slot-value` can be found on page 29.) First the class of the object is consulted to determine whether the slot exists and what its location is; then the slot is fetched out of the instance.

We can design a simple protocol for these operations by placing each under the direct control of a generic function. For example, the protocol for controlling `slot-value` is:

(`slot-value-using-class` ⟨*class*⟩ ⟨*instance*⟩ ⟨*slot-name*⟩) This generic function provides the behavior of the function `slot-value`. When `slot-value` is called, it calls this generic function; ⟨*instance*⟩ and ⟨*slot-name*⟩ are the arguments to `slot-value`. ⟨*class*⟩ is the class of ⟨*instance*⟩. The value returned by this generic function is returned by `slot-value`. The standard method can be overridden.

Modifying Closette to support this new protocol requires redefining `slot-value` to call `slot-value-using-class`. The body of the standard method is unchanged from the original definition of `slot-value`.

```
(defun slot-value (instance slot-name)
  (slot-value-using-class (class-of instance)
                          instance
                          slot-name)))
(defgeneric slot-value-using-class (class instance slot-name))
```

```
(defmethod slot-value-using-class ((class standard-class)
                                   instance
                                   slot-name)
  (let* ((location (slot-location class slot-name))
         (local-slots (std-instance-local-slots instance))
         (val (slot-contents local-slots location)))
    (if (eq secret-unbound-value val)
        (error "The slot ~S is unbound in the object ~S."
               slot-name instance)
        val)))
```

The modifications for (setf slot-value), slot-boundp and slot-makunbound are similar.

3.7.1   Monitoring Slot Access

Using this last protocol, the user can easily define an extension which records all slot accesses.

```
(defclass monitored-class (standard-class) ())
```

A before-method on each slot access generic function records the accesses.

```
(defmethod slot-value-using-class :before
           ((class monitored-class) instance slot-name)
  (note-operation instance slot-name 'slot-value))

(defmethod (setf slot-value-using-class) :before
           (new-value (class monitored-class)
            instance slot-name)
  (note-operation instance slot-name 'set-slot-value))

(defmethod slot-boundp-using-class :before
           ((class monitored-class) instance slot-name)
  (note-operation instance slot-name 'slot-boundp))

(defmethod slot-makunbound-using-class :before
           ((class monitored-class) instance slot-name)
  (note-operation instance slot-name 'slot-makunbound))
```

The functions that manipulate access history are as follows:

```
(let ((history-list ()))

  (defun note-operation (instance slot-name operation)
    (push '(,operation ,instance ,slot-name) history-list)
    (values))

  (defun reset-slot-access-history ()
    (setq history-list ())
    (values))

  (defun slot-access-history ()
    (reverse history-list))
  )
```

Testing of slot monitoring confirms that it behaves as desired.

```
(defclass foo ()
    ((slot1 :accessor foo-slot1 :initarg :slot1)
     (slot2 :accessor foo-slot2 :initform 200))
  (:metaclass monitored-class))

⟹ (reset-slot-access-history)
⟹ (setq i (make-instance 'foo :slot1 100))
#<FOO 381312>
⟹ (setf (slot-value i 'slot1) (foo-slot2 i))
200
⟹ (incf (foo-slot1 i))
201

⟹ (slot-access-history)
((SET-SLOT-VALUE #<FOO 381312> SLOT1)      ;From initialization
 (SLOT-BOUNDP #<FOO 381312> SLOT2)         ;From initialization
 (SET-SLOT-VALUE #<FOO 381312> SLOT2)      ;From initialization
 (SLOT-VALUE #<FOO 381312> SLOT2)          ;From foo-slot2
 (SET-SLOT-VALUE #<FOO 381312> SLOT1)      ;From setf
 (SLOT-VALUE #<FOO 381312> SLOT1)          ;From incf foo-slot1
 (SET-SLOT-VALUE #<FOO 381312> SLOT1))     ;From incf foo-slot1
```

3.8   Instance Allocation

Finally, we look at an example in which the user's need is not to change the behavior of the language, but rather to adjust the implementation tradeoffs for application-specific performance reasons. Imagine a situation in which the user defines a class with a large number of slots (several hundred or even a thousand). Further imagine that the typical usage pattern of this class is that there are a large number of instances, but in any given instance only a small number of the slots are actually used. In this scenario, the implementation strategy we have chosen in Closette—in which storage is allocated for every slot as soon as the instance is created—is inappropriate. It will cause a great deal of needless storage to be allocated, and may well lead to paging and other virtual memory problems.

This pattern of class definition and instance usage is common in knowledge representation applications, and languages tailored to these applications typically provide *dynamic* slots to handle it. Storage for a dynamic slot is not actually allocated until the first time the slot is used. Access to these slots tends to be somewhat slower because of the more complex scheme required to find the storage.

We can easily envision dynamic slots as an extension to CLOS. For simplicity, we will work with an extension in which all the slots of a given class are dynamic (Exercise 3.4 explores a more selective variant).

```
(defclass biggy ()
      (a1 b1 c1 d1 e1 f1 g1 h1 i1 j1 k1 l1 m1
       n1 o1 p1 q1 r1 s1 t1 u1 v1 w1 x1 y1 z1
       a2 b2 c2 d2 e2 f2 g2 h2 i2 j2 k2 l2 m2
       n2 o2 p2 q2 r2 s2 t2 u2 v2 w2 x2 y2 z2
       a3 b3 c3 d3 e3 f3 g3 h3 i3 j3 k3 l3 m3
       n3 o3 p3 q3 r3 s3 t3 u3 v3 w3 x3 y3 z3
       a4 b4 c4 d4 e4 f4 g4 h4 i4 j4 k4 l4 m4
       n4 o4 p4 q4 r4 s4 t4 u4 v4))
   (:metaclass dynamic-slot-class))
```

With the existing protocol, the user could try to implement dynamic slots by defining a specialized method on `compute-slots` that simply ignores all the slots of the class, choosing instead to return only a single slot. This single slot would be used for a sparse structure containing the values of all the other slots. Specialized methods on `slot-value-using-class` et al. would be defined to access this sparse structure. From the point of view of the function `allocate-instance` it would appear that instances of the class **biggy** have one slot rather than 100, so the instances would be smaller in the way we desire.

Unfortunately, this approach does not work properly. The problem is that it violates an important consistency constraint between two parts of the protocol: **compute-slots** now claims that instances have only a single slot, while **slot-value** et al. recognize all the original slot names as well. The fact is that many different parts of the implementation use the result of **compute-slots** (which they access via **class-slots**) to find out what slots a class has. Besides **allocate-instance**, these include: **shared-initialize**, to determine how to initialize or reinitialize the instance; and **change-class**, to identify which slot values are to be carried over to the new instance. If the user defines methods which present inconsistent views of a class's slots, these other language operations will no longer behave appropriately.

If we want the user to be able to control the way slots are stored, a more direct protocol is required. Consulting the model backstage architecture, we can see that there are actually two slot-like concepts. The first is the on-stage slots themselves and the second is the backstage slot storage. The correspondence between these two layers is maintained by the slot access generic functions and the backstage function **allocate-instance**.

Providing the user with control over this correspondence must be done carefully. We are working at a very low level, and we must be careful not to overly constrain the implementor by documenting arbitrary implementation details. In particular, it would not be appropriate to document the low-level representation of instances and slot storage (**std-instance-slots**, **slot-contents** etc.) as part of the protocol.

The solution we will use is to design the protocol so that the user can, on a per-slot basis, disable the implementation's slot storage mechanism. Once this is done, the storage for the slot can be implemented in whatever way is appropriate. This allows the user to control slot storage without having to know the details of the implementation's storage strategy.

We will do this by adding a new property to direct and effective slot definitions, called **:allocation**, which indicates how storage for the slot is handled. The default value of this property is **:instance**, which causes the standard methods on **allocate-instance**, **slot-value-using-class** et al. to treat the slot in the usual way. Any other value causes these methods to ignore the slot, allowing specialized methods to handle it instead. This property is carried over from direct to effective slot definitions, with the most specific direct slot's allocation prevailing.

(**allocate-instance** ⟨*class*⟩) This generic function is called to allocate a new instance of the class metaobject ⟨*class*⟩. The result returned is the new instance. For each slot in the class, **slot-definition-allocation** is called to determine how its storage

should be allocated. The standard method on `allocate-instance` will only allocate
storage for slots with `:instance` allocation; all other allocations are ignored. The
standard method cannot be overridden.

(`slot-definition-allocation` ⟨*slot-definition*⟩) This function is called to return the
allocation of a slot. The default value is `:instance`.

We also need to revise the specification of `slot-value-using-class` et al. If the
standard method of these generic functions is run, and the allocation of the slot is not
`:instance`, an error is signaled. A specialized method must handle these slots first, and
not invoke `call-next-method`.

Again, the changes to Closette are minor. The function `allocate-instance` (p. 28)
becomes a generic function. The standard method allocates storage only for those slots
with `:instance` allocation. The appropriate behavior for `slot-value-using-class` et
al. can be achieved simply by modifying the internal function `slot-location`.

```
(defgeneric allocate-instance (class))
(defmethod allocate-instance ((class standard-class))
  (allocate-std-instance
    class
    (allocate-slot-storage (count-if #'instance-slot-p
                                     (class-slots class))
                           secret-unbound-value)))

(defun slot-location (class slot-name)
  (let ((slot (find slot-name
                    (class-slots class)
                    :key #'slot-definition-name)))
    (if (null slot)
        (error "The slot ~S is missing from the class ~S."
               slot-name class)
        (let ((pos (position slot
                             (remove-if-not #'instance-slot-p
                                            (class-slots class)))))
          (if (null pos)
              (error "The slot ~S is not an instance~@
                      slot in the class ~S."
                     slot-name class)
              pos)))))
```

```
(defun instance-slot-p (slot)
  (eq (slot-definition-allocation slot) ':instance))
```

Returning to the dynamic slot example, the user code can now be written properly. The standard storage allocation can be completely overridden; storage for the slots can be allocated, as it is needed, in a table external to the instance.

Setting the allocation of each effective slot definition to :dynamic causes the standard method on allocate-instance not to allocate storage for any slots, resulting in instances that are as small as possible. The actual slot values are stored in a table external to the instance. Specialized methods on the slot access generic functions access the values from the table.

```
(defclass dynamic-slot-class (standard-class) ())
```

A specialized method on compute-effective-slot-definition marks all the slots.

```
(defmethod compute-effective-slot-definition
            ((class dynamic-slot-class) direct-slots)
  (let ((slot (call-next-method)))
    (setf (slot-definition-allocation slot) ':dynamic)
    slot))

(defun dynamic-slot-p (slot)
  (eq (slot-definition-allocation slot) ':dynamic))
```

When an instance is created, storage needs to be allocated in the external table; this is done by a specialized method on allocate-instance.

```
(defmethod allocate-instance ((class dynamic-slot-class))
  (let ((instance (call-next-method)))
    (allocate-table-entry instance)
    instance))
```

Methods must also be defined on the various slot access generic functions. If the slot does not exist, call-next-method is used to invoke the standard method and thereby the standard behavior for signaling that the slot is missing. (Only slot-value-using-class is shown; the other methods are similar.)

```
(defmethod slot-value-using-class ((class dynamic-slot-class)
                                    instance slot-name)
  (let ((slot (find slot-name (class-slots class)
                    :key #'slot-definition-name)))
    (if slot
        (read-dynamic-slot-value instance slot-name)
        (call-next-method)))))
```

The dynamic slot value table can be implemented in any number of ways; the scheme shown here is a hash table keyed on the instance. The table entries are sparse alists of slot values keyed on slot name; unbound slots are not explicitly represented.[7]

```
(let ((table (make-hash-table :test #'eq)))

  (defun allocate-table-entry (instance)
    (setf (gethash instance table) ()))

  (defun read-dynamic-slot-value (instance slot-name)
    (let* ((alist (gethash instance table))
           (entry (assoc slot-name alist)))
      (if (null entry)
          (error "The slot ~S is unbound in the object ~S."
                 slot-name instance))
      (cdr entry)))

  (defun write-dynamic-slot-value (new-value instance slot-name)
    (let* ((alist (gethash instance table))
           (entry (assoc slot-name alist)))
      (if (null entry)
          (push '(,slot-name . ,new-value)
                (gethash instance table))
          (setf (cdr entry) new-value))
      new-value))
```

---

[7]One problem with this scheme is that it can prevent the garbage collection of instances since the table will contain pointers to all such instances. Many modern Common Lisp implementations provide "weak pointers" or other facilities which can be used to address this problem.

```
(defun dynamic-slot-boundp (instance slot-name)
  (let* ((alist (gethash instance table))
         (entry (assoc slot-name alist)))
    (not (null entry))))

(defun dynamic-slot-makunbound (instance slot-name)
  (let* ((alist (gethash instance table))
         (entry (assoc slot-name alist)))
    (unless (null entry)
      (setf (gethash instance table)
            (delete entry alist)))))
  instance)
)
```

In essence, this extension has usurped the standard slot allocation behavior, and moved slot storage outside of the instances. A similar approach was used in [Paepcke 90] to extend CLOS to store instances in an object-oriented database.

Exercise 3.4 As implemented, `dynamic-slot-class` marks all of its slots as being dynamic. In some situations, this extension would be more useful if it were possible to mark only selected slots as dynamic.

Modify the implementation of `dynamic-slot-class` so that dynamic allocation can be selected on a per-slot basis. For example, in the definition

```
(defclass movable-rectangle (rectangle)
    ((previous-height :allocation :dynamic)
     (previous-width :allocation :dynamic))
  (:metaclass dynamic-slot-class))
```

the class has four slots: `height`, `width`, `previous-height` and `previous-width`. The first should have `:instance` allocation and the last two, which presumably would be used in only a small number of instances, should have `:dynamic` allocation.

Assume that `defclass` handles the `:allocation` option, and provides a default value for it when it is not provided.

Exercise 3.5 Another feature of full CLOS which was left out of our subset is the ability to define slots which are shared across all the instances of a given class. With a class slot, a call to slot-value on any instance of the class reads the same location. If the value is changed via one instance, all instances see the new value. For example:

```
(defclass labeled-rectangle (rectangle)
    ((font :initform 'old-english-12
           :allocation :class))
  (:metaclass class-slot-class))

(setq lr1 (make-instance 'labeled-rectangle))
(setq lr2 (make-instance 'labeled-rectangle))

⟹ (slot-value lr1 'font)
OLD-ENGLISH-12
⟹ (setf (slot-value lr1 'font) 'times-roman-10)
TIMES-ROMAN-10
⟹ (slot-value 'lr2 'font)
TIMES-ROMAN-10
```

Implement a new class metaobject class, class-slot-class, which supports this behavior. Note that the initialization form of a class slot should be evaluated at the time the class is defined.

Suppose a user wanted both class and dynamic slots together. One appealing way to define this behavior would be as a subclass of both dynamic-slot-class and class-slot-class. For example:

```
(defclass both-slots-class (dynamic-slot-class class-slot-class)
    ())
```

Does this produce the desired behavior? If so, why? If not, why not?

3.9   Summary

The evolving metaobject protocol is an object-oriented implementation of the CLOS language. This makes it possible to use specialization to define variant languages with different behavior or implementation characteristics. By providing users with a metaobject protocol we are, in effect, giving them not just the single point in language design space represented by the standard language, but also a surrounding region of language design space. By selecting other points in the region, users can obtain compatibility with other languages, add special features, or tune performance characteristics to meet their needs.

As with all other language design, there are a number of basic criteria that govern metaobject protocol design. We can see now what these are, and how our approach meets them.

- *Portability* stems from the fact that the metaobject protocols have been designed and documented in a way that allows it to be supported by all implementations of the language. When the user creates a language extension, they do so without resorting to implementation-specific details or hooks.
- Object-oriented techniques provide two kinds of *control* over the effect of any user extension:
  - *Scope* control is made possible by representing the program as a network of meta-objects, and arranging for the behavior of a metaobject to depend on its class. Non-standard behavior can be selected in a user-defined class like `rectangle` without affecting system-defined classes such as `standard-object`. Moreover, different parts of the user's program can use different language extensions.
  - *Operation* control refers to the way in which, when defining an extension, it is possible to adjust the behavior of some operations without affecting the behavior of others. For example, it is possible to change the inheritance rules without affecting slot access behavior.
- Together, operation and scope control mean that conceptually orthogonal language extensions can be naturally *composed*. For example, we can define a class that both supports dynamic slots and uses the Flavors inheritance rules by defining a new class metaobject class that is a subclass of the two classes that implement those two behaviors.
- Language extensions defined by the user *interoperate* with each other and with the standard language. In essence, this interoperability stems from our decision to limit extensibility to a delineated sub-region rather than to the whole of language design space. All the languages within the region share the same basic concepts, differing only in how those concepts are interpreted. For example, any CLOS extension supports a basic notion of slots, although the inheritance rules, storage allocation, and other aspects of the slots may vary.
- *Efficiency* is a topic about which we will say more in the next chapter, but already we can see how it stems from operation control and careful protocol design. For example, in the class precedence list case, we balanced the protocol so that it gave users the power they needed while still providing the implementor with basic guarantees on the behavior of any language extension. This allows the implementor to use memoization and other optimization techniques not only for the standard language, but also for any user-defined extensions.

4 Protocol Design

In practice, designing metaobject protocols is more difficult than the previous chapters might suggest. Developing a protocol that is simultaneously powerful, easy to use, and efficient involves a number of issues that have not yet been considered. These issues— many of which are common to all object-oriented protocol design—are the focus of this chapter. We will illustrate some common protocol design techniques, and also point out common pitfalls.

This chapter continues the evolutionary approach and the use of a staged sequence of examples. But now, given that the basic structure of metaobject protocols has been established, the approach will shift somewhat. We will start by sketching a simple meta-object protocol for controlling the behavior of generic functions and methods. This initial protocol, however, will suffer from a number of problems. We will use the example-driven approach to expose these problems, to discuss the underlying issues of metaobject protocol design, and to incrementally improve the protocol.

4.1 A Simple Generic Function Invocation Protocol

The metaobject protocols to be developed in this chapter will operate on generic function and method metaobjects. As with the class-based protocols of the last chapter, users will need to be able to control the class of the generic function and method metaobjects used to represent their programs. An extension to `defgeneric`, similar to the `:metaclass` option previously added to `defclass`, makes this convenient. The form

```
(defgeneric paint (x)
  (:generic-function-class specialized-generic-function)
  (:method-class specialized-method))
```

now specifies that the class of the `paint` generic function metaobject should be `specialized-generic-function` and that when `defmethod` is used to define methods on this generic function, the resulting method metaobjects should be instances of `specialized-method`.

To support this, `defgeneric` must pass all the options it receives on to `ensure-generic-function`; for example, the expansion of the above form is:

```
(ensure-generic-function 'paint
  :lambda-list '(x)
  :generic-function-class (find-class 'specialized-generic-function)
  :method-class (find-class 'specialized-method))
```

After providing reasonable default values for the :generic-function-class and :method-class options, ensure-generic-function makes an instance of the specified class. All the options are passed along as initialization arguments. Initialization of the generic function records the value of the :method-class option; it can be accessed later with generic-function-method-class. (These minor changes are reflected by the implementation in Appendix D.)

4.1.1 Generic Function Invocation

In Chapter 2 we developed metaobject protocols that make it possible for users to write tools that analyze the static structure of their program. But often, tools are required to analyze the program's dynamic behavior as well. Consider a simple performance analysis in which we search for parts of the program where performance is critical by counting how often specific generic functions and methods are called.

In Closette, the relevant backstage architecture is modeled by these five functions (indentation reflects the calling relationship from main to subfunctions):

```
apply-generic-function
    compute-applicable-methods-using-classes
        method-more-specific-p
    apply-methods
        apply-method
```

The events we would like to count correspond directly to apply-generic-function and apply-method. By making these functions generic, we can give the user the functionality required to support the counting behavior.

(apply-generic-function ⟨gf⟩ ⟨args⟩) Applies a generic function to arguments.
(apply-method ⟨method⟩ ⟨args⟩ ⟨next-methods⟩) Applies a method to arguments and a list of next methods.

The changes to Closette are minor. The code in the bodies of the two new standard methods (i.e., the methods specialized to standard-generic-function and standard-method) is unchanged from the code in the bodies of the original definitions of apply-generic-function and apply-method (pages 40 and 44, respectively).

4.1.2 Example: Counting Invocations

Given this new metaobject protocol, the user code for counting generic function calls is straightforward. A specialized generic function class and a specialized method on apply-generic-function are all that is required:

```
(defclass counting-gf (standard-generic-function)
    ((call-count :initform 0 :accessor call-count)))

(defmethod apply-generic-function :before
          ((gf counting-gf) args)
  (incf (call-count gf)))
```

Counting method calls is done similarly:

```
(defclass counting-method (standard-method)
    ((call-count :initform 0 :accessor call-count)))

(defmethod apply-method :before
          ((method counting-method) args next-methods)
  (incf (call-count method)))
```

The behavior of this extension can be seen in the following example:

```
(defgeneric ack (x)
  (:generic-function-class counting-gf)
  (:method-class counting-method))
(defmethod ack :before ((x standard-object)) nil)
(defmethod ack (x) t)

⟹ (ack (make-instance 'standard-object))
T
⟹ (ack 1)
T
⟹ (call-count #'ack)
2
⟹ (mapcar #'(lambda (method)
                (list (generate-defmethod method)
                      (call-count method)))
          (generic-function-methods #'ack))
(((DEFMETHOD ACK :BEFORE ((X STANDARD-OBJECT))) 1)
 ((DEFMETHOD ACK (X)) 2))
```

Exercise 4.1 Show how the same basic approach can be used to make generic functions that can be traced. For example,

```
(defgeneric foo (...)
  (:generic-function-class traceable-gf))
```

should indicate that `foo` is traceable, and

```
(trace-generic-function 'foo t)
```

should turn tracing on. Subsequent calls to `foo` should cause information about the call—the arguments passed and the eventual return value—to be printed to the stream `*trace-output*`. The tracing should be turned off by:

```
(trace-generic-function 'foo nil)
```

4.2   Functional and Procedural Protocols

The approach to counting invocations illustrated above is more convenient than the traditional scheme of adding extra statements to method bodies. This is an example of how, by providing a second organizational structure through which to affect the behavior of the program, the metaobject protocol makes it possible to say in one place what would otherwise have to be spread out among a number of places.

Because these counters are intended to paint an accurate picture of the dynamic characteristics of the program, we must pay careful attention to the specification of **apply-generic-function** and **apply-method**. In particular, in order to guarantee that the example code accurately counts the number of times a generic function has been called, it is essential that the protocol specification stipulate that **apply-generic-function** be called *each and every time* a generic function is invoked. Similar considerations apply to **apply-method** and method invocation.

Notice, however, that this requirement contrasts with a property that some of the protocols developed in the last chapter were designed to allow, namely memoizability. For example, **compute-class-precedence-list** was expressly designed so that it would *not* be necessary to call it every time a class's precedence list was needed; instead, the user was told that this generic function would be consulted only the *first* time a class's class precedence list was needed. Each subsequent time, the initial value would be reused.

We can make sense of this disparity by distinguishing between *procedural* and *functional* protocols.

In a functional protocol, such as **compute-class-precedence-list** and **compute-slots**, a function is called to compute a result, which is then used by other parts of the system to produce the intended behavior. Calling a functional protocol, in other words, can affect the overall behavior of a system, but it does not produce that behavior directly. Rather, it produces a result that is in turn used by other parts of the system, to produce the intended behavior, at appropriate times, and in appropriate places.

This aspect of functional protocols allows us to place two useful limits on their expressive power. First, because the effect is only made visible through the mediation of other parts of the system, the power is inherently limited by the behavioral repertoire of the clients of the result in question. Second, the specification of functional protocols can impose additional constraints on the result. For example, we placed such limitations on the results of `compute-class-precedence-list`, so as to be able to assure its clients of the persistence of certain basic properties. Furthermore, because these restrictions have the effect of limiting the context on which functional protocols can depend, they guarantee that the results can be memoized. The implementor can easily arrange to monitor those limited parts of the context that might invalidate any results that have previously been cached.

Procedural protocols, on the other hand, such as `finalize-inheritance`, `slot-value-using-class`, and, of course, `apply-generic-function` and `apply-method`, are called to perform some action—that is, to directly produce some part of the total system behavior. As a result, the specification of a procedural protocol tends to place fewer restrictions on the activity of the function, but more restrictions on exactly when it is called.

Because the effect of a procedural protocol is direct, and is expressed procedurally, such protocols tend to put more power in the hands of the user. By the same token, however, their results cannot generally be memoized. In general this makes sense, since causing behavior, not producing an answer, is a procedural protocol's primary purpose. In Section 4.4, however, we will see a way to separate the direct effect and procedural expressiveness of such protocols, which will allow us to develop a third kind of protocol, essentially a partially memoizable procedural protocol, which will be appropriate in certain specialized situations.

4.2.1 Documenting Generic Functions vs Methods

A general issue in the design of object-oriented protocols is whether the specification should be phrased in terms of restrictions on the behavior of generic functions or on the behavior of their standard methods. The specification of a generic function governs all its methods, system and user-defined alike. The specification of a standard method does not restrict user-defined methods on the generic function. There are times and places for both.

For example, the specification of `apply-generic-function` states that all ensuing explicit method invocations use `apply-method` (our call counting example depends on this). Since this constraint applies to the generic function as a whole, user-supplied methods must also obey it even when it might be more convenient not to. This means that user code that relies on `apply-method` (such as call counting) can be combined with user code that specializes `apply-generic-function` and still work properly.

On the other hand, constraints placed by the protocol specification on standard methods are weaker, but nevertheless useful. For example, the specification for the standard method for `slot-value-using-class` states that an error is signaled if the slot is currently unbound. Because this constraint does not apply to the generic function as a whole, the user is free to write specialized methods for `slot-value-using-class` that take some sort of corrective action when an unbound slot is accessed.

Knowing the behavior of the standard method amounts to knowing the unspecialized behavior of the generic function. This is the behavior not only of standard metaobjects, but also specialized metaobjects for which this generic function has not been specialized. It is also the behavior produced by `call-next-method` when it is used to invoke the standard method.

4.2.2 Overriding the Standard Method

The before- and after-methods of CLOS are especially well-suited to constructing specializable procedural protocols, because they allow easy placement of additional activities before or after the activity of the primary method. However, because neither before- nor after-methods have any say in what other methods run, and because neither can inspect or affect the result returned by the primary method, they can only be used to *supplement* the behavior of the standard method. If it is necessary to *override* the behavior of the standard primary method, a specialized primary method must be used.

As an example of a primary method overriding a standard method, consider the following optimistic technique for streamlining generic function invocation. We will assume that the generic function is always called with valid arguments, that is, there is always an applicable method. This means that if the generic function has only a single primary method, the method lookup process can be elided—the single method can always be used. A similar, but somewhat more robust technique can be used to produce a CLOS delivery compiler, that is, a compiler which assumes that the program is no longer going to change and so precomputes method lookups wherever possible.

The following class and method definitions implement this "trusting" behavior:

```
(defclass trusting-gf (standard-generic-function) ())
```

```
(defmethod apply-generic-function ((gf trusting-gf) args)
  (let ((methods (generic-function-methods gf)))
    (if (and (= (length methods) 1)
             (primary-method-p (car methods)))
        (apply-method (car methods) args ())
        (call-next-method)))))
```

Notice that this code does not require trusting generic functions to have only a single primary method; instead, it merely tests for that special case and relies on `call-next-method` to take care of more complex cases. Moreover, even in the special case, the replacement activity still obeys the general constraint that each and every method invocation uses `apply-method`. We can combine our previous counting code with the new trusting lookup code and obtain a class of generic function with both behaviors:

```
(defclass trusting-counting-gf (trusting-gf counting-gf) ())
```

This example raises a question however: when should a protocol allow methods—the standard method in particular—to be overridden by more specialized methods, and under what circumstances should overriding be prohibited?

When allowing users to override the standard method, we must be sure that they will be able to write their method so as to properly fulfill the restrictions on the generic function as a whole. In the above example, the restrictions on `apply-generic-function` are simple enough that the user code was easy to write—this is an example where it seems reasonable to allow specialized methods to override the standard method.

But there are situations in which it is not appropriate to document the standard method in sufficient sufficient detail for the user to be able to properly override it. For example, the standard method for `finalize-inheritance` shouldn't be overridden, since in order to leave the implementor room to perform other operations when a class is finalized, the activities it carries out are only partially specified. If a specialized method could legally prevent the standard method from running, then the standard method would not be a suitable place for the implementation to place operations that need to be carried out whenever the generic function is called.

Notice that prohibiting the overriding of the standard method effectively prohibits all method overriding, since each specialized primary method is required to invoke `call-next-method`. Prohibiting overriding thus guarantees that each and every applicable primary method will be run each time the generic function is called.[1]

---

[1] CLOS's method combination facility provides a powerful mechanism for simplifying the documentation of this sort of protocol. An appropriate method combination can be used to regulate the interaction between user

4.2.3   Example: Encapsulated Methods

This example extends encapsulated classes, which we saw earlier in Exercise 3.2, to be
more compatible with Common Objects. Encapsulated classes provide a way to define
slots that are proprietary to a class; different classes in the inheritance hierarchy can have
slots of the same name without those slots being coalesced. In our original example, the
proprietary nature of the slots was reflected in the fact that access to the slot required
not just the name of the slot but also the identity of the class to which it belongs.

But in languages which use encapsulated classes, it is common to enforce the proprietary nature of private slots by requiring that access be made only from within the body
of methods defined on their class. An *encapsulated method* is one that provides this
access mechanism. Within the body of an encapsulated method specialized to an encapsulated class, the form (`slot` '⟨*slot-name*⟩) can be used to refer to the class's private
slot named ⟨*slot-name*⟩. This extension is demonstrated in the following example:

```
(defclass c1 ()
    ((foo :initform 100))
  (:metaclass encapsulated-class))
(defclass c2 (c1)
    ((foo :initform 200))
  (:metaclass encapsulated-class))

(defgeneric f1 (x)
  (:generic-function-class encapsulating-gf)
  (:method-class encapsulated-method))

(defmethod f1 ((y c1))
  (1- (slot 'foo)))
(defmethod f1 ((z c2))
  (1+ (slot 'foo)))
```

Within the body of the encapsulated method specialized to c1, the form (`slot` 'foo)
accesses the slot named foo, private to the class c1, of the argument to f1. On the other
hand, within the body of the method specialized to c2, the same form accesses the slot
named foo that is private to c2.

⟹ (f1 (make-instance 'c1))
99

---

and standard methods, and guarantee that certain methods cannot be overridden. For example, in this case
we could document that `finalize-inheritance` used `progn` method combination which would ensure that all
applicable methods always run.

$\Longrightarrow$ (f1 (make-instance 'c2))
201

In our earlier example, where encapsulated methods were not available, those two
methods would have been written:

```
(defmethod f1 ((y c1))
  (1- (private-slot-value y 'foo (find-class 'c1))))
(defmethod f1 ((z c2))
  (1+ (private-slot-value z 'foo (find-class 'c2))))
```

These examples suggest that `slot` be defined in terms of the `private-slot-value`
function mentioned previously. At each `slot` form, we will need access to two pieces of
information: the class the encapsulated method is specialized to, and the value of the
method's first argument. This access is most easily provided by introducing a lexical
definition of `slot` into the scope of the method's body, in exactly the way `call-next-`
`method` and `next-method-p` were handled. That is, we want to have the same effect
as:

```
(defmethod f1 ((y c1))
  (flet ((slot (slot-name)
           (private-slot-value y slot-name (find-class 'c1))))
    (1- (slot 'foo))))
(defmethod f1 ((z c2))
  (flet ((slot (slot-name)
           (private-slot-value z slot-name (find-class 'c2))))
    (1+ (slot 'foo))))
```

Lexical definitions for (`setf slot`) would be handled analogously.[2]

---

[2]It might appear that a simpler solution would be to arrange for `apply-method` to use special variables to
pass the information needed to `slot`.

```
(proclaim '(special *specializer* *argument*))

(defmethod apply-method ((method encapsulated-method) args next-methods)
  (let ((*specializer* (first (method-specializers method)))
        (*argument* (first args)))
    (call-next-method)))

(defun slot (slot-name)
  (private-slot-value *argument* slot-name *specializer*))
```

This approach cannot be used, however, because in the presence of functional arguments, dynamic mechanisms
cannot be reliably substituted for lexical ones—this is related to the well-known "funarg" problem.

In the current protocol, the only way to introduce new lexical definitions into the
scope of the body of an encapsulated method is with a specialized, overriding, method
on **apply-method**. But, because overriding the standard method means taking over *all*
its responsibilities, the overriding method will have to do a great deal more than just
handle the two new lexical function bindings. For the Closette implementation we have
now, the complete method that the user needs to be able to write is:

```
(defmethod apply-method
           ((method encapsulated-method) args next-methods)
   (eval (method-body method)
         (add-function-bindings
           '(slot (setf slot) call-next-method next-method-p)
           (list
             #'(lambda (slot-name)
                 (private-slot-value
                   (car args)
                   slot-name
                   (car (method-specializers method))))
             #'(lambda (new-value slot-name)
                 (setf (private-slot-value
                          (car args)
                          slot-name
                          (car (method-specializers method)))
                       new-value))
             #'(lambda (&rest cnm-args)
                 (if (null next-methods)
                     (error "No next method for the~@
                             generic-function ~S."
                            (method-generic-function method))
                     (apply-methods
                       (method-generic-function method)
                       (or cnm-args args)
                       next-methods)))
             #'(lambda () (not (null next-methods))))
           (add-variable-bindings (method-lambda-list method)
                                  args
                                  (method-environment method)))))
```

Making it possible for the user to write this method places a significant burden on all involved—protocol designer, implementor and user alike.

First, the protocol designer must specify an enormous amount of detail about the behavior of the standard method on `apply-method`: that `call-next-method` and `next-method-p` must be introduced; the existence of `apply-methods` and that `call-next-method` must use it to properly handle the next methods; that lexical function bindings are performed with `add-function-bindings`; that variable bindings are performed with `add-variable-bindings`; and that `eval` must be called to actually run the method body.

Specifying this detail results in a corresponding lack of freedom for the implementor. The implementor must not only provide the required functionality under the required names, but also lose the standard method on `apply-method` as a place to put implementation-specific code that is certain not to be overridden.

Finally, even with the detailed specification, writing the method is a lot of work for the user. It certainly seems to be more work than is appropriate for the simple task of adding two lexical function bindings to the scope of method bodies. In addition, two user programs, both of which override the standard method on `apply-method` (suppose each adds a distinct lexical function), cannot be combined easily.

If as protocol designers, we expect that adding new lexical bindings will be a common activity, we can easily provide this capability by extending the protocol with a new subprotocol under `apply-method`.

(`extra-function-bindings` ⟨*method*⟩ ⟨*arguments*⟩ ⟨*next-methods*⟩) This generic function is a specializable functional protocol that returns a list of (⟨*function-name*⟩ ⟨*function-value*⟩) pairs. All primary methods of the generic function `apply-method` are required to consult `extra-function-bindings` to find out what extra lexical function bindings should be added to the scope of a method before executing it. The standard method on `extra-function-bindings` may not overriden; instead, user methods are free to add whatever new they wish onto the result of the standard method.

We implement this new protocol as follows:

```
(defgeneric extra-function-bindings (method args next-methods))
```

The standard method for `extra-function-bindings` returns entries for `call-next-method` and `next-method-p`:

```
(defmethod extra-function-bindings
           ((method standard-method) args next-methods)
  (list
    (list 'call-next-method
          #'(lambda (&rest cnm-args)
              (if (null next-methods)
                  (error "No next method for the~@
                          generic-function ~S."
                         (method-generic-function method))
                  (apply-methods (method-generic-function method)
                                 (or cnm-args args)
                                 next-methods))))
    (list 'next-method-p
          #'(lambda () (not (null next-methods))))))
```

The standard method for `apply-method` must be modified to call `extra-function-bindings`:

```
(defmethod apply-method ((method standard-method) args next-methods)
  (let ((extra-fn-bindings
          (extra-function-bindings method args next-methods)))
    (eval (method-body method)
          (add-function-bindings
            (mapcar #'car extra-fn-bindings)
            (mapcar #'cadr extra-fn-bindings)
            (add-variable-bindings (method-lambda-list method)
                                   args
                                   (method-environment method))))))
```

Given this new protocol, encapsulated methods can be implemented with a specialized, but non-overriding, method on **extra-function-bindings**:

```
(defmethod extra-function-bindings
           ((method encapsulated-method) args next-methods)
  (list*
    (list 'slot
          #'(lambda (slot-name)
              (private-slot-value
                (car args)
                slot-name
                (car (method-specializers method)))))
    (list '(setf slot)
          #'(lambda (new-value slot-name)
              (setf (private-slot-value
                      (car args)
                      slot-name
                      (car (method-specializers method)))
                    new-value)))
    (call-next-method)))
```

We have given the procedural protocol **apply-method** a functional subprotocol **extra-function-bindings**. By mandating that all methods for **apply-method** call **extra-function-bindings**, and that the standard method on **extra-function-bindings** not be overridden (nor its result discarded), we arrive at a reliable way for an open-ended set of function bindings to be added to a method body's lexical environment.

4.3   Layered Protocols

There is a more general technique at work here, called *protocol layering*, based on the idea of taking a large, complex portion of the protocol and splitting it into pieces, requiring that the main generic function call subsidiary generic functions to do parts of the overall task. Then, even though each generic function supports extensibility along only a single dimension, the combination supports extensibility along multiple dimensions. For example, **apply-method** makes it convenient to add extra activities, like call counting, to the basic activity of applying a method, while **extra-function-bindings** makes it easy to introduce extra lexical bindings into the scope of the method body. Another benefit is that, when necessary, it is easier to override methods on the main generic function because more of the subtasks have corresponding subprotocols. For example, an overriding method on **apply-method** can simply call **extra-function-bindings** rather than having to write it from scratch.

It is a general characteristic of layered protocols that the upper layers (e.g., **apply-method**) tend to provide more powerful access than the lower layers (e.g., **extra-function-bindings**). With this power comes responsibility for a number of things that may be unrelated to the aspect that is to be changed. Lower layer protocols, on the other hand, tend to be more focused and easier to use.

Protocol layering is a powerful tool for helping protocol designers meet the needs of their users. Lower-level, highly-focused layers provide easy handles for what we expect to be common needs. Higher-level protocols are a fallback strategy; they may be more difficult to use, but they give the user more complete power.

Armed with this technique, we can now revise the protocol to introduce appropriate layers between **apply-generic-function** at the top and **apply-method** at (or near) the bottom. As we saw earlier, this middle realm breaks cleanly into three tasks: determining which methods are applicable to given argument classes (**compute-applicable-methods-using-classes**), arranging them in decreasing order of specificity (**method-more-specific-p**), and applying the methods in the order dictated by the individual methods' qualifiers (**apply-methods**). Simple protocols for each are as follows (these are sketches only):

(**compute-applicable-methods-using-classes** ⟨*gf*⟩ ⟨*required-classes*⟩) A functional protocol that returns the list of methods applicable to the given argument classes. Once the applicable methods are computed, **method-more-specific-p** is called to assist in the ordering of the resulting list of methods. This function is called by the standard method of **apply-generic-function**. This is a non-specializable protocol; that is, the user may call it, but should only specialize **method-more-specific-p**.[3]

(**method-more-specific-p** ⟨*gf*⟩ ⟨*method1*⟩ ⟨*method2*⟩ ⟨*required-classes*⟩) A functional protocol that determines whether the first method is more specific than the second relative to the given argument classes. Methods on this generic function may only specialize the first argument. The standard method may be overridden.

(**apply-methods** ⟨*gf*⟩ ⟨*args*⟩ ⟨*methods*⟩) A procedural protocol specialized on the first argument that orchestrates the application of the methods (using **apply-method**) to the given arguments. This generic function is called by the standard method of **apply-generic-function**. The standard method may be overridden.

---

[3]In the full MOP, which provides support for **eql** specializers, this is a specializable generic function.

In summary, the full set of layered protocols within generic function invocation is:

`apply-generic-function`	procedural	overridable
`compute-applicable-methods-using-classes`	functional	non-specializable
`method-more-specific-p`	functional	overridable
`apply-methods`	procedural	overridable
`apply-method`	procedural	overridable
`extra-function-bindings`	functional	non-overridable

4.3.1 Revised Definitions

For convenience, we give the definitions of `apply-generic-function`, `compute-applicable-methods-using-classes`, `method-more-specific-p`, and `apply-methods` corresponding to the current protocol are given in this section. The definitions of `apply-method` and `extra-function-bindings` can be found on page 118.

```
(defgeneric apply-generic-function (gf args))
(defmethod apply-generic-function ((gf standard-generic-function) args)
  (let ((applicable-methods
          (compute-applicable-methods-using-classes
            gf (mapcar #'class-of (required-portion gf args)))))
    (if (null applicable-methods)
        (error "No matching method for the~@
                generic function ~S,~@
                when called with arguments ~:S." gf args)
        (apply-methods gf args applicable-methods))))

(defun compute-applicable-methods-using-classes (gf required-classes)
  (sort
    (copy-list
      (remove-if-not #'(lambda (method)
                         (every #'subclassp
                                required-classes
                                (method-specializers method)))
                     (generic-function-methods gf)))
    #'(lambda (m1 m2)
        (method-more-specific-p gf m1 m2 required-classes))))

(defgeneric method-more-specific-p
            (gf method1 method2 required-classes))
```

```
(defmethod method-more-specific-p
           ((gf standard-generic-function)
            method1 method2 required-classes)
  (mapc #'(lambda (spec1 spec2 arg-class)
            (unless (eq spec1 spec2)
              (return-from method-more-specific-p
                (sub-specializer-p spec1 spec2 arg-class))))
        (method-specializers method1)
        (method-specializers method2)
        required-classes)
  nil)

(defgeneric apply-methods (gf args methods))
(defmethod apply-methods
           ((gf standard-generic-function) args methods)
  (let ((primaries (remove-if-not #'primary-method-p methods))
        (befores (remove-if-not #'before-method-p methods))
        (afters (remove-if-not #'after-method-p methods)))
    (when (null primaries)
      (error "No primary methods for the~@
              generic function ~S." gf))
    (dolist (before befores)
      (apply-method before args ()))
    (multiple-value-prog1
      (apply-method (car primaries) args (cdr primaries))
      (dolist (after (reverse afters))
        (apply-method after args ())))))
```

4.3.2 Example: Method Combination

Our CLOS subset includes only a simplified version of the full method combination
facility. Our methods have qualifiers, which indicate how they should be combined, but
we have only supported before- and after-methods. Full CLOS also has around-methods
(using the :around qualifier) which have a higher precedence than all applicable primary,
before-, and after-methods. When a generic function is called, the most specific around-
method is invoked first; when it calls call-next-method the next most specific one is
invoked and so on. When there are no more around-methods, call-next-method runs
the remaining before-, after- and primary methods as usual.

Using the protocol we have just developed, it is an easy matter to add around-methods to our CLOS subset.

```
(defclass gf-with-arounds (standard-generic-function) ())

(defun around-method-p (method)
  (equal '(:around) (method-qualifiers method)))

(defmethod apply-methods ((gf gf-with-arounds) args methods)
  (let ((around (find-if #'around-method-p methods)))
    (if around
        (apply-method around args (remove around methods))
        (call-next-method))))
```

The full CLOS method combination facility also supports a wide variety of special-purpose ways of combining primary methods. For instance, it is sometimes more useful to treat each primary method as a supplier of a portion of the result; i.e., invoke all applicable primary methods, appending together their results. Although the same effect can be achieved using normal primary methods with bodies like

```
(append ⟨list⟩ (if (next-method-p) (call-next-method) ()))
```

an extension can be defined which better localizes this behavior. Generic functions with **append** combination support only primary methods. When they are invoked, all the applicable methods are run, and the results are appended together.

```
(defclass gf-with-append (standard-generic-function) ())

(defmethod apply-methods ((gf gf-with-append) args methods)
  (mapappend #'(lambda (method)
                 (apply-method method args ()))
             methods))
```

The function **extra-function-bindings** is a ready example of where this form of method combination could have been used to gather together lexical function bindings from the various specialized methods.

Exercise 4.2 Unlike most other object-oriented languages, CLOS supports *multi-methods*, which are methods specialized in more than one argument position.

When there is only a single specialized argument position, two applicable methods can be directly ordered by comparing their specializers with respect to the class of the argument at hand using `sub-specializer-p`. But when there are multiple specialized argument positions, a more complex ordering scheme is needed. By default, CLOS uses left-to-right lexicographic ordering; i.e., based on the specializer ordering of the leftmost argument position with different specializers. However, full CLOS also provides an `:argument-precedence-order` option on the generic function definition that allows the user to specify a permutation of the required arguments; this permutation is used rather than the default left-to-right ordering. This particular feature was omitted from our CLOS subset, but it can easily be accommodated by the protocols just introduced. Define a new generic function metaobject class `apo-gf` so that, for example, the definition

```
(defgeneric draw (object stream)
  (:generic-function-class apo-gf)
  (:argument-precedence-order (stream object)))
```

indicates that for the purposes of ordering the applicable methods, the second argument position should be considered before the first.

Exercise 4.3 In the Beta programming language [Kristensen et al. 87], ordering of applicable methods is handled differently. Methods from superclasses are executed *before* methods from subclasses; i.e., the first method run is the method from the highest superclass. Within the body of a method, a call to `inner` is similar to a call to `call-next-method` except that it calls the next *more* specific method. Unlike `call-next-method`, `inner` accepts no arguments, and if called when there are no more methods, returns false rather than signaling an error.

Define specialized generic function and method metaobject classes which invoke methods in this order. Also implement `inner` so that it has the specified behavior. (You need only support primary methods.)

Exercise 4.4 We have now seen how several features of full CLOS, originally left out of our subset, can be added back using the metaobject protocol (default initialization arguments, around-methods, other kinds of method combinations, and argument precedence order). This brings up the question of how the presence of a metaobject protocol might affect the design of the standard language. In particular, can metaobject protocols be used to make language definitions smaller?

Pick a programming language with which you are familiar, and look for features which, given an appropriate metaobject protocol, need not be part of the standard language. What criteria are you using to make your decisions? One additional possibility is for certain features to be included as part of a library of specialized metaobject classes. What features would you put into such a library?

4.4   Improving Performance

As we have designed it, the generic function invocation protocol severely impairs the implementor's ability to optimize generic function invocation. The root of the problem is that our protocol provides little opportunity for memoization in the generic function invocation process; most of the generic functions in the protocol are procedural and must be called during each generic function invocation. Fortunately, the performance characteristics of generic function invocation can be greatly improved by careful redesign of the relevant protocols. The same basic technique can be applied in three different places: `apply-generic-function`, `apply-method`, and `apply-methods`.

4.4.1   Effective Method Functions

Consider `apply-methods`, calls to which lie directly along the execution path of generic function invocation (it is called from `apply-generic-function` and from `call-next-method`). This means that the performance of generic function invocation is limited by the performance of `apply-methods`; if `apply-methods` does a lot of work, generic function invocation cannot help but be slow.

In traditional language implementations, the implementor would not be constrained to implement `apply-methods` literally. If it were too expensive to call `apply-methods`, the implementation could be rewritten to dispense with it, and do things some faster way. But this is not a traditional language; `apply-methods` is a procedural generic function in our documented metaobject protocol. The implementor is not free to dispense with calls to it. Moreover, since it is procedural protocol, clever memoization is not an option.

Our solution will be to redesign the protocol, splitting the activity of `apply-methods` into two parts. One part will be functional; as a result it will be memoizable and won't need to be called during each generic function invocation. The second part will be procedural, and will remain on the direct execution path. Having made the division, we will then be able to improve performance by moving as much of the activity as possible out of the second part and into the first.

Notice that the ⟨*args*⟩ argument to `apply-methods` is simply passed along to `apply-method`; it is not used in deciding the order in which the methods are invoked. This means, in effect, that the work being done by `apply-methods` is actually a function of only the ⟨*generic-function*⟩ and ⟨*methods*⟩ arguments. It is a simple matter to rewrite `apply-method` as a two-argument function that returns a function as a result.[4] We call these functional results *effective method functions*, and the function that computes them `compute-effective-method-function`. We then rewrite calls of the form:

---

[4]Many will recognize this as the standard functional programming technique of *currying*, applied to the middle argument position of `apply-methods`.

```
(apply-methods ⟨gf⟩ ⟨args⟩ ⟨methods⟩)
```

as

```
(funcall (compute-effective-method-function ⟨gf⟩ ⟨methods⟩)
         ⟨args⟩)
```

The standard method for this new generic function can be derived directly from the standard method for apply-methods (p. 122):

```
(defgeneric compute-effective-method-function (gf methods))
(defmethod compute-effective-method-function
             ((gf standard-generic-function) methods)
  #'(lambda (args)
      (let ((primaries (remove-if-not #'primary-method-p methods))
            (befores (remove-if-not #'before-method-p methods))
            (afters (remove-if-not #'after-method-p methods)))
        (when (null primaries)
          (error "No primary methods for the~@
                  generic function ~S." gf))
        (dolist (before befores)
          (apply-method before args ()))
        (multiple-value-prog1
          (apply-method (car primaries) args (cdr primaries))
          (dolist (after (reverse afters))
            (apply-method after args ()))))))
```

By constraining the context compute-effective-method-function may use in computing its result to just its two arguments, we make it memoizable.[5] Given a generic function, a list of methods and a list of arguments, the implementation must call the effective method function; but, if an effective method function has previously been computed for that generic function and list of methods, the implementation is free to reuse it.

Separating the original behavior of apply-method into a memoizable part and a part that is on the direct execution path provides the opportunity for performance improvement. To take advantage of it, we must actually move as many activities as possible out of the critical path. Looking at the above method, we can see that there is no reason to sift through the list of applicable methods every time the effective method function is

---

[5]In the full MOP, the corresponding contextual constraints are somewhat more complex. Redefinition of the generic function requires that any memoized effective method function be discarded.

called; instead, it can be done in advance. The check to ensure that there is at least one primary method can also be done in advance. This can be expressed by rearranging the above method, pulling code from inside the **lambda** to outside it:

```
(defmethod compute-effective-method-function
          ((gf standard-generic-function) methods)
  (let ((primaries (remove-if-not #'primary-method-p methods))
        (befores (remove-if-not #'before-method-p methods))
        (reverse-afters
          (reverse (remove-if-not #'after-method-p methods))))
    (when (null primaries)
      (error "No primary methods for the~@
              generic function ~S." gf))
    #'(lambda (args)
        (dolist (before befores)
          (apply-method before args ()))
        (multiple-value-prog1
          (apply-method
            (car primaries) args (cdr primaries))
          (dolist (after reverse-afters)
            (apply-method after args ())))))))
```

4.4.2   Method Functions

The above technique can also be profitably applied to **apply-method**. Instead of mandating that the generic function **apply-method** be invoked every time a method is applied, this procedural protocol is replaced by a functional protocol, **compute-method-function**, that computes a *method function* which will be called whenever the method is invoked. We re-express:

(apply-method ⟨*method*⟩ ⟨*args*⟩ ⟨*next-methods*⟩)

as

(funcall (compute-method-function ⟨*method*⟩)
         ⟨*args*⟩
         ⟨*next-methods*⟩)

In this case, the opportunity for memoization is straightforward. The method functions, being a function of only the method, can be computed once and stored with the method metaobject.[6]

It is still possible to use this new protocol to count calls to methods, although we can't use a before-method as we did with `apply-method`. In the following method, `call-next-method` is first used to obtain the standard method function. Then a new method function is returned which first increments the call count, and then calls the standard method function.

```
(defmethod compute-method-function ((method counting-method))
  (let ((normal-method-function (call-next-method)))
    #'(lambda (args next-methods)
        (incf (call-count method))
        (funcall normal-method-function args next-methods))))
```

4.4.3 Discriminating Functions

Finally, this technique can be applied to `apply-generic-function`. Again, we divide the procedural protocol into a functional protocol that returns a function which will itself be called whenever the generic function is invoked. These functions are called *discriminating functions* because their primary task is to discriminate on the arguments to determine which methods are to be applied. The generic function that computes them is called `compute-discriminating-function`. We re-express the root call:

(apply-generic-function ⟨*gf*⟩ ⟨*args*⟩)

as

(apply (compute-discriminating-function ⟨*gf*⟩) ⟨*args*⟩)

The standard method on this new generic function returns a function that does what the standard method on `apply-generic-function` (p. 121) did:

---

[6]The standard method in Appendix D explains what else this involves. To allow real CLOS implementations to compile code during file compilation, the full MOP adjusts this protocol even further.

```
(defgeneric compute-discriminating-function (gf))
(defmethod compute-discriminating-function
          ((gf standard-generic-function))
  #'(lambda (&rest args)
      (let ((applicable-methods
              (compute-applicable-methods-using-classes
                gf
                (mapcar #'class-of
                        (required-portion gf args)))))
        (if (null applicable-methods)
            (error "No matching method for the~@
                    generic function ~S,~@
                    when called with arguments ~:S." gf args)
            (apply-methods gf args applicable-methods)))))
```

To make this protocol memoizable, we restrict `compute-discriminating-function`
to depend only on the class of the generic function and its set of methods. Whenever a
method is added to the generic function, a new discriminating function must be computed
and stored. Since discriminating functions accept the same arguments as the generic
function itself, the implementation is free to arrange for calls to a generic function to go
straight to its discriminating function.

Again, call-counting in this new framework can be done quite simply:

```
(defmethod compute-discriminating-function ((gf counting-gf))
  (let ((normal-dfun (call-next-method)))
    #'(lambda (&rest args)
        (incf (call-count gf))
        (apply normal-dfun args))))
```

4.4.4 Streamlined Generic Function Invocation

We now present, from the perspective of the implementor, a more in-depth look at the
freedom this revised protocol offers. We will show one way to take advantage of this
freedom to optimize the performance of generic function invocation.

The optimization strategy is based on memoization, as allowed by the protocol, of
three values: effective method functions, method functions and discriminating functions.

Memoization of discriminating functions is done when the generic function metaobject
is first created. The discriminating function is stored, and we arrange for all calls to the
generic function to go directly to the discriminating function.

Memoization of method functions is done similarly. When the method metaobject is initialized, `compute-method-function` is called and the resulting method function is saved and used for all subsequent calls to the method.

The more complex case is memoization of effective method functions. This is done on a per generic function basis, using a table which maps from classes of arguments to effective method functions (along the lines of Exercise 1.1).

The "fast path" sequence of activities for a call to a generic function, from the time the discriminating function is entered, is: get the classes of the arguments, use them as the key to find an effective method function in the primary table, and apply the effective method function to the arguments. In this way, the discrimination overhead is reduced to that of determining the classes of the arguments, performing the table lookup and calling the effective method function.

The slower path is taken when an effective method function can't be found in the table; this involves finding out what methods are applicable to this class of argument and then computing an effective method function for that list of applicable methods. It is only along this route that `compute-applicable-methods-using-classes`, `method-more-specific-p`, and `compute-effective-method-function` are called.

Our implementation involves replacing the previous method on `compute-discriminating-function`:

```
(defmethod compute-discriminating-function
          ((gf standard-generic-function))
  (let ((classes-to-emf-table (make-hash-table :test #'equal)))
    #'(lambda (&rest args)
        (let* ((classes (mapcar #'class-of
                                (required-portion gf args)))
               (emfun (gethash classes classes-to-emf-table nil)))
          (if emfun
            (funcall emfun args)
            (slow-method-lookup gf args classes classes-to-emf-table))))))
```

```
(defun slow-method-lookup
        (gf args classes classes-to-emf-table)
  (let* ((applicable-methods
            (compute-applicable-methods-using-classes gf classes))
         (emfun
            (compute-effective-method-function
              gf applicable-methods)))
    (setf (gethash classes classes-to-emf-table) emfun)
    (funcall emfun args)))
```

A number of issues remain to fully optimize generic function invocation. First, there are a number of calls to **apply-methods**, which we have not yet converted into memoized calls to **compute-effective-method-function**. These are all related to **call-next-method**; they include the call from within the body of **call-next-method** itself and the call from within the body of effective method functions. (The code in Appendix D reflects these further optimizations.)

Another important optimization is that table lookups should be based only on the arguments which are actually specialized instead of on all required arguments. A related issue is the design of the table data structures and the hashing strategy used within them. While we have not discussed these, the discussion above is indicative of the basic structure of an optimized implementation strategy; similar approaches have proven effective in several full CLOS implementations [Dussud 89, Moon 86, Kiczales&Rodriguez 90].

4.5   Protocol Design Summary

We have explored some (but certainly not all) of the issues that face designers of meta-object protocols and object-oriented protocols in general. It is instructive to recap the major points about protocol design:

- There are two broad categories of object-oriented protocols: functional and procedural. Functional protocols can be designed to make memoization possible while allowing the user to control what answer is computed. On the other hand, memoization is not possible with procedural protocols, where the operative notion is one of temporal predictability. Procedural protocols can be designed so that the user can reliably predict when certain activities will take place in relation to other significant activities. Procedural protocols that allow some activities to be overridden are more flexible, but less predictable, than ones that allow new activities to augment existing ones but not to replace them.

- Providing several layers of protocols makes customizing the implementation easier. The lower layer protocols make it easy to make small changes to particular aspects. The higher layer protocols are used to make more sweeping changes, but are inevitably more complex. On the other hand, by being defined at a higher level, they generally avoid having to deal with details of concern to the lower layers.

- Procedural protocols that lie along the execution critical path can be pulled apart into a functional protocol that computes a procedure. The procedure gets called on the critical path; computing the procedure itself can either be done once and cached, or moved off the critical path entirely by precomputing it.

Exercise 4.5 We began the chapter with a simple metaobject protocol for controlling generic function invocation: the generic functions `apply-generic-function` and `apply-method`. Now, these have been replaced by `compute-discriminating-function` and `compute-method-function`.

One way to view the original protocol is to see that its generic functions were *directly* implementing the basic operations of generic function invocation. From this same perspective, the generic functions in the revised protocol can be seen as returning functional results which directly implement the same basic operations.

A further step in this same direction would be to have the generic functions in the protocol return *source code* which, when compiled, would directly implement the basic operations. In such a protocol, the specialized method for counting generic functions might be as follows:

```
(defmethod compute-discriminating-lambda ((gf counting-gf))
  (let ((normal-lambda (call-next-method)))
    '(lambda (&rest args)
       (incf (call-count ',gf))
       (apply #',normal-lambda args))))
```

Design and implement the rest of this protocol in terms of the protocol we have already developed. Evaluate your design by considering how it supports each of the examples we have seen.

II A METAOBJECT PROTOCOL FOR CLOS

In this part of the book, we provide the detailed specification of a metaobject protocol for CLOS. Our work with this protocol has always been rooted in our own implementation of CLOS, PCL. This has made it possible for us to have a user community, which in turn has provided us with feedback on this protocol as it has evolved. As a result, much of the design presented here is well-tested and stable. As this is being written, those parts have been implemented not only in PCL, but in at least three other CLOS implementations we know of. Other parts of the protocol, even though they have been implemented in one form or another in PCL and other implementations, are less well worked out. Work remains to improve not only the ease of use of these protocols, but also the balance they provide between user extensibility and implementor freedom.

In preparing this specification, it is our hope that it will provide a basis for the users and implementors who wish to work with a metaobject protocol for CLOS. This document should not be construed as any sort of final word or standard, but rather only as documentation of what has been done so far. We look forward to seeing the improvements, both small and large, which we hope this publication will catalyze.

To this end, for Part II only (chapters 5 and 6), we grant permission to prepare revisions or other derivative works including any amount of the original text. We ask only that you properly acknowledge the source of the original text and explicitly allow subsequent revisions and derivative works under the same terms. To further facilitate improvements in this work, we have made the electronic source for these chapters publicly available; it can be accessed by anonymous FTP from the `/pcl/mop` directory on `arisia.xerox.com`.

In addition to the valuable feedback from users of PCL, the protocol design presented here has benefited from detailed comments and suggestions by the following people: Kim Barrett, Scott Cyphers, Harley Davis, Patrick Dussud, John Foderaro, Richard P. Gabriel, David Gray, David A. Moon, Andreas Paepcke, Chris Richardson, Walter van Roggen, and Jon L. White. We are very grateful to each of them. Any remaining errors, inconsistencies or design deficiencies are the responsibility of the authors alone.

5 Concepts

5.1 Introduction

The CLOS Specification [X3J13, CLtLII] describes the standard Programmer Interface for the Common Lisp Object System (CLOS). This document extends that specification by defining a metaobject protocol for CLOS—that is, a description of CLOS itself as an extensible CLOS program. In this description, the fundamental elements of CLOS programs (classes, slot definitions, generic functions, methods, specializers and method combinations) are represented by first-class objects. The behavior of CLOS is provided by these objects, or, more precisely, by methods specialized to the classes of these objects.

Because these objects represent pieces of CLOS programs, and because their behavior provides the behavior of the CLOS language itself, they are considered meta-level objects or metaobjects. The protocol followed by the metaobjects to provide the behavior of CLOS is called the CLOS Metaobject Protocol (MOP).

5.2 Metaobjects

For each kind of program element there is a corresponding *basic metaobject class*. These are the classes: **class**, **slot-definition**, **generic-function**, **method** and **method-combination**. A *metaobject class* is a subclass of exactly one of these classes. The results are undefined if an attempt is made to define a class that is a subclass of more than one basic metaobject class. A *metaobject* is an instance of a metaobject class.

Each metaobject represents one program element. Associated with each metaobject is the information required to serve its role. This includes information that might be provided directly in a user interface macro such as **defclass** or **defmethod**. It also includes information computed indirectly from other metaobjects such as that computed from class inheritance or the full set of methods associated with a generic function.

Much of the information associated with a metaobject is in the form of connections to other metaobjects. This interconnection means that the role of a metaobject is always based on that of other metaobjects. As an introduction to this interconnected structure, this section presents a partial enumeration of the kinds of information associated with each kind of metaobject. More detailed information is presented later.

5.2.1 Classes

A *class metaobject* determines the structure and the default behavior of its instances. The following information is associated with class metaobjects:

- The name, if there is one, is available as an object.
- The direct subclasses, direct superclasses and class precedence list are available as lists of class metaobjects.
- The slots defined directly in the class are available as a list of direct slot definition metaobjects. The slots which are accessible in instances of the class are available as a list of effective slot definition metaobjects.
- The documentation is available as a string or **nil**.
- The methods which use the class as a specializer, and the generic functions associated with those methods are available as lists of method and generic function metaobjects respectively.

5.2.2   Slot Definitions

A *slot definition metaobject* contains information about the definition of a slot. There are two kinds of slot definition metaobjects. A direct slot definition metaobject is used to represent the direct definition of a slot in a class. This corresponds roughly to the slot specifiers found in **defclass** forms. An effective slot definition metaobject is used to represent information, including inherited information, about a slot which is accessible in instances of a particular class.

Associated with each class metaobject is a list of direct slot definition metaobjects representing the slots defined directly in the class. Also associated with each class metaobject is a list of effective slot definition metaobjects representing the set of slots accessible in instances of that class.

The following information is associated with both direct and effective slot definitions metaobjects:

- The name, allocation, and type are available as forms that could appear in a **defclass** form.
- The initialization form, if there is one, is available as a form that could appear in a **defclass** form. The initialization form together with its lexical environment is available as a function of no arguments which, when called, returns the result of evaluating the initialization form in its lexical environment. This is called the *initfunction* of the slot.
- The slot filling initialization arguments are available as a list of symbols.
- The documentation is available as a string or **nil**.

Certain other information is only associated with direct slot definition metaobjects. This information applies only to the direct definition of the slot in the class (it is not inherited).

- The function names of those generic functions for which there are automatically generated reader and writer methods. This information is available as lists of function names. Any accessors specified in the **defclass** form are broken down into their equivalent readers and writers in the direct slot definition.

Information, including inherited information, which applies to the definition of a slot in a particular class in which it is accessible is associated only with effective slot definition metaobjects.

- For certain slots, the location of the slot in instances of the class is available.

5.2.3   Generic Functions

A *generic function metaobject* contains information about a generic function over and above the information associated with each of the generic function's methods.

- The name is available as a function name.
- The methods associated with the generic function are available as a list of method metaobjects.
- The default class for this generic function's method metaobjects is available as a class metaobject.
- The lambda list is available as a list.
- The method combination is available as a method combination metaobject.
- The documentation is available as a string or **nil**.
- The argument precedence order is available as a permutation of those symbols from the lambda list which name the required arguments of the generic function.
- The declarations are available as a list of declarations.
    Terminology Note:
    There is some ambiguity in Common Lisp about the terms used to identify the various parts of **declare** special forms. In this document, the term *declaration* is used to refer to an object that could be an argument to a **declare** special form. For example, in the special form (**declare** (**special *g1***)), the list (**special *g1***) is a declaration.

5.2.4   Methods

A *method metaobject* contains information about a specific method.

- The qualifiers are available as a list of of non-null atoms.
- The lambda list is available as a list.
- The specializers are available as a list of specializer metaobjects.
- The function is available as a function. This function can be applied to arguments and a list of next methods using **apply** or **funcall**.

- When the method is associated with a generic function, that generic function metaobject is available. A method can be associated with at most one generic function at a time.
- The documentation is available as a string or **nil**.

5.2.5 Specializers

A specializer metaobject represents the specializers of a method. Class metaobjects are themselves specializer metaobjects. A special kind of specializer metaobject is used for **eql** specializers.

5.2.6 Method Combinations

A *method combination metaobject* represents the information about the method combination being used by a generic function.

Note:
This document does not specify the structure of method combination metaobjects.

5.3 Inheritance Structure of Metaobject Classes

The inheritance structure of the specified metaobject classes is shown in Table 5.1.

Each class marked with a "∗" is an *abstract class* and is not intended to be instantiated. The results are undefined if an attempt is made to make an instance of one of these classes with **make-instance**.

The classes **standard-class**, **standard-direct-slot-definition**, **standard-effective-slot-definition**, **standard-method**, **standard-reader-method**, **standard-writer-method** and **standard-generic-function** are called *standard metaobject classes*. For each kind of metaobject, this is the class the user interface macros presented in the CLOS Specification use by default. These are also the classes on which user specializations are normally based.

The classes **built-in-class**, **funcallable-standard-class** and **forward-referenced-class** are special-purpose class metaobject classes. Built-in classes are instances of the class **built-in-class**. The class **funcallable-standard-class** provides a special kind of instances described in the section called "Funcallable Instances." When the definition of a class references another class which has not yet been defined, an instance of **forward-referenced-class** is used as a stand-in until the class is actually defined.

The class **standard-object** is the *default direct superclass* of the class **standard-class**. When an instance of the class **standard-class** is created, and no direct superclasses are explicitly specified, it defaults to the class **standard-object**. In this way, any

Metaobject Class	Direct Superclasses
standard-object	(t)
funcallable-standard-object	(standard-object function)
* metaobject	(standard-object)
* generic-function	(metaobject funcallable-standard-object)
standard-generic-function	(generic-function)
* method	(metaobject)
standard-method	(method)
* standard-accessor-method	(standard-method)
standard-reader-method	(standard-accessor-method)
standard-writer-method	(standard-accessor-method)
* method-combination	(metaobject)
* slot-definition	(metaobject)
* direct-slot-definition	(slot-definition)
* effective-slot-definition	(slot-definition)
* standard-slot-definition	(slot-definition)
standard-direct-slot-definition	(standard-slot-definition direct-slot-definition)
standard-effective-slot-definition	(standard-slot-definition effective-slot-definition)
* specializer	(metaobject)
eql-specializer	(specializer)
* class	(specializer)
built-in-class	(class)
forward-referenced-class	(class)
standard-class	(class)
funcallable-standard-class	(class)

Table 5.1 Direct superclass relationships among the specified metaobject classes. The class of every class shown is **standard-class** except for the class **t** which is an instance of the class **built-in-class** and the classes **generic-function** and **standard-generic-function** which are instances of the class **funcallable-standard-class**.

behavior associated with the class **standard-object** will be inherited, directly or indirectly, by all instances of the class **standard-class**. A subclass of **standard-class** may have a different class as its default direct superclass, but that class must be a subclass of the class **standard-object**.

The same is true for **funcallable-standard-class** and **funcallable-standard-object**.

The class **specializer** captures only the most basic behavior of method specializers, and is not itself intended to be instantiated. The class **class** is a direct subclass of **specializer** reflecting the property that classes by themselves can be used as method specializers. The class **eql-specializer** is used for **eql** specializers.

5.3.1   Implementation and User Specialization

The purpose of the Metaobject Protocol is to provide users with a powerful mechanism for extending and customizing the basic behavior of the Common Lisp Object System. As an object-oriented description of the basic CLOS behavior, the Metaobject Protocol makes it possible to create these extensions by defining specialized subclasses of existing metaobject classes.

The Metaobject Protocol provides this capability without interfering with the implementor's ability to develop high-performance implementations. This balance between user extensibility and implementor freedom is mediated by placing explicit restrictions on each. Some of these restrictions are general—they apply to the entire class graph and the applicability of all methods. These are presented in this section.

The following additional terminology is used to present these restrictions:

- Metaobjects are divided into three categories. Those defined in this document are called *specified*; those defined by an implementation but not mentioned in this document are called *implementation-specific*; and those defined by a portable program are called *portable*.
- A class I is *interposed* between two other classes C_1 and C_2 if and only if there is some path, following direct superclasses, from the class C_1 to the class C_2 which includes I.
- A method is *specialized to* a class if and only if that class is in the list of specializers associated with the method; and the method is in the list of methods associated with some generic function.
- In a given implementation, a specified method is said to have been *promoted* if and only if the specializers of the method, $S_1 \ldots S_n$, are defined in this specification as the classes $C_1 \ldots C_n$, but in the implementation, one or more of the specializers S_i, is a superclass of the class given in the specification C_i.
- For a given generic function and set of arguments, a method M_2 *extends* a method M_1 if and only if:

(i) M_1 and M_2 are both associated with the given generic function,

(ii) M_1 and M_2 are both applicable to the given arguments,

(iii) the specializers and qualifiers of the methods are such that when the generic function is called, M_2 is executed before M_1,

(iv) M_1 will be executed if and only if **call-next-method** is invoked from within the body of M_2 and

(v) **call-next-method** is invoked from within the body of M_2, thereby causing M_1 to be executed.

- For a given generic function and set of arguments, a method M_2 *overrides* a method M_1 if and only if conditions i through iv above hold and

(v′) **call-next-method** is not invoked from within the body of M_2, thereby preventing M_1 from being executed.

Restrictions on Implementations   Implementations are allowed latitude to modify the structure of specified classes and methods. This includes: the interposition of implementation-specific classes; the promotion of specified methods; and the consolidation of two or more specified methods into a single method specialized to interposed classes.

Any such modifications are permitted only so long as for any portable class C_p that is a subclass of one or more specified classes $C_0 \ldots C_i$, the following conditions are met:

- In the actual class precedence list of C_p, the classes $C_0 \ldots C_i$ must appear in the same order as they would have if no implementation-specific modifications had been made.
- The method applicability of any specified generic function must be the same in terms of behavior as it would have been had no implementation-specific changes been made. This includes specified generic functions that have had portable methods added. In this context, the expression "the same in terms of behavior" means that methods with the same behavior as those specified are applicable, and in the same order.
- No portable class C_p may inherit, by virtue of being a direct or indirect subclass of a specified class, any slot for which the name is a symbol accessible in the **common-lisp-user** package or exported by any package defined in the ANSI Common Lisp standard.
- Implementations are free to define implementation-specific before- and after-methods on specified generic functions. Implementations are also free to define implementation-specific around-methods with extending behavior.

Restrictions on Portable Programs   Portable programs are allowed to define subclasses of specified classes, and are permitted to define methods on specified generic

functions, with the following restrictions. The results are undefined if any of these restrictions is violated.

- Portable programs must not redefine any specified classes, generic functions, methods
  or method combinations. Any method defined by a portable program on a specified
  generic function must have at least one specializer that is neither a specified class nor
  an **eql** specializer whose associated value is an instance of a specified class.
- Portable programs may define methods that extend specified methods unless the description of the specified method explicitly prohibits this. Unless there is a specific
  statement to the contrary, these extending methods must return whatever value was
  returned by the call to **call-next-method**.
- Portable programs may define methods that override specified methods only when the
  description of the specified method explicitly allows this. Typically, when a method is
  allowed to be overridden, a small number of related methods will need to be overridden
  as well.

  An example of this is the specified methods on the generic functions **add-dependent**, **remove-dependent** and **map-dependents**. Overriding a specified method on
  one of these generic functions requires that the corresponding method on the other
  two generic functions be overridden as well.
- Portable methods on specified generic functions specialized to portable metaobject
  classes must be defined before any instances of those classes (or any subclasses) are
  created, either directly or indirectly by a call to **make-instance**. Methods can be defined after instances are created by **allocate-instance** however. Portable metaobject
  classes cannot be redefined.

  Implementation Note:

  The purpose of this last restriction is to permit implementations to provide performance optimizations by analyzing, at the time the first instance of a metaobject
  class is initialized, what portable methods will be applicable to it. This can make
  it possible to optimize calls to those specified generic functions which would have
  no applicable portable methods.

  Note:

  The specification technology used in this document needs further development. The
  concepts of object-oriented protocols and subclass specialization are intuitively familiar to programmers of object-oriented systems; the protocols presented here fit
  quite naturally into this framework. Nonetheless, in preparing this document, we
  have found it difficult to give specification-quality descriptions of the protocols in
  a way that makes it clear what extensions users can and cannot write. Object-
  oriented protocol specification is inherently about specifying leeway, and this seems
  difficult using current technology.

5.4   Processing of the User Interface Macros

A list in which the first element is one of the symbols **defclass**, **defmethod**, **defgeneric**, **define-method-combination**, **generic-function**, **generic-flet** or **generic-labels**, and which has proper syntax for that macro is called a *user interface macro form*. This document provides an extended specification of the **defclass**, **defmethod** and **defgeneric** macros.

The user interface macros **defclass**, **defgeneric** and **defmethod** can be used not only to define metaobjects that are instances of the corresponding standard metaobject class, but also to define metaobjects that are instances of appropriate portable metaobject classes. To make it possible for portable metaobject classes to properly process the information appearing in the macro form, this document provides a limited specification of the processing of these macro forms.

User interface macro forms can be *evaluated* or *compiled* and later *executed*. The effect of evaluating or executing a user interface macro form is specified in terms of calls to specified functions and generic functions which provide the actual behavior of the macro. The arguments received by these functions and generic functions are derived in a specified way from the macro form.

Converting a user interface macro form into the arguments to the appropriate functions and generic functions has two major aspects: the conversion of the macro argument syntax into a form more suitable for later processing, and the processing of macro arguments which are forms to be evaluated (including method bodies).

In the syntax of the **defclass** macro, the *initform* and *default-initarg-initial-value-form* arguments are forms which will be evaluated one or more times after the macro form is evaluated or executed. Special processing must be done on these arguments to ensure that the lexical scope of the forms is captured properly. This is done by building a function of zero arguments which, when called, returns the result of evaluating the form in the proper lexical environment.

In the syntax of the **defmethod** macro the *form** argument is a list of forms that comprise the body of the method definition. This list of forms must be processed specially to capture the lexical scope of the macro form. In addition, the lexical functions available only in the body of methods must be introduced. To allow this and any other special processing (such as slot access optimization), a specializable protocol is used for processing the body of methods. This is discussed in the section "Processing Method Bodies."

5.4.1 Compile-file Processing of the User Interface Macros

It is common practice for Common Lisp compilers, while processing a file or set of files, to maintain information about the definitions that have been compiled so far. Among other things, this makes it possible to ensure that a global macro definition (**defmacro** form) which appears in a file will affect uses of the macro later in that file. This information about the state of the compilation is called the *compile-file environment*.

When compiling files containing CLOS definitions, it is useful to maintain certain additional information in the compile-file environment. This can make it possible to issue various kinds of warnings (e.g., lambda list congruence) and to do various performance optimizations that would not otherwise be possible.

At this time, there is such significant variance in the way existing Common Lisp implementations handle compile-file environments that it would be premature to specify this mechanism. Consequently, this document specifies only the behavior of evaluating or executing user interface macro forms. What functions and generic functions are called during compile-file processing of a user interface macro form is not specified. Implementations are free to define and document their own behavior. Users may need to check implementation-specific behavior before attempting to compile certain portable programs.

5.4.2 The defclass Macro

The evaluation or execution of a **defclass** form results in a call to the **ensure-class** function. The arguments received by **ensure-class** are derived from the **defclass** form in a defined way. The exact macro-expansion of the **defclass** form is not defined, only the relationship between the arguments to the **defclass** macro and the arguments received by the **ensure-class** function. Examples of typical **defclass** forms and sample expansions are shown in Figures 5.1 and 5.2.

- The *name* argument to **defclass** becomes the value of the first argument to **ensure-class**. This is the only positional argument accepted by **ensure-class**; all other arguments are keyword arguments.
- The *direct-superclasses* argument to **defclass** becomes the value of the **:direct-superclasses** keyword argument to **ensure-class**.
- The *direct slots* argument to **defclass** becomes the value of the **:direct-slots** keyword argument to **ensure-class**. Special processing of this value is done to regularize the form of each slot specification and to properly capture the lexical scope of the initialization forms. This is done by converting each slot specification to a property list called a *canonicalized slot specification*. The resulting list of canonicalized slot specifications is the value of the **:direct-slots** keyword argument.

```
(defclass plane (moving-object graphics-object)
    ((altitude :initform 0 :accessor plane-altitude)
     (speed))
  (:default-initargs :engine *jet*))

(ensure-class 'plane
  ':direct-superclasses '(moving-object graphics-object)
  ':direct-slots (list (list ':name 'altitude
                             ':initform '0
                             ':initfunction #'(lambda () 0)
                             ':readers '(plane-altitude)
                             ':writers '((setf plane-altitude)))
                       (list ':name 'speed))
  ':direct-default-initargs (list (list ':engine
                                        '*jet*
                                        #'(lambda () *jet*)))))
```

Figure 5.1 A **defclass** form with standard slot and class options and an expansion of it that would result in the proper call to **ensure-class**.

Canonicalized slot specifications are later used as the keyword arguments to a generic function which will, in turn, pass them to **make-instance** for use as a set of initialization arguments. Each canonicalized slot specification is formed from the corresponding slot specification as follows:

- The name of the slot is the value of the **:name** property. This property appears in every canonicalized slot specification.
- When the **:initform** slot option is present in the slot specification, then both the **:initform** and **:initfunction** properties are present in the canonicalized slot specification. The value of the **:initform** property is the initialization form. The value of the **:initfunction** property is a function of zero arguments which, when called, returns the result of evaluating the initialization form in its proper lexical environment.

    If the **:initform** slot option is not present in the slot specification, then either the **:initfunction** property will not appear, or its value will be false. In such cases, the value of the **:initform** property, or whether it appears, is unspecified.
- The value of the **:initargs** property is a list of the values of each **:initarg** slot option. If there are no **:initarg** slot options, then either the **:initargs** property will not appear or its value will be the empty list.

```
(defclass sst (plane)
    ((mach mag-step 2
           locator sst-mach
           locator mach-location
           :reader mach-speed
           :reader mach))
  (:metaclass faster-class)
  (another-option foo bar))

(ensure-class 'sst
  ':direct-superclasses '(plane)
  ':direct-slots (list (list ':name 'mach
                             ':readers '(mach-speed mach)
                             'mag-step '2
                             'locator '(sst-mach mach-location)))
  ':metaclass 'faster-class
  'another-option '(foo bar))
```

Figure 5.2 A **defclass** form with non-standard class and slot options, and an expansion of it which results in the proper call to **ensure-class**. Note that the order of the slot options has not affected the order of the properties in the canonicalized slot specification, but has affected the order of the elements in the lists which are the values of those properties.

- The value of the **:readers** property is a list of the values of each **:reader** and **:accessor** slot option. If there are no **:reader** or **:accessor** slot options, then either the **:readers** property will not appear or its value will be the empty list.
- The value of the **:writers** property is a list of the values specified by each **:writer** and **:accessor** slot option. The value specified by a **:writer** slot option is just the value of the slot option. The value specified by an **:accessor** slot option is a two element list: the first element is the symbol **setf**, the second element is the value of the slot option. If there are no **:writer** or **:accessor** slot options, then either the **:writers** property will not appear or its value will be the empty list.
- The value of the **:documentation** property is the value of the **:documentation** slot option. If there is no **:documentation** slot option, then either the **:documentation** property will not appear or its value will be false.
- All other slot options appear as the values of properties with the same name as the slot option. Note that this includes not only the remaining standard slot options (**:allocation** and **:type**), but also any other options and values appearing in the

slot specification. If one of these slot options appears more than once, the value of the property will be a list of the specified values.

- An implementation is free to add additional properties to the canonicalized slot specification provided these are not symbols accessible in the **common-lisp-user** package, or exported by any package defined in the ANSI Common Lisp standard.

Returning to the correspondence between arguments to the **defclass** macro and the arguments received by the **ensure-class** function:

- The *default initargs* class option, if it is present in the **defclass** form, becomes the value of the :**direct-default-initargs** keyword argument to **ensure-class**. Special processing of this value is done to properly capture the lexical scope of the default value forms. This is done by converting each default initarg in the class option into a *canonicalized default initarg*. The resulting list of canonicalized default initargs is the value of the :**direct-default-initargs** keyword argument to **ensure-class**.

  A canonicalized default initarg is a list of three elements. The first element is the name; the second is the actual form itself; and the third is a function of zero arguments which, when called, returns the result of evaluating the default value form in its proper lexical environment.

- The *metaclass* class option, if it is present in the **defclass** form, becomes the value of the :**metaclass** keyword argument to **ensure-class**.

- The *documentation* class option, if it is present in the **defclass** form, becomes the value of the :**documentation** keyword argument to **ensure-class**.

- Any other class options become the value of keyword arguments with the same name. The value of the keyword argument is the tail of the class option. An error is signaled if any class option appears more than once in the **defclass** form.

In the call to **ensure-class**, every element of its arguments appears in the same left-to-right order as the corresponding element of the **defclass** form, except that the order of the properties of canonicalized slot specifications is unspecified. The values of properties in canonicalized slot specifications do follow this ordering requirement. Other ordering relationships in the keyword arguments to **ensure-class** are unspecified.

The result of the call to **ensure-class** is returned as the result of evaluating or executing the **defclass** form.

5.4.3   The defmethod Macro

The evaluation or execution of a **defmethod** form requires first that the body of the method be converted to a method function. This process is described in the next section. The result of this process is a method function and a set of additional initialization arguments to be used when creating the new method. Given these two values, the evaluation or execution of a **defmethod** form proceeds in three steps.

The first step ensures the existence of a generic function with the specified name. This is done by calling the function **ensure-generic-function**. The first argument in this call is the generic function name specified in the **defmethod** form.

The second step is the creation of the new method metaobject by calling **make-instance**. The class of the new method metaobject is determined by calling **generic-function-method-class** on the result of the call to **ensure-generic-function** from the first step.

The initialization arguments received by the call to **make-instance** are as follows:

- The value of the **:qualifiers** initialization argument is a list of the qualifiers which appeared in the **defmethod** form. No special processing is done on these values. The order of the elements of this list is the same as in the **defmethod** form.

- The value of the **:lambda-list** initialization argument is the unspecialized lambda list from the **defmethod** form.

- The value of the **:specializers** initialization argument is a list of the specializers for the method. For specializers which are classes, the specializer is the class metaobject itself. In the case of **eql** specializers, it will be an **eql-specializer** metaobject obtained by calling **intern-eql-specializer** on the result of evaluating the **eql** specializer form in the lexical environment of the **defmethod** form.

- The value of the **:function** initialization argument is the method function.

- The value of the **:declarations** initialization argument is a list of the declarations from the **defmethod** form. If there are no declarations in the macro form, this initialization argument either doesn't appear, or appears with a value of the empty list.

- The value of the **:documentation** initialization argument is the documentation string from the **defmethod** form. If there is no documentation string in the macro form this initialization argument either doesn't appear, or appears with a value of false.

- Any other initialization argument produced in conjunction with the method function are also included.

- The implementation is free to include additional initialization arguments provided these are not symbols accessible in the **common-lisp-user** package, or exported by any package defined in the ANSI Common Lisp standard.

In the third step, **add-method** is called to add the newly created method to the set of methods associated with the generic function metaobject.

```
(defmethod move :before ((p position) (l (eql 0))
                         &optional (visiblyp t)
                         &key color)
  (set-to-origin p)
  (when visiblyp (show-move p 0 color)))

(let ((#:g001 (ensure-generic-function 'move)))
  (add-method #:g001
    (make-instance (generic-function-method-class #:g001)
                   ':qualifiers '(:before)
                   ':specializers (list (find-class 'position)
                                        (intern-eql-specializer 0))
                   ':lambda-list '(p l &optional (visiblyp t)
                                        &key color)
                   ':function (function method-lambda)
                   'additional-initarg-1 't
                   'additional-initarg-2 '39)))
```

Figure 5.3 An example **defmethod** form and one possible correct expansion. In the expansion, *method-lambda* is the result of calling **make-method-lambda** as described in the section "Processing Method Bodies". The initargs appearing after **:function** are assumed to be additional initargs returned from the call to **make-method-lambda**.

The result of the call to **add-method** is returned as the result of evaluating or executing the **defmethod** form.

An example showing a typical **defmethod** form and a sample expansion is shown in Figure 5.3. The processing of the method body for this method is shown in Figure 5.4.

5.4.4   Processing Method Bodies

Before a method can be created, the list of forms comprising the method body must be converted to a method function. This conversion is a two step process.

Note:

The body of methods can also appear in the **:initial-methods** option of **defgeneric** forms. Initial methods are not considered by any of the protocols specified in this document.

The first step occurs during macro-expansion of the macro form. In this step, the method lambda list, declarations and body are converted to a lambda expression called

```
(let ((gf (ensure-generic-function 'move)))
  (make-method-lambda
    gf
    (class-prototype (generic-function-method-class gf))
    '(lambda (p 1 &optional (visiblyp t) &key color)
       (set-to-origin p)
       (when visiblyp (show-move p 0 color)))
    environment))
```

Figure 5.4 During macro-expansion of the **defmethod** macro shown in Figure 5.3, code similar to this would be run to produce the method lambda and additional initargs. In this example, *environment* is the macroexpansion environment of the **defmethod** macro form.

a *method lambda*. This conversion is based on information associated with the generic function definition in effect at the time the macro form is expanded.

The generic function definition is obtained by calling **ensure-generic-function** with a first argument of the generic function name specified in the macro form. The **:lambda-list** keyword argument is not passed in this call.

Given the generic function, production of the method lambda proceeds by calling **make-method-lambda**. The first argument in this call is the generic function obtained as described above. The second argument is the result of calling **class-prototype** on the result of calling **generic-function-method-class** on the generic function. The third argument is a lambda expression formed from the method lambda list, declarations and body. The fourth argument is the macro-expansion environment of the macro form; this is the value of the **&environment** argument to the **defmethod** macro.

The generic function **make-method-lambda** returns two values. The first is the method lambda itself. The second is a list of initialization arguments and values. These are included in the initialization arguments when the method is created.

In the second step, the method lambda is converted to a function which properly captures the lexical scope of the macro form. This is done by having the method lambda appear in the macro-expansion as the argument of the **function** special form. During the subsequent evaluation of the macro-expansion, the result of the **function** special form is the method function.

5.4.5   The defgeneric Macro

The evaluation or execution of a **defgeneric** form results in a call to the **ensure-generic-function** function. The arguments received by **ensure-generic-function** are derived from the **defgeneric** form in a defined way. As with **defclass** and **defmethod**, the exact macro-expansion of the **defgeneric** form is not defined, only the relationship between the arguments to the macro and the arguments received by **ensure-generic-function**.

- The *function-name* argument to **defgeneric** becomes the first argument to **ensure-generic-function**. This is the only positional argument accepted by **ensure-generic-function**; all other arguments are keyword arguments.
- The *lambda-list* argument to **defgeneric** becomes the value of the **:lambda-list** keyword argument to **ensure-generic-function**.
- For each of the options **:argument-precedence-order**, **:documentation**, **:generic-function-class** and **:method-class**, the value of the option becomes the value of the keyword argument with the same name. If the option does not appear in the macro form, the keyword argument does not appear in the resulting call to **ensure-generic-function**.
- For the option **declare**, the list of declarations becomes the value of the **:declarations** keyword argument. If the **declare** option does not appear in the macro form, the **:declarations** keyword argument does not appear in the call to **ensure-generic-function**.
- The handling of the **:method-combination** option is not specified.

The result of the call to **ensure-generic-function** is returned as the result of evaluating or executing the **defgeneric** form.

5.5   Subprotocols

This section provides an overview of the Metaobject Protocols. The detailed behavior of each function, generic function and macro in the Metaobject Protocol is presented in Chapter 6. The remainder of this chapter is intended to emphasize connections among the parts of the Metaobject Protocol, and to provide some examples of the kinds of specializations and extensions the protocols are designed to support.

5.5.1   Metaobject Initialization Protocols

Like other objects, metaobjects can be created by calling **make-instance**. The initialization arguments passed to **make-instance** are used to initialize the metaobject in the usual way. The set of legal initialization arguments, and their interpretation, depends on the kind of metaobject being created. Implementations and portable programs are free to extend the set of legal initialization arguments. Detailed information about the initialization of each kind of metaobject are provided in Chapter 6; this section provides an overview and examples of this behavior.

Initialization of Class Metaobjects Class metaobjects created with **make-instance** are usually *anonymous*; that is, they have no proper name. An anonymous class metaobject can be given a proper name using (setf **find-class**) and (setf **class-name**).

When a class metaobject is created with **make-instance**, it is initialized in the usual way. The initialization arguments passed to **make-instance** are use to establish the definition of the class. Each initialization argument is checked for errors and associated with the class metaobject. The initialization arguments correspond roughly to the arguments accepted by the **defclass** macro, and more closely to the arguments accepted by the **ensure-class** function.

Some class metaobject classes allow their instances to be redefined. When permissible, this is done by calling **reinitialize-instance**. This is discussed in the next section.

An example of creating an anonymous class directly using **make-instance** follows:

```
(flet ((zero () 0)
       (propellor () *propellor*))
  (make-instance 'standard-class
    :name '(my-class foo)
    :direct-superclasses (list (find-class 'plane)
                               another-anonymous-class)
    :direct-slots '((:name x
                     :initform 0
                     :initfunction ,#'zero
                     :initargs (:x)
                     :readers (position-x)
                     :writers ((setf position-x)))
                    (:name y
                     :initform 0
                     :initfunction ,#'zero
                     :initargs (:y)
                     :readers (position-y)
                     :writers ((setf position-y))))
    :direct-default-initargs '((:engine *propellor* ,#'propellor))))
```

Reinitialization of Class Metaobjects Some class metaobject classes allow their instances to be reinitialized. This is done by calling **reinitialize-instance**. The initialization arguments have the same interpretation as in class initialization.

If the class metaobject was finalized before the call to **reinitialize-instance**, **finalize-inheritance** will be called again once all the initialization arguments have been processed and associated with the class metaobject. In addition, once finalization is complete, any dependents of the class metaobject will be updated by calling **update-dependent**.

Initialization of Generic Function and Method Metaobjects An example of creating a generic function and a method metaobject, and then adding the method to the generic function is shown below. This example is comparable to the method definition shown in Figure 5.3.

```
(let* ((gf (make-instance 'standard-generic-function
                          :lambda-list '(p 1 &optional visiblyp &key)))
       (method-class (generic-function-method-class gf)))
  (multiple-value-bind (lambda initargs)
      (make-method-lambda
        gf
        (class-prototype method-class)
        '(lambda (p 1 &optional (visiblyp t) &key color)
           (set-to-origin p)
           (when visiblyp (show-move p 0 color)))
        nil)
    (add-method gf
                (apply #'make-instance method-class
                       :function (compile nil lambda)
                       :specializers (list (find-class 'position)
                                           (intern-eql-specializer 0))
                       :qualifiers ()
                       :lambda-list '(p 1 &optional (visiblyp t)
                                      &key color)
                       initargs))))
```

5.5.2   Class Finalization Protocol

Class *finalization* is the process of computing the information a class inherits from its superclasses and preparing to actually allocate instances of the class. The class finalization process includes computing the class's class precedence list, the full set of slots accessible in instances of the class and the full set of default initialization arguments for the class. These values are associated with the class metaobject and can be accessed by calling the appropriate reader. In addition, the class finalization process makes decisions about how instances of the class will be implemented.

To support forward-referenced superclasses, and to account for the fact that not all classes are actually instantiated, class finalization is not done as part of the initialization of the class metaobject. Instead, finalization is done as a separate protocol, invoked by calling the generic function **finalize-inheritance**. The exact point at which **finalize-inheritance** is called depends on the class of the class metaobject; for **standard-class** it is called sometime after all the classes superclasses are defined, but no later than when the first instance of the class is allocated (by **allocate-instance**).

The first step of class finalization is computing the class precedence list. Doing this first allows subsequent steps to access the class precedence list. This step is performed by calling the generic function **compute-class-precedence-list**. The value returned from this call is associated with the class metaobject and can be accessed by calling the **class-precedence-list** generic function.

The second step is computing the full set of slots that will be accessible in instances of the class. This step is performed by calling the generic function **compute-slots**. The result of this call is a list of effective slot definition metaobjects. This value is associated with the class metaobject and can be accessed by calling the **class-slots** generic function.

The behavior of **compute-slots** is itself layered, consisting of calls to **effective-slot-definition-class** and **compute-effective-slot-definition**.

The final step of class finalization is computing the full set of initialization arguments for the class. This is done by calling the generic function **compute-default-initargs**. The value returned by this generic function is associated with the class metaobject and can be accessed by calling **class-default-initargs**.

If the class was previously finalized, **finalize-inheritance** may call **make-instances-obsolete**. The circumstances under which this happens are describe in the section of the CLOS specification called "Redefining Classes."

Forward-referenced classes, which provide a temporary definition for a class which has been referenced but not yet defined, can never be finalized. An error is signalled if **finalize-inheritance** is called on a forward-referenced class.

5.5.3   Instance Structure Protocol

The instance structure protocol is responsible for implementing the behavior of the slot access functions like **slot-value** and **(setf slot-value)**.

For each CLOS slot access function other than **slot-exists-p**, there is a corresponding generic function which actually provides the behavior of the function. When called, the slot access function finds the pertinent effective slot definition metaobject, calls the corresponding generic function and returns its result. The arguments passed on to the generic function include one additional value, the class of the *object* argument, which always immediately precedes the *object* argument.

The correspondences between slot access function and underlying slot access generic function are as follows:

Slot Access Function	Corresponding Slot Access Generic Function
slot-boundp	slot-boundp-using-class
slot-makunbound	slot-makunbound-using-class
slot-value	slot-value-using-class
(setf slot-value)	(setf slot-value-using-class)

At the lowest level, the instance structure protocol provides only limited mechanisms for portable programs to control the implementation of instances and to directly access the storage associated with instances without going through the indirection of slot access. This is done to allow portable programs to perform certain commonly requested slot access optimizations.

In particular, portable programs can control the implementation of, and obtain direct access to, slots with allocation :**instance** and type **t**. These are called *directly accessible slots*.

The relevant specified around-method on **compute-slots** determines the implementation of instances by deciding how each slot in the instance will be stored. For each directly accessible slot, this method allocates a *location* and associates it with the effective slot definition metaobject. The location can be accessed by calling the **slot-definition-location** generic function. Locations are non-negative integers. For a given class, the locations increase consecutively, in the order that the directly accessible slots appear in the list of effective slots. (Note that here, the next paragraph, and the specification of this around-method are the only places where the value returned by **compute-slots** is described as a list rather than a set.)

Given the location of a directly accessible slot, the value of that slot in an instance can be accessed with the appropriate accessor. For **standard-class**, this accessor is the function **standard-instance-access**. For **funcallable-standard-class**, this accessor is the function **funcallable-standard-instance-access**. In each case, the arguments to the accessor are the instance and the slot location, in that order. See the definition of each accessor in Chapter 6 for additional restrictions on the use of these function.

Portable programs are permitted to affect and rely on the allocation of locations only in the following limited way: By first defining a portable primary method on **compute-slots** which orders the returned value in a predictable way, and then relying on the defined behavior of the specified around-method to assign locations to all directly accessible slots.

Portable programs may compile-in calls to low-level accessors which take advantage of
the resulting predictable allocation of slot locations.

Example:

The following example shows the use of this mechanism to implement a new class
metaobject class, **ordered-class** and class option **:slot-order**. This option provides
control over the allocation of slot locations. In this simple example implementation,
the **:slot-order** option is not inherited by subclasses; it controls only instances of the
class itself.

```
(defclass ordered-class (standard-class)
    ((slot-order :initform ()
                 :initarg :slot-order
                 :reader class-slot-order)))

(defmethod compute-slots ((class ordered-class))
  (let ((order (class-slot-order class)))
    (sort (copy-list (call-next-method))
          #'(lambda (a b)
              (< (position (slot-definition-name a) order)
                 (position (slot-definition-name a) order))))))
```

Following is the source code the user of this extension would write. Note that because
the code above doesn't implement inheritance of the **:slot-order** option, the function
distance must not be called on instances of subclasses of **point**; it can only be called
on instances of **point** itself.

```
(defclass point ()
    ((x :initform 0)
     (y :initform 0))
  (:metaclass ordered-class)
  (:slot-order x y))

(defun distance (point)
  (sqrt (/ (+ (expt (standard-instance-access point 0) 2)
              (expt (standard-instance-access point 1) 2))
           2.0)))
```

In more realistic uses of this mechanism, the calls to the low-level instance structure
accessors would not actually appear textually in the source program, but rather would
be generated by a meta-level analysis program run during the process of compiling
the source program.

5.5.4   Funcallable Instances

Instances of classes which are themselves instances of **funcallable-standard-class** or
one of its subclasses are called *funcallable instances*. Funcallable instances can only be
created by **allocate-instance (funcallable-standard-class)**.

Like standard instances, funcallable instances have slots with the normal behavior.
They differ from standard instances in that they can be used as functions as well; that
is, they can be passed to **funcall** and **apply**, and they can be stored as the definition
of a function name. Associated with each funcallable instance is the function which it
runs when it is called. This function can be changed with **set-funcallable-instance-
function**.

Example:

The following simple example shows the use of funcallable instances to create a simple,
defstruct-like facility. (Funcallable instances are useful when a program needs to
construct and maintain a set of functions and information about those functions.
They make it possible to maintain both as the same object rather than two separate
objects linked, for example, by hash tables.)

```
(defclass constructor ()
    ((name :initarg :name :accessor constructor-name)
     (fields :initarg :fields :accessor constructor-fields))
  (:metaclass funcallable-standard-class))

(defmethod initialize-instance :after ((c constructor) &key)
  (with-slots (name fields) c
    (set-funcallable-instance-function
      c
      #'(lambda ()
          (let ((new (make-array (1+ (length fields)))))
            (setf (aref new 0) name)
            new)))))

(setq c1 (make-instance 'constructor
                        :name 'position :fields '(x y)))
#<CONSTRUCTOR 262437>

(setq p1 (funcall c1))
#<ARRAY 3 263674>
```

5.5.5   Generic Function Invocation Protocol

Associated with each generic function is its discriminating function. Each time the generic function is called, the discriminating function is called to provide the behavior of the generic function. The discriminating function receives the full set of arguments received by the generic function. It must lookup and execute the appropriate methods, and return the appropriate values.

The discriminating function is computed by the highest layer of the generic function invocation protocol, **compute-discriminating-function**. Whenever a generic function metaobject is initialized, reinitialized, or a method is added or removed, the discriminating function is recomputed. The new discriminating function is then stored with **set-funcallable-instance-function**.

Discriminating functions call **compute-applicable-methods** and **compute-applicable-methods-using-classes** to compute the methods applicable to the generic functions arguments. Applicable methods are combined by **compute-effective-method** to produce an *effective method*. Provisions are made to allow memoization of the method applicability and effective methods computations. (See the description of **compute-discriminating-function** for details.)

The body of method definitions are processed by **make-method-lambda**. The result of this generic function is a lambda expression which is processed by either **compile** or the file compiler to produce a *method function*. The arguments received by the method function are controlled by the **call-method** forms appearing in the effective methods. By default, method functions accept two arguments: a list of arguments to the generic function, and a list of next methods. The list of next methods corresponds to the next methods argument to **call-method**. If **call-method** appears with additional arguments, these will be passed to the method functions as well; in these cases, **make-method-lambda** must have created the method lambdas to expect additional arguments.

5.5.6   Dependent Maintenance Protocol

It is convenient for portable metaobjects to be able to memoize information about other metaobjects, portable or otherwise. Because class and generic function metaobjects can be reinitialized, and generic function metaobjects can be modified by adding and removing methods, a means must be provided to update this memoized information.

The dependent maintenance protocol supports this by providing a way to register an object which should be notified whenever a class or generic function is modified. An object which has been registered this way is called a *dependent* of the class or generic function metaobject. The dependents of class and generic function metaobjects are maintained with **add-dependent** and **remove-dependent**. The dependents of a class or generic function metaobject can be accessed with **map-dependents**. Dependents are notified about a modification by calling **update-dependent**. (See the specification of **update-dependent** for detailed description of the circumstances under which it is called.)

To prevent conflicts between two portable programs, or between portable programs and the implementation, portable code must not register metaobjects themselves as dependents. Instead, portable programs which need to record a metaobject as a dependent, should encapsulate that metaobject in some other kind of object, and record that object as the dependent. The results are undefined if this restriction is violated.

Example:

This example shows a general facility for encapsulating metaobjects before recording them as dependents. The facility defines a basic kind of encapsulating object: an updater. Specializations of the basic class can be defined with appropriate special updating behavior. In this way, information about the updating required is associated with each updater rather than with the metaobject being updated.

Updaters are used to encapsulate any metaobject which requires updating when a given class or generic function is modified. The function **record-updater** is called to both create an updater and add it to the dependents of the class or generic function. Methods on the generic function **update-dependent**, specialized to the specific class of updater do the appropriate update work.

```
(defclass updater ()
    ((dependent :initarg :dependent :reader dependent)))

(defun record-updater (class dependee dependent &rest initargs)
    (let ((updater (apply #'make-instance class :dependent dependent
                                                initargs)))
      (add-dependent dependee updater)
      updater))
```

A **flush-cache-updater** simply flushes the cache of the dependent when it is updated.

```
(defclass flush-cache-updater (updater) ())

(defmethod update-dependent (dependee (updater flush-cache-updater)
                                       &rest args)
    (declare (ignore args))
    (flush-cache (dependent updater)))
```

6 Generic Functions and Methods

This chapter describes each of the functions and generic functions that make up the CLOS Metaobject Protocol. The descriptions appear in alphabetical order with the exception that all the reader generic functions for each kind of metaobject are grouped together. So, for example, **method-function** would be found with **method-qualifiers** and other method metaobject readers under "Readers for Method Metaobjects."

The description of functions follows the same form as used in the CLOS specification. The description of generic functions is similar to that in the CLOS specification, but some minor changes have been made in the way methods are presented.

The following is an example of the format for the syntax description of a generic function:

gf1

    x y &optional z &key k

This description indicates that **gf1** is a generic function with two required parameters, x and y, an optional parameter z and a keyword parameter k.

The description of a generic function includes a description of its behavior. This provides the general behavior, or protocol of the generic function. All methods defined on the generic function, both portable and specified, must have behavior consistent with this description.

Every generic function described in this section is an instance of the class **standard-generic-function** and uses standard method combination.

The description of a generic function also includes descriptions of the specified methods for that generic function. In the description of these methods, a *method signature* is used to describe the parameters and parameter specializers of each method. The following is an example of the format for a method signature:

gf1 *Primary Method*

    (x *class*) y &optional z &key k

This signature indicates that this primary method on the generic function **gf1** has two required parameters, named x and y. In addition, there is an optional parameter z and a keyword parameter k. This signature also indicates that the method's parameter specializers are the classes named **class** and **t**.

The description of each method includes a description of the behavior particular to that method.

An abbreviated syntax is used when referring to a method defined elsewhere in the document. This abbreviated syntax includes the name of the generic function, the qualifiers, and the parameter specializers. A reference to the method with the signature shown above is written as: **gf1 (class t)**.

---

add-dependent   *Generic Function*

SYNTAX
add-dependent
   metaobject dependent

ARGUMENTS
The *metaobject* argument is a class or generic function metaobject.
   The *dependent* argument is an object.

VALUES
The value returned by this generic function is unspecified.

PURPOSE
This generic function adds *dependent* to the dependents of *metaobject*. If *dependent* is already in the set of dependents it is not added again (no error is signaled).
   The generic function **map-dependents** can be called to access the set of dependents of a class or generic function. The generic function **remove-dependent** can be called to remove an object from the set of dependents of a class or generic function. The effect of calling **add-dependent** or **remove-dependent** while a call to **map-dependents** on the same class or generic function is in progress is unspecified.
   The situations in which **add-dependent** is called are not specified.

METHODS
add-dependent   *Primary Method*
   (*class* **standard-class**) *dependent*

No behavior is specified for this method beyond that which is specified for the generic function.
   This method cannot be overridden unless the following methods are overridden as well:
      remove-dependent (standard-class t)
      map-dependents (standard-class t)

add-dependent   *Primary Method*

   (*class* `funcallable-standard-class`) *dependent*

No behavior is specified for this method beyond that which is specified for the generic function.

This method cannot be overridden unless the following methods are overridden as well:

   remove-dependent (funcallable-standard-class t)

   map-dependents (funcallable-standard-class t)

add-dependent   *Primary Method*

   (*generic-function* `standard-generic-function`) *dependent*

No behavior is specified for this method beyond that which is specified for the generic function.

This method cannot be overridden unless the following methods are overridden as well:

   remove-dependent (standard-generic-function t)

   map-dependents (standard-generic-function t)

REMARKS

See the "Dependent Maintenance Protocol" section for remarks about the use of this facility.

---

add-direct-method   *Generic Function*

SYNTAX

add-direct-method

   specializer method

ARGUMENTS

The *specializer* argument is a specializer metaobject.

   The *method* argument is a method metaobject.

VALUES

The value returned by this generic function is unspecified.

PURPOSE

This generic function is called to maintain a set of backpointers from a specializer to the set of methods specialized to it. If *method* is already in the set, it is not added again (no error is signaled).

This set can be accessed as a list by calling the generic function **specializer-direct-methods**. Methods are removed from the set by **remove-direct-method**.

The generic function **add-direct-method** is called by **add-method** whenever a method is added to a generic function. It is called once for each of the specializers of the method. Note that in cases where a specializer appears more than once in the specializers of a method, this generic function will be called more than once with the same specializer as argument.

The results are undefined if the *specializer* argument is not one of the specializers of the *method* argument.

METHODS
add-direct-method   *Primary Method*
    (*specializer* `class`)
    (*method* `method`)

This method implements the behavior of the generic function for class specializers. No behavior is specified for this method beyond that which is specified for the generic function.

This method cannot be overridden unless the following methods are overridden as well:

> **remove-direct-method (class method)**
> **specializer-direct-generic-functions (class)**
> **specializer-direct-methods (class)**

add-direct-method   *Primary Method*
    (*specializer* `eql-specializer`)
    (*method* `method`)

This method implements the behavior of the generic function for **eql** specializers. No behavior is specified for this method beyond that which is specified for the generic function.

---

add-direct-subclass   *Generic Function*

SYNTAX
add-direct-subclass
    superclass subclass

ARGUMENTS
The *superclass* argument is a class metaobject.

The *subclass* argument is a class metaobject.

VALUES

The value returned by this generic function is unspecified.

PURPOSE

This generic function is called to maintain a set of backpointers from a class to its direct subclasses. This generic function adds *subclass* to the set of direct subclasses of *superclass*.

When a class is initialized, this generic function is called once for each direct superclass of the class.

When a class is reinitialized, this generic function is called once for each added direct superclass of the class. The generic function **remove-direct-subclass** is called once for each deleted direct superclass of the class.

METHODS

add-direct-subclass   *Primary Method*

    (*superclass* **class**)

    (*subclass* **class**)

No behavior is specified for this method beyond that which is specified for the generic function.

This method cannot be overridden unless the following methods are overridden as well:

    remove-direct-subclass (class class)

    class-direct-subclasses (class)

---

add-method   *Generic Function*

SYNTAX

add-method

    generic-function method

ARGUMENTS

The *generic-function* argument is a generic function metaobject.

The *method* argument is a method metaobject.

VALUES

The *generic-function* argument is returned.

PURPOSE

This generic function associates an unattached method with a generic function.

An error is signaled if the lambda list of the method is not congruent with the lambda list of the generic function. An error is also signaled if the method is already associated with some other generic function.

If the given method agrees with an existing method of the generic function on parameter specializers and qualifiers, the existing method is removed by calling **remove-method** before the new method is added. See the section of the CLOS Specification called "Agreement on Parameter Specializers and Qualifiers" for a definition of agreement in this context.

Associating the method with the generic function then proceeds in four steps: (i) add *method* to the set returned by **generic-function-methods** and arrange for **method-generic-function** to return *generic-function*; (ii) call **add-direct-method** for each of the method's specializers; (iii) call **compute-discriminating-function** and install its result with **set-funcallable-instance-function**; and (iv) update the dependents of the generic function.

The generic function **add-method** can be called by the user or the implementation.

METHODS

add-method   *Primary Method*
    (*generic-function* `standard-generic-function`)
    (*method* `standard-method`)

No behavior is specified for this method beyond that which is specified for the generic function.

---

allocate-instance   *Generic Function*

SYNTAX

allocate-instance
    class **&rest** *initargs*

ARGUMENTS

The *class* argument is a class metaobject.

The *initargs* argument consists of alternating initialization argument names and values.

VALUES

The value returned is a newly allocated instance of *class*.

PURPOSE

This generic function is called to create a new, uninitialized instance of a class. The interpretation of the concept of an "uninitialized" instance depends on the class metaobject class.

Before allocating the new instance, **class-finalized-p** is called to see if *class* has been finalized. If it has not been finalized, **finalize-inheritance** is called before the new instance is allocated.

METHODS

allocate-instance   *Primary Method*
    (*class* `standard-class`) **&rest** *initargs*

This method allocates storage in the instance for each slot with allocation **:instance**. These slots are unbound. Slots with any other allocation are ignored by this method (no error is signaled).

allocate-instance   *Primary Method*
    (*class* `funcallable-standard-class`) **&rest** *initargs*

This method allocates storage in the instance for each slot with allocation **:instance**. These slots are unbound. Slots with any other allocation are ignored by this method (no error is signaled).

The funcallable instance function of the instance is undefined—the results are undefined if the instance is applied to arguments before **set-funcallable-instance-function** has been used to set the funcallable instance function.

allocate-instance   *Primary Method*
    (*class* `built-in-class`) **&rest** *initargs*

This method signals an error.

---

class-...   *Generic Function*

The following generic functions are described together under "Readers for Class Metaobjects" (page 212): **class-default-initargs**, **class-direct-default-initargs**, **class-direct-slots**, **class-direct-subclasses**, **class-direct-superclasses**, **class-finalized-p**, **class-name**, **class-precedence-list**, **class-prototype** and **class-slots**.

---

compute-applicable-methods   *Generic Function*

SYNTAX
compute-applicable-methods
   generic-function arguments

ARGUMENTS
The *generic-function* argument is a generic function metaobject.
   The *arguments* argument is a list of objects.

VALUES
This generic function returns a possibly empty list of method metaobjects.

PURPOSE
This generic function determines the method applicability of a generic function given a list
of required arguments. The returned list of method metaobjects is sorted by precedence
order with the most specific method appearing first. If no methods are applicable to the
supplied arguments the empty list is returned.

When a generic function is invoked, the discriminating function must determine the
ordered list of methods applicable to the arguments. Depending on the generic function
and the arguments, this is done in one of three ways: using a memoized value; calling **compute-applicable-methods-using-classes**; or calling **compute-applicable-
methods**. (Refer to the description of **compute-discriminating-function** for the
details of this process.)

The *arguments* argument is permitted to contain more elements than the generic function accepts required arguments; in these cases the extra arguments will be ignored. An
error is signaled if *arguments* contains fewer elements than the generic function accepts
required arguments.

The list returned by this generic function will not be mutated by the implementation.
The results are undefined if a portable program mutates the list returned by this generic
function.

METHODS
compute-applicable-methods   *Primary Method*
   (*generic-function* `standard-generic-function`)
   arguments

   This method signals an error if any method of the generic function has a specializer
   which is neither a class metaobject nor an **eql** specializer metaobject.

Otherwise, this method computes the sorted list of applicable methods according to the rules described in the section of the CLOS Specification called "Method Selection and Combination."

This method can be overridden. Because of the consistency requirements between this generic function and **compute-applicable-methods-using-classes**, doing so may require also overriding **compute-applicable-methods-using-classes (standard-generic-function t)**.

compute-applicable-methods-using-classes   *Generic Function*

SYNTAX

compute-applicable-methods-using-classes

   generic-function classes

ARGUMENTS

The *generic-function* argument is a generic function metaobject.

The *classes* argument is a list of class metaobjects.

VALUES

This generic function returns two values. The first is a possibly empty list of method metaobjects. The second is either true or false.

PURPOSE

This generic function is called to attempt to determine the method applicability of a generic function given only the classes of the required arguments.

If it is possible to completely determine the ordered list of applicable methods based only on the supplied classes, this generic function returns that list as its first value and true as its second value. The returned list of method metaobjects is sorted by precedence order, the most specific method coming first. If no methods are applicable to arguments with the specified classes, the empty list and true are returned.

If it is not possible to completely determine the ordered list of applicable methods based only on the supplied classes, this generic function returns an unspecified first value and false as its second value.

When a generic function is invoked, the discriminating function must determine the ordered list of methods applicable to the arguments. Depending on the generic function and the arguments, this is done in one of three ways: using a memoized value; calling **compute-applicable-methods-using-classes**; or calling **compute-applicable-methods**. (Refer to the description of **compute-discriminating-function** for the details of this process.)

The following consistency relationship between **compute-applicable-methods-using-classes** and **compute-applicable-methods** must be maintained: for any given generic function and set of arguments, if **compute-applicable-methods-using-classes** returns a second value of true, the first value must be equal to the value that would be returned by a corresponding call to **compute-applicable-methods**. The results are undefined if a portable method on either of these generic functions causes this consistency to be violated.

The list returned by this generic function will not be mutated by the implementation. The results are undefined if a portable program mutates the list returned by this generic function.

METHODS

compute-applicable-methods-using-classes   *Primary Method*
    (*generic-function* `standard-generic-function`)
    classes

If any method of the generic function has a specializer which is neither a class metaobject nor an **eql** specializer metaobject, this method signals an error.

In cases where the generic function has no methods with **eql** specializers, or has no methods with **eql** specializers that could be applicable to arguments of the supplied classes, this method returns the ordered list of applicable methods as its first value and true as its second value.

Otherwise this method returns an unspecified first value and false as its second value.

This method can be overridden. Because of the consistency requirements between this generic function and **compute-applicable-methods**, doing so may require also overriding **compute-applicable-methods (standard-generic-function t)**.

REMARKS

This generic function exists to allow user extensions which alter method lookup rules, but which base the new rules only on the classes of the required arguments, to take advantage of the class-based method lookup memoization found in many implementations. (There is of course no requirement for an implementation to provide this optimization.)

Such an extension can be implemented by two methods, one on this generic function and one on **compute-applicable-methods**. Whenever the user extension is in effect, the first method will return a second value of true. This should allow the implementation to absorb these cases into its own memoization scheme.

To get appropriate performance, other kinds of extensions may require methods on **compute-discriminating-function** which implement their own memoization scheme.

---

compute-class-precedence-list   *Generic Function*

SYNTAX
compute-class-precedence-list
   class

ARGUMENTS
The *class* argument is a class metaobject.

VALUES
The value returned by this generic function is a list of class metaobjects.

PURPOSE
This generic-function is called to determine the class precedence list of a class.

The result is a list which contains each of *class* and its superclasses once and only once. The first element of the list is *class* and the last element is the class named **t**.

All methods on this generic function must compute the class precedence list as a function of the ordered direct superclasses of the superclasses of *class*. The results are undefined if the rules used to compute the class precedence list depend on any other factors.

When a class is finalized, **finalize-inheritance** calls this generic function and associates the returned value with the class metaobject. The value can then be accessed by calling **class-precedence-list**.

The list returned by this generic function will not be mutated by the implementation. The results are undefined if a portable program mutates the list returned by this generic function.

METHODS
compute-class-precedence-list   *Primary Method*
   (*class* **class**)

   This method computes the class precedence list according to the rules described in the section of the CLOS Specification called "Determining the Class Precedence List."

   This method signals an error if *class* or any of its superclasses is a forward referenced class.

   This method can be overridden.

---

compute-default-initargs   *Generic Function*

SYNTAX
compute-default-initargs
   class

ARGUMENTS
The *class* argument is a class metaobject.

VALUES
The value returned by this generic function is a list of canonicalized default initialization arguments.

PURPOSE
This generic-function is called to determine the default initialization arguments for a class.

The result is a list of canonicalized default initialization arguments, with no duplication among initialization argument names.

All methods on this generic function must compute the default initialization arguments as a function of only: (i) the class precedence list of *class*, and (ii) the direct default initialization arguments of each class in that list. The results are undefined if the rules used to compute the default initialization arguments depend on any other factors.

When a class is finalized, **finalize-inheritance** calls this generic function and associates the returned value with the class metaobject. The value can then be accessed by calling **class-default-initargs**.

The list returned by this generic function will not be mutated by the implementation. The results are undefined if a portable program mutates the list returned by this generic function.

METHODS
compute-default-initargs   *Primary Method*
   (*class* `standard-class`)

compute-default-initargs   *Primary Method*
   (*class* `funcallable-standard-class`)

These methods compute the default initialization arguments according to the rules described in the section of the CLOS Specification called "Defaulting of Initialization Arguments."

These methods signal an error if *class* or any of its superclasses is a forward referenced class.

These methods can be overridden.

---

compute-discriminating-function   *Generic Function*

SYNTAX
compute-discriminating-function
   generic-function

ARGUMENTS
The *generic-function* argument is a generic function metaobject.

VALUES
The value returned by this generic function is a function.

PURPOSE
This generic function is called to determine the discriminating function for a generic function. When a generic function is called, the *installed* discriminating function is called with the full set of arguments received by the generic function, and must implement the behavior of calling the generic function: determining the ordered set of applicable methods, determining the effective method, and running the effective method.

To determine the ordered set of applicable methods, the discriminating function first calls **compute-applicable-methods-using-classes**. If **compute-applicable-methods-using-classes** returns a second value of false, the discriminating function then calls **compute-applicable-methods**.

When **compute-applicable-methods-using-classes** returns a second value of true, the discriminating function is permitted to memoize the first returned value as follows. The discriminating function may reuse the list of applicable methods without calling **compute-applicable-methods-using-classes** again provided that:

(i) the generic function is being called again with required arguments which are instances of the same classes,

(ii) the generic function has not been reinitialized,

(iii) no method has been added to or removed from the generic function,

(iv) for all the specializers of all the generic function's methods which are classes, their class precedence lists have not changed and

(v) for any such memoized value, the class precedence list of the class of each of the required arguments has not changed.

Determination of the effective method is done by calling **compute-effective-method**. When the effective method is run, each method's function is called, and receives as arguments: (i) a list of the arguments to the generic function, and (ii) whatever other arguments are specified in the **call-method** form indicating that the method should be called. (See **make-method-lambda** for more information about how method functions are called.)

The generic function **compute-discriminating-function** is called, and its result installed, by **add-method**, **remove-method**, **initialize-instance** and **reinitialize-instance**.

METHODS

compute-discriminating-function   *Primary Method*
  (*generic-function* `standard-generic-function`)

No behavior is specified for this method beyond that specified for the generic function. This method can be overridden.

---

compute-effective-method   *Generic Function*

SYNTAX

compute-effective-method
  generic-function method-combination methods

ARGUMENTS

The *generic-function* argument is a generic function metaobject.

The *method-combination* argument is a method combination metaobject.

The *methods* argument is a list of method metaobjects.

VALUES

This generic function returns two values. The first is an effective method, the second is a list of effective method options.

PURPOSE

This generic function is called to determine the effective method from a sorted list of method metaobjects.

An effective method is a form that describes how the applicable methods are to be combined. Inside of effective method forms are **call-method** forms which indicate that a particular method is to be called. The arguments to the **call-method** form indicate exactly how the method function of the method should be called. (See **make-method-lambda** for more details about method functions.)

An effective method option has the same interpretation and syntax as either the
:arguments or the **:generic-function** option in the long form of **define-method-combination**.

More information about the form and interpretation of effective methods and effective
method options can be found under the description of the **define-method-combination**
macro in the CLOS specification.

This generic function can be called by the user or the implementation. It is called by
discriminating functions whenever a sorted list of applicable methods must be converted
to an effective method.

METHODS

compute-effective-method   *Primary Method*

  (*generic-function* `standard-generic-function`)
  method-combination
  methods

This method computes the effective method according to the rules of the method
combination type implemented by *method-combination*.

This method can be overridden.

---

compute-effective-slot-definition   *Generic Function*

SYNTAX

compute-effective-slot-definition

  class name direct-slot-definitions

ARGUMENTS

The *class* argument is a class metaobject.

The *name* argument is a slot name.

The *direct-slot-definitions* argument is an ordered list of direct slot definition metaobjects. The most specific direct slot definition metaobject appears first in the list.

VALUES

The value returned by this generic function is an effective slot definition metaobject.

PURPOSE

This generic function determines the effective slot definition for a slot in a class. It is
called by **compute-slots** once for each slot accessible in instances of *class*.

This generic function uses the supplied list of direct slot definition metaobjects to
compute the inheritance of slot properties for a single slot. The returned effective slot

definition represents the result of computing the inheritance. The name of the new effective slot definition is the same as the name of the direct slot definitions supplied.

The class of the effective slot definition metaobject is determined by calling **effective-slot-definition-class**. The effective slot definition is then created by calling **make-instance**. The initialization arguments passed in this call to **make-instance** are used to initialize the new effective slot definition metaobject. See "Initialization of Slot Definition Metaobjects" for details.

METHODS

compute-effective-slot-definition   *Primary Method*

    (*class* `standard-class`)

    name

    direct-slot-definitions

This method implements the inheritance and defaulting of slot options following the rules described in the "Inheritance of Slots and Options" section of the CLOS Specification.

This method can be extended, but the value returned by the extending method must be the value returned by this method.

compute-effective-slot-definition   *Primary Method*

    (*class* `funcallable-standard-class`)

    name

    direct-slot-definitions

This method implements the inheritance and defaulting of slot options following the rules described in the "Inheritance of Slots and Options" section of the CLOS Specification.

This method can be extended, but the value returned by the extending method must be the value returned by this method.

---

compute-slots   *Generic Function*

SYNTAX

compute-slots

    class

ARGUMENTS

The *class* argument is a class metaobject.

VALUES
The value returned is a set of effective slot definition metaobjects.

PURPOSE
This generic function computes a set of effective slot definition metaobjects for the class *class*. The result is a list of effective slot definition metaobjects: one for each slot that will be accessible in instances of *class*.

This generic function proceeds in 3 steps:

The first step collects the full set of direct slot definitions from the superclasses of *class*.

The direct slot definitions are then collected into individual lists, one list for each slot name associated with any of the direct slot definitions. The slot names are compared with **eql**. Each such list is then sorted into class precedence list order. Direct slot definitions coming from classes earlier in the class precedence list of *class* appear before those coming from classes later in the class precedence list. For each slot name, the generic function **compute-effective-slot-definition** is called to compute an effective slot definition. The result of **compute-slots** is a list of these effective slot definitions, in unspecified order.

In the final step, the location for each effective slot definition is set. This is done by specified around-methods; portable methods cannot take over this behavior. For more information on the slot definition locations, see the section "Instance Structure Protocol."

The list returned by this generic function will not be mutated by the implementation. The results are undefined if a portable program mutates the list returned by this generic function.

METHODS

compute-slots   *Primary Method*
    (*class* `standard-class`)

  This method implements the specified behavior of the generic function.
  This method can be overridden.

compute-slots   *Primary Method*
    (*class* `funcallable-standard-class`)

  This method implements the specified behavior of the generic function.
  This method can be overridden.

compute-slots   *Around-Method*
  (*class* `standard-class`)

This method implements the specified behavior of computing and storing slot locations.
This method cannot be overridden.

compute-slots   *Around-Method*
  (*class* `funcallable-standard-class`)

This method implements the specified behavior of computing and storing slot locations.
This method cannot be overridden.

---

direct-slot-definition-class   *Generic Function*

SYNTAX
direct-slot-definition-class
  class **&rest** *initargs*

ARGUMENTS
The *class* argument is a class metaobject.
  The *initargs* argument is a set of initialization arguments and values.

VALUES
The value returned is a subclass of the class **direct-slot-definition**.

PURPOSE
When a class is initialized, each of the canonicalized slot specifications must be converted
to a direct slot definition metaobject. This generic function is called to determine the
class of that direct slot definition metaobject.
  The *initargs* argument is simply the canonicalized slot specification for the slot.

METHODS
direct-slot-definition-class   *Primary Method*
  (*class* `standard-class`)
  &rest *initargs*

This method returns the class **standard-direct-slot-definition**.
  This method can be overridden.

direct-slot-definition-class   *Primary Method*
  (*class* `funcallable-standard-class`)
  &rest *initargs*

This method returns the class **standard-direct-slot-definition**.
This method can be overridden.

---

effective-slot-definition-class   *Generic Function*

SYNTAX
effective-slot-definition-class
  class **&rest** *initargs*

ARGUMENTS
The *class* argument is a class metaobject.
  The *initargs* argument is a set of initialization arguments and values.

VALUES
The value returned is a subclass of the class **effective-slot-definition-class**.

PURPOSE
This generic function is called by **compute-effective-slot-definition** to determine the
class of the resulting effective slot definition metaobject. The *initargs* argument is the
set of initialization arguments and values that will be passed to **make-instance** when
the effective slot definition metaobject is created.

METHODS
effective-slot-definition-class   *Primary Method*
  (*class* `standard-class`)
  &rest initargs

This method returns the class **standard-effective-slot-definition**.
This method can be overridden.

effective-slot-definition-class   *Primary Method*
  (*class* `funcallable-standard-class`)
  &rest initargs

This method returns the class **standard-effective-slot-definition**.
This method can be overridden.

---

ensure-class   *Function*

SYNTAX
ensure-class
   name &key &allow-other-keys

ARGUMENTS
The *name* argument is a symbol.

Some of the keyword arguments accepted by this function are actually processed by
ensure-class-using-class, others are processed during initialization of the class metaobject (as described in the section called "Initialization of Class Metaobjects").

VALUES
The result is a class metaobject.

PURPOSE
This function is called to define or redefine a class with the specified name, and can be
called by the user or the implementation. It is the functional equivalent of **defclass**, and
is called by the expansion of the **defclass** macro.

The behavior of this function is actually implemented by the generic function **ensure-
class-using-class**. When **ensure-class** is called, it immediately calls **ensure-class-
using-class** and returns that result as its own.

The first argument to **ensure-class-using-class** is computed as follows:

- If *name* names a class (**find-class** returns a class when called with *name*) use that
  class.
- Otherwise use **nil**.

The second argument is *name*. The remaining arguments are the complete set of keyword
arguments received by the **ensure-class** function.

ensure-class-using-class   *Generic Function*

SYNTAX

ensure-class-using-class

   class name **&key** `:direct-default-initargs :direct-slots`
                      `:direct-superclasses :name`
                      `:metaclass`

   &allow-other-keys

ARGUMENTS

The *class* argument is a class metaobject or **nil**.

The *name* argument is a class name.

The **:metaclass** argument is a class metaobject class or a class metaobject class name. If this argument is not supplied, it defaults to the class named **standard-class**. If a class name is supplied, it is interpreted as the class with that name. If a class name is supplied, but there is no such class, an error is signaled.

The **:direct-superclasses** argument is a list of which each element is a class metaobject or a class name. An error is signaled if this argument is not a proper list.

For the interpretation of additional keyword arguments, see "Initialization of Class Metaobjects" (page 193).

VALUES

The result is a class metaobject.

PURPOSE

This generic function is called to define or modify the definition of a named class. It is called by the **ensure-class** function. It can also be called directly.

The first step performed by this generic function is to compute the set of initialization arguments which will be used to create or reinitialize the named class. The initialization arguments are computed from the full set of keyword arguments received by this generic function as follows:

- The **:metaclass** argument is not included in the initialization arguments.
- If the **:direct-superclasses** argument was received by this generic function, it is converted into a list of class metaobjects. This conversion does not affect the structure of the supplied **:direct-superclasses** argument. For each element in the **:direct-superclasses** argument:

  - If the element is a class metaobject, that class metaobject is used.

- If the element names a class, that class metaobject is used.
- Otherwise an instance of the class **forward-referenced-class** is created and used. The proper name of the newly created forward referenced class metaobject is set to *name*.

- All other keyword arguments are included directly in the initialization arguments.

If the *class* argument is **nil**, a new class metaobject is created by calling the **make-instance** generic function with the value of the :metaclass argument as its first argument, and the previously computed initialization arguments. The proper name of the newly created class metaobject is set to *name*. The newly created class metaobject is returned.

If the *class* argument is a forward referenced class, **change-class** is called to change its class to the value specified by the :metaclass argument. The class metaobject is then reinitialized with the previously initialization arguments. (This is a documented violation of the general constraint that **change-class** not be used with class metaobjects.)

If the class of the *class* argument is not the same as the class specified by the :metaclass argument, an error is signaled.

Otherwise, the class metaobject *class* is redefined by calling the **reinitialize-instance** generic function with *class* and the initialization arguments. The *class* argument is then returned.

METHODS
ensure-class-using-class   *Primary Method*
    (*class* class)
    name
    &key :metaclass
        :direct-superclasses

    &allow-other-keys

This method implements the behavior of the generic function in the case where the *class* argument is a class.

This method can be overridden.

ensure-class-using-class   *Primary Method*

   (*class* `forward-referenced-class`)

   name

   `&key :metaclass`

        `:direct-superclasses`

   `&allow-other-keys`

This method implements the behavior of the generic function in the case where the *class* argument is a forward referenced class.

ensure-class-using-class   *Primary Method*

   (*class* `null`)

   name

   `&key :metaclass`

        `:direct-superclasses`

   `&allow-other-keys`

This method implements the behavior of the generic function in the case where the *class* argument is **nil**.

---

ensure-generic-function   *Function*

SYNTAX

ensure-generic-function

   function-name `&key &allow-other-keys`

ARGUMENTS

The *function-name* argument is a symbol or a list of the form (`setf` *symbol*).

Some of the keyword arguments accepted by this function are actually processed by **ensure-generic-function-using-class**, others are processed during initialization of the generic function metaobject (as described in the section called "Initialization of Generic Function Metaobjects").

VALUES

The result is a generic function metaobject.

PURPOSE

This function is called to define a globally named generic function or to specify or modify options and declarations that pertain to a globally named generic function as a whole. It can be called by the user or the implementation.

It is the functional equivalent of **defgeneric**, and is called by the expansion of the **defgeneric** and **defmethod** macros.

The behavior of this function is actually implemented by the generic function **ensure-generic-function-using-class**. When **ensure-generic-function** is called, it immediately calls **ensure-generic-function-using-class** and returns that result as its own.

The first argument to **ensure-generic-function-using-class** is computed as follows:

- If *function-name* names a non-generic function, a macro, or a special form, an error is signaled.
- If *function-name* names a generic function, that generic function metaobject is used.
- Otherwise, **nil** is used.

The second argument is *function-name*. The remaining arguments are the complete set of keyword arguments received by **ensure-generic-function**.

---

ensure-generic-function-using-class   *Generic Function*

SYNTAX

ensure-generic-function-using-class

    generic-function

    function-name

    &key `:argument-precedence-order` `:declarations`

            `:documentation` `:generic-function-class`

            `:lambda-list` `:method-class`

            `:method-combination` `:name`

    &allow-other-keys

ARGUMENTS

The *generic-function* argument is a generic function metaobject or **nil**.

The *function-name* argument is a symbol or a list of the form (`setf` *symbol*).

The **:generic-function-class** argument is a class metaobject or a class name. If it is not supplied, it defaults to the class named **standard-generic-function**. If a class name is supplied, it is interpreted as the class with that name. If a class name is supplied, but there is no such class, an error is signaled.

For the interpretation of additional keyword arguments, see "Initialization of Generic Function Metaobjects" (page 197).

VALUES

The result is a generic function metaobject.

PURPOSE

The generic function **ensure-generic-function-using-class** is called to define or modify the definition of a globally named generic function. It is called by the **ensure-generic-function** function. It can also be called directly.

The first step performed by this generic function is to compute the set of initialization arguments which will be used to create or reinitialize the globally named generic function. These initialization arguments are computed from the full set of keyword arguments received by this generic function as follows:

- The **:generic-function-class** argument is not included in the initialization arguments.
- If the **:method-class** argument was received by this generic function, it is converted into a class metaobject. This is done by looking up the class name with **find-class**. If there is no such class, an error is signalled.
- All other keyword arguments are included directly in the initialization arguments.

If the *generic-function* argument is **nil**, an instance of the class specified by the **:generic-function-class** argument is created by calling **make-instance** with the previously computed initialization arguments. The function name *function-name* is set to name the generic function. The newly created generic function metaobject is returned.

If the class of the *generic-function* argument is not the same as the class specified by the **:generic-function-class** argument, an error is signaled.

Otherwise the generic function *generic-function* is redefined by calling the **reinitialize-instance** generic function with *generic-function* and the initialization arguments. The *generic-function* argument is then returned.

METHODS

ensure-generic-function-using-class   *Primary Method*
 (*generic-function* `generic-function`)
 function-name
 &key `:generic-function-class`

 &allow-other-keys

This method implements the behavior of the generic function in the case where *function-name* names an existing generic function.

This method can be overridden.

ensure-generic-function-using-class   *Primary Method*
    (*generic-function* `null`)
    function-name
    `&key` `:generic-function-class`

    `&allow-other-keys`

This method implements the behavior of the generic function in the case where *function-name* names no function, generic function, macro or special form.

---

eql-specializer-object   *Function*

SYNTAX
eql-specializer-object
    eql-specializer

ARGUMENTS
The *eql-specializer* argument is an **eql** specializer metaobject.

VALUES
The value returned by this function is an object.

PURPOSE
This function returns the object associated with *eql-specializer* during initialization. The value is guaranteed to be **eql** to the value originally passed to **intern-eql-specializer**, but it is not necessarily **eq** to that value.

    This function signals an error if *eql-specializer* is not an **eql** specializer.

---

extract-lambda-list   *Function*

SYNTAX
extract-lambda-list
    specialized-lambda-list

ARGUMENTS
The *specialized-lambda-list* argument is a specialized lambda list as accepted by **defmethod**.

VALUES
The result is an unspecialized lambda list.

PURPOSE
This function takes a specialized lambda list and returns the lambda list with the specializers removed. This is a non-destructive operation. Whether the result shares any structure with the argument is unspecified.

   If the *specialized-lambda-list* argument does not have legal syntax, an error is signaled. This syntax checking does not check the syntax of the actual specializer names, only the syntax of the lambda list and where the specializers appear.

EXAMPLES
```
(extract-lambda-list '((p position)))          ==> (P)

(extract-lambda-list '((p position) x y))      ==> (P X Y)

(extract-lambda-list '(a (b (eql x)) c &rest i)) ==> (A B C &OPTIONAL I)
```

---

extract-specializer-names   *Function*

SYNTAX
extract-specializer-names
   specialized-lambda-list

ARGUMENTS
The *specialized-lambda-list* argument is a specialized lambda list as accepted by **defmethod**.

VALUES
The result is a list of specializer names.

PURPOSE
This function takes a specialized lambda list and returns its specializer names. This is a non-destructive operation. Whether the result shares structure with the argument is unspecified. The results are undefined if the result of this function is modified.

   The result of this function will be a list with a number of elements equal to the number of required arguments in *specialized-lambda-list*. Specializers are defaulted to the symbol **t**.

   If the *specialized-lambda-list* argument does not have legal syntax, an error is signaled. This syntax checking does not check the syntax of the actual specializer names, only the syntax of the lambda list and where the specializers appear.

EXAMPLES

```
(extract-specializer-names '((p position)))           ==> (POSITION)

(extract-specializer-names '((p position) x y))       ==> (POSITION T T)

(extract-specializer-names '(a (b (eql x)) c &rest i)) ==> (T (EQL X) T)
```

---

finalize-inheritance   *Generic Function*

SYNTAX

finalize-inheritance
   class

ARGUMENTS

The *class* argument is a class metaobject.

VALUES

The value returned by this generic function is unspecified.

PURPOSE

This generic function is called to finalize a class metaobject. This is described in the Section named "Class Finalization Protocol."

   After **finalize-inheritance** returns, the class metaobject is finalized and the result of calling **class-finalized-p** on the class metaobject will be true.

METHODS

finalize-inheritance   *Primary Method*
   (*class* standard-class)

finalize-inheritance   *Primary Method*
   (*class* funcallable-standard-class)

   No behavior is specified for these methods beyond that which is specified for the generic function.

finalize-inheritance   *Primary Method*
   (*class* forward-referenced-class)

   This method signals an error.

find-method-combination   *Generic Function*

SYNTAX

find-method-combination

   generic-function

   method-combination-type-name

   method-combination-options

ARGUMENTS

The *generic-function* argument is a generic function metaobject.

   The *method-combination-type-name* argument is a symbol which names a type of method combination.

   The *method-combination-options* argument is a list of arguments to the method combination type.

VALUES

The value returned by this generic function is a method combination metaobject.

PURPOSE

This generic function is called to determine the method combination object used by a generic function.

REMARKS

Further details of method combination metaobjects are not specified.

funcallable-standard-instance-access   *Function*

SYNTAX

funcallable-standard-instance-access

   instance location

ARGUMENTS

The *instance* argument is an object.

   The *location* argument is a slot location.

VALUES

The result of this function is an object.

PURPOSE

This function is called to provide direct access to a slot in an instance. By usurping the normal slot lookup protocol, this function is intended to provide highly optimized access to the slots associated with an instance.

The following restrictions apply to the use of this function:

- The *instance* argument must be a funcallable instance (it must have been returned by **allocate-instance (funcallable-standard-class)**).
- The *instance* argument cannot be an non-updated obsolete instance.
- The *location* argument must be a location of one of the directly accessible slots of the instance's class.
- The slot must be bound.

The results are undefined if any of these restrictions are not met.

---

generic-function-...   *Generic Function*

The following generic functions are described together under "Readers for Generic Function Metaobjects" (page 216): **generic-function-argument-precedence-order**, **generic-function-declarations**, **generic-function-lambda-list**, **generic-function-method-class**, **generic-function-method-combination**, **generic-function-methods** and **generic-function-name**.

Initialization of Class Metaobjects

A class metaobject can be created by calling **make-instance**. The initialization arguments establish the definition of the class. A class metaobject can be redefined by calling **reinitialize-instance**. Some classes of class metaobject do not support redefinition; in these cases, **reinitialize-instance** signals an error.

Initialization of a class metaobject must be done by calling **make-instance** and allowing it to call **initialize-instance**. Reinitialization of a class metaobject must be done by calling **reinitialize-instance**. Portable programs must not call **initialize-instance** directly to initialize a class metaobject. Portable programs must not call **shared-initialize** directly to initialize or reinitialize a class metaobject. Portable programs must not call **change-class** to change the class of any class metaobject or to turn a non-class object into a class metaobject.

Since metaobject classes may not be redefined, no behavior is specified for the result of calls to **update-instance-for-redefined-class** on class metaobjects. Since the class of class metaobjects may not be changed, no behavior is specified for the result of calls to **update-instance-for-different-class** on class metaobjects.

During initialization or reinitialization, each initialization argument is checked for errors and then associated with the class metaobject. The value can then be accessed by calling the appropriate accessor as shown in Table 6.1.

This section begins with a description of the error checking and processing of each initialization argument. This is followed by a table showing the generic functions that can be used to access the stored initialization arguments. Initialization behavior specific to the different specified class metaobject classes comes next. The section ends with a set of restrictions on portable methods affecting class metaobject initialization and reinitialization.

In these descriptions, the phrase "this argument defaults to *value*" means that when that initialization argument is not supplied, initialization or reinitialization is performed as if *value* had been supplied. For some initialization arguments this could be done by the use of default initialization arguments, but whether it is done this way is not specified. Implementations are free to define default initialization arguments for specified class metaobject classes. Portable programs are free to define default initialization arguments for portable subclasses of the class **class**.

Unless there is a specific note to the contrary, then during reinitialization, if an initialization argument is not supplied, the previously stored value is left unchanged.

- The **:direct-default-initargs** argument is a list of canonicalized default initialization arguments.

An error is signaled if this value is not a proper list, or if any element of the list is not a canonicalized default initialization argument.

If the class metaobject is being initialized, this argument defaults to the empty list.

- The **:direct-slots** argument is a list of canonicalized slot specifications.

An error is signaled if this value is not a proper list or if any element of the list is not a canonicalized slot specification.

After error checking, this value is converted to a list of direct slot definition metaobjects before it is associated with the class metaobject. Conversion of each canonicalized slot specification to a direct slot definition metaobject is a two-step process. First, the generic function **direct-slot-definition-class** is called with the class metaobject and the canonicalized slot specification to determine the class of the new direct slot definition metaobject; this permits both the class metaobject and the canonicalized slot specification to control the resulting direct slot definition metaobject class. Second, **make-instance** is applied to the direct slot definition metaobject class and the canonicalized slot specification. This conversion could be implemented as shown in the following code:

```
(defun convert-to-direct-slot-definition (class canonicalized-slot)
  (apply #'make-instance
         (apply #'direct-slot-definition-class
                class canonicalized-slot)
         canonicalized-slot))
```

If the class metaobject is being initialized, this argument defaults to the empty list.

Once the direct slot definition metaobjects have been created, the specified reader and writer methods are created. The generic functions **reader-method-class** and **writer-method-class** are called to determine the classes of the method metaobjects created.

- The **:direct-superclasses** argument is a list of class metaobjects. Classes which do not support multiple inheritance signal an error if the list contains more than one element.

An error is signaled if this value is not a proper list or if **validate-superclass** applied to *class* and any element of this list returns false.

When the class metaobject is being initialized, and this argument is either not supplied or is the empty list, this argument defaults as follows: if the class is an instance of **standard-class** or one of its subclasses the default value is a list of the class **standard-object**; if the class is an instance of **funcallable-standard-class** or one of its subclasses the default value is list of the class **funcallable-standard-object**.

After any defaulting of the value, the generic function **add-direct-subclass** is called once for each element of the list.

When the class metaobject is being reinitialized and this argument is supplied, the generic function **remove-direct-subclass** is called once for each class metaobject in the previously stored value but not in the new value; the generic function **add-direct-subclass** is called once for each class metaobject in the new value but not in the previously stored value.

- The **:documentation** argument is a string or **nil**.

  An error is signaled if this value is not a string or **nil**.

  If the class metaobject is being initialized, this argument defaults to **nil**.

- The **:name** argument is an object.

  If the class is being initialized, this argument defaults to **nil**.

After the processing and defaulting of initialization arguments described above, the value of each initialization argument is associated with the class metaobject. These values can then be accessed by calling the corresponding generic function. The correspondences are as follows:

Initialization Argument	Generic Function
:direct-default-initargs	class-direct-default-initargs
:direct-slots	class-direct-slots
:direct-superclasses	class-direct-superclasses
:documentation	documentation
:name	class-name

Table 6.1 Initialization arguments and accessors for class metaobjects.

Instances of the class **standard-class** support multiple inheritance and reinitialization. Instances of the class **funcallable-standard-class** support multiple inheritance and reinitialization. For forward referenced classes, all of the initialization arguments default to **nil**.

Since built-in classes cannot be created or reinitialized by the user, an error is signaled if **initialize-instance** or **reinitialize-instance** are called to initialize or reinitialize a derived instance of the class **built-in-class**.

METHODS
It is not specified which methods provide the initialization and reinitialization behavior described above. Instead, the information needed to allow portable programs to specialize

this behavior is presented as a set of restrictions on the methods a portable program can define. The model is that portable initialization methods have access to the class metaobject when either all or none of the specified initialization has taken effect.

These restrictions govern the methods that a portable program can define on the generic functions **initialize-instance**, **reinitialize-instance**, and **shared-initialize**. These restrictions apply only to methods on these generic functions for which the first specializer is a subclass of the class **class**. Other portable methods on these generic functions are not affected by these restrictions.

- Portable programs must not define methods on **shared-initialize**.
- For **initialize-instance** and **reinitialize-instance**:

  - Portable programs must not define primary methods.
  - Portable programs may define around-methods, but these must be extending, not overriding methods.
  - Portable before-methods must assume that when they are run, none of the initialization behavior described above has been completed.
  - Portable after-methods must assume that when they are run, all of the initialization behavior described above has been completed.

    The results are undefined if any of these restrictions are violated.

Initialization of Generic Function Metaobjects

A generic function metaobject can be created by calling **make-instance**. The initialization arguments establish the definition of the generic function. A generic function metaobject can be redefined by calling **reinitialize-instance**. Some classes of generic function metaobject do not support redefinition; in these cases, **reinitialize-instance** signals an error.

Initialization of a generic function metaobject must be done by calling **make-instance** and allowing it to call **initialize-instance**. Reinitialization of a generic-function metaobject must be done by calling **reinitialize-instance**. Portable programs must not call **initialize-instance** directly to initialize a generic function metaobject. Portable programs must not call **shared-initialize** directly to initialize or reinitialize a generic function metaobject. Portable programs must not call **change-class** to change the class of any generic function metaobject or to turn a non-generic-function object into a generic function metaobject.

Since metaobject classes may not be redefined, no behavior is specified for the result of calls to **update-instance-for-redefined-class** on generic function metaobjects. Since the class of a generic function metaobject may not be changed, no behavior is specified for the results of calls to **update-instance-for-different-class** on generic function metaobjects.

During initialization or reinitialization, each initialization argument is checked for errors and then associated with the generic function metaobject. The value can then be accessed by calling the appropriate accessor as shown in Table 6.2.

This section begins with a description of the error checking and processing of each initialization argument. This is followed by a table showing the generic functions that can be used to access the stored initialization arguments. The section ends with a set of restrictions on portable methods affecting generic function metaobject initialization and reinitialization.

In these descriptions, the phrase "this argument defaults to *value*" means that when that initialization argument is not supplied, initialization or reinitialization is performed as if *value* had been supplied. For some initialization arguments this could be done by the use of default initialization arguments, but whether it is done this way is not specified. Implementations are free to define default initialization arguments for specified generic function metaobject classes. Portable programs are free to define default initialization arguments for portable subclasses of the class **generic-function**.

Unless there is a specific note to the contrary, then during reinitialization, if an initialization argument is not supplied, the previously stored value is left unchanged.

- The **:argument-precedence-order** argument is a list of symbols.

  An error is signaled if this argument appears but the **:lambda-list** argument does not appear. An error is signaled if this value is not a proper list or if this value is not a permutation of the symbols from the required arguments part of the **:lambda-list** initialization argument.

  When the generic function is being initialized or reinitialized, and this argument is not supplied, but the **:lambda-list** argument is supplied, this value defaults to the symbols from the required arguments part of the **:lambda-list** argument, in the order they appear in that argument. If neither argument is supplied, neither are initialized (see the description of **:lambda-list**.)

- The **:declarations** argument is a list of declarations.

  An error is signaled if this value is not a proper list or if each of its elements is not a legal declaration.

  When the generic function is being initialized, and this argument is not supplied, it defaults to the empty list.

- The **:documentation** argument is a string or **nil**.

  An error is signaled if this value is not a string or **nil**.

  If the generic function is being initialized, this argument defaults to **nil**.

- The **:lambda-list** argument is a lambda list.

  An error is signaled if this value is not a proper generic function lambda list.

  When the generic function is being initialized, and this argument is not supplied, the generic function's lambda list is not initialized. The lambda list will be initialized later, either when the first method is added to the generic function, or a later reinitialization of the generic function.

- The **:method-combination** argument is a method combination metaobject.

- The **:method-class** argument is a class metaobject.

  An error is signaled if this value is not a subclass of the class **method**.

  When the generic function is being initialized, and this argument is not supplied, it defaults to the class **standard-method**.

- The **:name** argument is an object.

  If the generic function is being initialized, this argument defaults to **nil**.

After the processing and defaulting of initialization arguments described above, the value of each initialization argument is associated with the generic function metaobject. These values can then be accessed by calling the corresponding generic function. The correspondences are as follows:

Initialization Argument	Generic Function
:argument-precedence-order	generic-function-argument-precedence-order
:declarations	generic-function-declarations
:documentation	documentation
:lambda-list	generic-function-lambda-list
:method-combination	generic-function-method-combination
:method-class	generic-function-method-class
:name	generic-function-name

Table 6.2 Initialization arguments and accessors for generic function metaobjects.

METHODS

It is not specified which methods provide the initialization and reinitialization behavior described above. Instead, the information needed to allow portable programs to specialize this behavior is presented as a set of restrictions on the methods a portable program can define. The model is that portable initialization methods have access to the generic function metaobject when either all or none of the specified initialization has taken effect.

These restrictions govern the methods that a portable program can define on the generic functions **initialize-instance**, **reinitialize-instance**, and **shared-initialize**. These restrictions apply only to methods on these generic functions for which the first specializer is a subclass of the class **generic-function**. Other portable methods on these generic functions are not affected by these restrictions.

- Portable programs must not define methods on **shared-initialize**.
- For **initialize-instance** and **reinitialize-instance**:

  - Portable programs must not define primary methods.
  - Portable programs may define around-methods, but these must be extending, not overriding methods.
  - Portable before-methods must assume that when they are run, none of the initialization behavior described above has been completed.
  - Portable after-methods must assume that when they are run, all of the initialization behavior described above has been completed.

The results are undefined if any of these restrictions are violated.

Initialization of Method Metaobjects

A method metaobject can be created by calling **make-instance**. The initialization arguments establish the definition of the method. A method metaobject cannot be redefined; calling **reinitialize-instance** signals an error.

Initialization of a method metaobject must be done by calling **make-instance** and allowing it to call **initialize-instance**. Portable programs must not call **initialize-instance** directly to initialize a method metaoject. Portable programs must not call **shared-initialize** directly to initialize a method metaobject. Portable programs must not call **change-class** to change the class of any method metaobject or to turn a non-method object into a method metaobject.

Since metaobject classes may not be redefined, no behavior is specified for the result of calls to **update-instance-for-redefined-class** on method metaobjects. Since the class of a method metaobject cannot be changed, no behavior is specified for the result of calls to **update-instance-for-different-class** on method metaobjects.

During initialization, each initialization argument is checked for errors and then associated with the method metaobject. The value can then be accessed by calling the appropriate accessor as shown in Table 6.3.

This section begins with a description of the error checking and processing of each initialization argument. This is followed by a table showing the generic functions that can be used to access the stored initialization arguments. The section ends with a set of restrictions on portable methods affecting method metaobject initialization.

In these descriptions, the phrase "this argument defaults to *value*" means that when that initialization argument is not supplied, initialization is performed as if *value* had been supplied. For some initialization arguments this could be done by the use of default initialization arguments, but whether it is done this way is not specified. Implementations are free to define default initialization arguments for specified method metaobject classes. Portable programs are free to define default initialization arguments for portable subclasses of the class **method**.

- The **:qualifiers** argument is a list of method qualifiers. An error is signaled if this value is not a proper list, or if any element of the list is not a non-null atom. This argument defaults to the empty list.
- The **:lambda-list** argument is the unspecialized lambda list of the method. An error is signaled if this value is not a proper lambda list. If this value is not supplied, an error is signaled.
- The **:specializers** argument is a list of the specializer metaobjects for the method. An error is signaled if this value is not a proper list, or if the length of the list differs from

the number of required arguments in the **:lambda-list** argument, or if any element of the list is not a specializer metaobject. If this value is not supplied, an error is signaled.

- The **:function** argument is a method function. It must be compatible with the methods on **compute-effective-method** defined for this class of method and generic function with which it will be used. That is, it must accept the same number of arguments as all uses of **call-method** that will call it supply. (See **compute-effective-method** for more information.) An error is signaled if this argument is not supplied.

- When the method being initialized is an instance of a subclass of **standard-accessor-method**, the **:slot-definition** initialization argument must be provided. Its value is the direct slot definition metaobject which defines this accessor method. An error is signaled if the value is not an instance of a subclass of **direct-slot-definition**.

- The **:documentation** argument is a string or **nil**. An error is signaled if this value is not a string or **nil**. This argument defaults to **nil**.

After the processing and defaulting of initialization arguments described above, the value of each initialization argument is associated with the method metaobject. These values can then be accessed by calling the corresponding generic function. The correspondences are as follows:

Initialization Argument	Generic Function
:qualifiers	method-qualifiers
:lambda-list	method-lambda-list
:specializers	method-specializers
:function	method-function
:slot-definition	accessor-method-slot-definition
:documentation	documentation

Table 6.3 Initialization arguments and accessors for method metaobjects.

METHODS

It is not specified which methods provide the initialization behavior described above. Instead, the information needed to allow portable programs to specialize this behavior is presented in as a set of restrictions on the methods a portable program can define. The model is that portable initialization methods have access to the method metaobject when either all or none of the specified initialization has taken effect.

These restrictions govern the methods that a portable program can define on the generic functions **initialize-instance**, **reinitialize-instance**, and **shared-initialize**. These restrictions apply only to methods on these generic functions for which the first specializer is a subclass of the class **method**. Other portable methods on these generic functions are not affected by these restrictions.

- Portable programs must not define methods on **shared-initialize** or **reinitialize-instance**.
- For **initialize-instance**:

  - Portable programs must not define primary methods.
  - Portable programs may define around-methods, but these must be extending, not overriding methods.
  - Portable before-methods must assume that when they are run, none of the initialization behavior described above has been completed.
  - Portable after-methods must assume that when they are run, all of the initialization behavior described above has been completed.

The results are undefined if any of these restrictions are violated.

Initialization of Slot Definition Metaobjects

A slot definition metaobject can be created by calling **make-instance**. The initialization arguments establish the definition of the slot definition. A slot definition metaobject cannot be redefined; calling **reinitialize-instance** signals an error.

Initialization of a slot definition metaobject must be done by calling **make-instance** and allowing it to call **initialize-instance**. Portable programs must not call **initialize-instance** directly to initialize a slot definition metaobject. Portable programs must not call **shared-initialize** directly to initialize a slot definition metaobject. Portable programs must not call **change-class** to change the class of any slot definition metaobject or to turn a non-slot-definition object into a slot definition metaobject.

Since metaobject classes may not be redefined, no behavior is specified for the result of calls to **update-instance-for-redefined-class** on slot definition metaobjects. Since the class of a slot definition metaobject cannot be changed, no behavior is specified for the result of calls to **update-instance-for-different-class** on slot definition metaobjects.

During initialization, each initialization argument is checked for errors and then associated with the slot definition metaobject. The value can then be accessed by calling the appropriate accessor as shown in Table 6.4.

This section begins with a description of the error checking and processing of each initialization argument. This is followed by a table showing the generic functions that can be used to access the stored initialization arguments.

In these descriptions, the phrase "this argument defaults to *value*" means that when that initialization argument is not supplied, initialization is performed as if *value* had been supplied. For some initialization arguments this could be done by the use of default initialization arguments, but whether it is done this way is not specified. Implementations are free to define default initialization arguments for specified slot definition metaobject classes. Portable programs are free to define default initialization arguments for portable subclasses of the class **slot-definition**.

- The **:name** argument is a slot name. An error is signaled if this argument is not a symbol which can be used as a variable name. An error is signaled if this argument is not supplied.
- The **:initform** argument is a form. The **:initform** argument defaults to **nil**. An error is signaled if the **:initform** argument is supplied, but the **:initfunction** argument is not supplied.

- The **:initfunction** argument is a function of zero arguments which, when called, evaluates the **:initform** in the appropriate lexical environment. The **:initfunction** argument defaults to false. An error is signaled if the **:initfunction** argument is supplied, but the **:initform** argument is not supplied.
- The **:type** argument is a type specifier name. An error is signaled otherwise. The **:type** argument defaults to the symbol **t**.
- The **:allocation** argument is a symbol. An error is signaled otherwise. The **:allocation** argument defaults to the symbol **:instance**.
- The **:initargs** argument is a list of symbols. An error is signaled if this argument is not a proper list, or if any element of this list is not a symbol. The **:initargs** argument defaults to the empty list.
- The **:readers** argument is a list of function names. An error is signaled if it is not a proper list, or if any element is not a valid function name. It defaults to the empty list. An error is signaled if this argument is supplied and the metaobject is not a direct slot definition.
- The **:writers** argument is a list of function names. An error is signaled if it is not a proper list, or if any element is not a valid function name. It defaults to the empty list. An error is signaled if this argument is supplied and the metaobject is not a direct slot definition.
- The **:documentation** argument is a string or **nil**. An error is signaled otherwise. The **:documentation** argument defaults to **nil**.

After the processing and defaulting of initialization arguments described above, the value of each initialization argument is associated with the slot definition metaobject. These values can then be accessed by calling the corresponding generic function. The correspondences are as follows:

Initialization Argument	Generic Function
:name	slot-definition-name
:initform	slot-definition-initform
:initfunction	slot-definition-initfunction
:type	slot-definition-type
:allocation	slot-definition-allocation
:initargs	slot-definition-initargs
:readers	slot-definition-readers
:writers	slot-definition-writers
:documentation	documentation

Table 6.4 Initialization arguments and accessors for slot definition metaobjects.

METHODS

It is not specified which methods provide the initialization and reinitialization behavior described above. Instead, the information needed to allow portable programs to specialize this behavior is presented as a set of restrictions on the methods a portable program can define. The model is that portable initialization methods have access to the slot definition metaobject when either all or none of the specified initialization has taken effect.

These restrictions govern the methods that a portable program can define on the generic functions **initialize-instance**, **reinitialize-instance**, and **shared-initialize**. These restrictions apply only to methods on these generic functions for which the first specializer is a subclass of the class **slot-definition**. Other portable methods on these generic functions are not affected by these restrictions.

- Portable programs must not define methods on **shared-initialize** or **reinitialize-instance**.
- For **initialize-instance**:

  - Portable programs must not define primary methods.
  - Portable programs may define around-methods, but these must be extending, not overriding methods.
  - Portable before-methods must assume that when they are run, none of the initialization behavior described above has been completed.
  - Portable after-methods must assume that when they are run, all of the initialization behavior described above has been completed.

The results are undefined if any of these restrictions are violated.

---

intern-eql-specializer   *Function*

SYNTAX

intern-eql-specializer
  object

ARGUMENTS

The *object* argument is any Lisp object.

VALUES

The result is the **eql** specializer metaobject for *object*.

PURPOSE

This function returns the unique **eql** specializer metaobject for *object*, creating one if necessary. Two calls to **intern-eql-specializer** with **eql** arguments will return the same (i.e., **eq**) value.

REMARKS

The result of calling **eql-specializer-object** on the result of a call to **intern-eql-specializer** is only guaranteed to be **eql** to the original *object* argument, not necessarily **eq**.

---

make-instance   *Generic Function*

SYNTAX

make-instance
  class **&rest** *initargs*

ARGUMENTS

The *class* argument is a class metaobject or a class name.
  The *initargs* argument is a list of alternating initialization argument names and values.

VALUES

The result is a newly allocated and initialized instance of *class*.

PURPOSE

The generic function **make-instance** creates and returns a new instance of the given class. Its behavior and use is described in the CLOS specification.

Methods

make-instance   *Primary Method*

   (*class* symbol) &rest *initargs*

This method simply invokes **make-instance** recursively on the arguments (find-class *class*) and *initargs*.

make-instance   *Primary Method*

   (*class* standard-class) &rest *initargs*

make-instance   *Primary Method*

   (*class* funcallable-standard-class) &rest *initargs*

These methods implement the behavior of **make-instance** described in the CLOS specification section named "Object Creation and Initialization."

---

make-method-lambda   *Generic Function*

Syntax

make-method-lambda

   generic-function method lambda-expression environment

Arguments

The *generic-function* argument is a generic function metaobject.

   The *method* argument is a (possibly uninitialized) method metaobject.

   The *lambda-expression* argument is a lambda expression.

   The *environment* argument is the same as the **&environment** argument to macro expansion functions.

Values

This generic function returns two values. The first is a lambda expression, the second is a list of initialization arguments and values.

Purpose

This generic function is called to produce a lambda expression which can itself be used to produce a method function for a method and generic function with the specified classes. The generic function and method the method function will be used with are not required to be the given ones. Moreover, the method metaobject may be uninitialized.

   Either the function **compile**, the special form **function** or the function **coerce** must be used to convert the lambda expression a method function. The method function itself can be applied to arguments with **apply** or **funcall**.

When a method is actually called by an effective method, its first argument will be a list of the arguments to the generic function. Its remaining arguments will be all but the first argument passed to **call-method**. By default, all method functions must accept two arguments: the list of arguments to the generic function and the list of next methods.

For a given generic function and method class, the applicable methods on **make-method-lambda** and **compute-effective-method** must be consistent in the following way: each use of **call-method** returned by the method on **compute-effective-method** must have the same number of arguments, and the method lambda returned by the method on **make-method-lambda** must accept a corresponding number of arguments.

Note that the system-supplied implementation of **call-next-method** is not required to handle extra arguments to the method function. Users who define additional arguments to the method function must either redefine or forego **call-next-method**. (See the example below.)

When the method metaobject is created with **make-instance**, the method function must be the value of the **:function** initialization argument. The additional initialization arguments, returned as the second value of this generic function, must also be passed in this call to **make-instance**.

METHODS

make-method-lambda   *Primary Method*

(*generic-function* `standard-generic-function`)
(*method* `standard-method`)
lambda-expression
environment

This method returns a method lambda which accepts two arguments, the list of arguments to the generic function, and the list of next methods. What initialization arguments may be returned in the second value are unspecified.

This method can be overridden.

Example:

This example shows how to define a kind of method which, from within the body of the method, has access to the actual method metaobject for the method. This simplified code overrides whatever method combination is specified for the generic function, implementing a simple method combination supporting only primary methods, **call-next-method** and **next-method-p**. (In addition, its a simplified version of **call-next-method** which does no error checking.)

Notice that the extra lexical function bindings get wrapped around the body before **call-next-method** is called. In this way, the user's definition of **call-next-method** and **next-method-p** are sure to override the system's definitions.

```
(defclass my-generic-function (standard-generic-function)
    ()
  (:default-initargs :method-class (find-class 'my-method)))

(defclass my-method (standard-method) ())

(defmethod make-method-lambda ((gf my-generic-function)
                               (method my-method)
                               lambda-expression
                               environment)
  (declare (ignore environment))
  `(lambda (args next-methods this-method)
     (,(call-next-method gf method
          `(lambda ,(cadr lambda-expression)
             (flet ((this-method () this-method)
                    (call-next-method (&rest cnm-args)
                      (funcall (method-function (car next-methods))
                               (or cnm-args args)
                               (cdr next-methods)
                               (car next-methods)))
                    (next-method-p ()
                      (not (null next-methods))))
               ,@(cddr lambda-expression)))
          environment)
       args next-methods)))

(defmethod compute-effective-method ((gf my-generic-function)
                                     method-combination
                                     methods)
  `(call-method ,(car methods) ,(cdr methods) ,(car methods)))
```

map-dependents   *Generic Function*

SYNTAX

map-dependents

   metaobject function

ARGUMENTS

The *metaobject* argument is a class or generic function metaobject.

   The *function* argument is a function which accepts one argument.

VALUES

The value returned is unspecified.

PURPOSE

This generic function applies *function* to each of the dependents of *metaobject*. The order in which the dependents are processed is not specified, but *function* is applied to each dependent once and only once. If, during the mapping, **add-dependent** or **remove-dependent** is called to alter the dependents of *metaobject*, it is not specified whether the newly added or removed dependent will have *function* applied to it.

METHODS

map-dependents   *Primary Method*

   (*metaobject* **standard-class**) *function*

   This method has no specified behavior beyond that which is specified for the generic function.

   This method cannot be overridden unless the following methods are overridden as well:

      add-dependent (standard-class t)
      remove-dependent (standard-class t)

map-dependents   *Primary Method*

   (*metaobject* **funcallable-standard-class**) *function*

   This method has no specified behavior beyond that which is specified for the generic function.

   This method cannot be overridden unless the following methods are overridden as well:

      add-dependent (funcallable-standard-class t)
      remove-dependent (funcallable-standard-class t)

map-dependents   *Primary Method*
    (*metaobject* `standard-generic-function`) *function*

This method has no specified behavior beyond that which is specified for the generic function.

This method cannot be overridden unless the following methods are overridden as well:

    add-dependent (standard-generic-function t)
    remove-dependent (standard-generic-function t)

REMARKS
See the "Dependent Maintenance Protocol" section for remarks about the use of this facility.

---

method-...   *Generic Function*

The following generic functions are described together under "Readers for Method Metaobjects" (page 218): **method-function**, **method-generic-function**, **method-lambda-list**, **method-specializers**, **method-qualifiers** and **accessor-method-slot-definition**.

Readers for Class Metaobjects

In this and the immediately following sections, the "reader" generic functions which simply return information associated with a particular kind of metaobject are presented together. General information is presented first, followed by a description of the purpose of each, and ending with the specified methods for these generic functions.

The reader generic functions which simply return information associated with class metaobjects are presented together in this section.

Each of the reader generic functions for class metaobjects has the same syntax, accepting one required argument called *class*, which must be an class metaobject; otherwise, an error is signaled. An error is also signaled if the class metaobject has not been initialized.

These generic functions can be called by the user or the implementation.

For any of these generic functions which returns a list, such lists will not be mutated by the implementation. The results are undefined if a portable program allows such a list to be mutated.

class-default-initargs   *Generic Function*

    class

Returns a list of the default initialization arguments for *class*. Each element of this list is a canonicalized default initialization argument. The empty list is returned if *class* has no default initialization arguments.

During finalization **finalize-inheritance** calls **compute-default-initargs** to compute the default initialization arguments for the class. That value is associated with the class metaobject and is returned by **class-default-initargs**.

This generic function signals an error if *class* has not been finalized.

class-direct-default-initargs   *Generic Function*

    class

Returns a list of the direct default initialization arguments for *class*. Each element of this list is a canonicalized default initialization argument. The empty list is returned if *class* has no direct default initialization arguments. This is the defaulted value of the **:direct-default-initargs** initialization argument that was associated with the class during initialization or reinitialization.

class-direct-slots   *Generic Function*

   class

Returns a set of the direct slots of *class*. The elements of this set are direct slot definition metaobjects. If the class has no direct slots, the empty set is returned. This is the defaulted value of the **:direct-slots** initialization argument that was associated with the class during initialization and reinitialization.

class-direct-subclasses   *Generic Function*

   class

Returns a set of the direct subclasses of *class*. The elements of this set are class metaobjects that all mention this class among their direct superclasses. The empty set is returned if *class* has no direct subclasses. This value is maintained by the generic functions **add-direct-subclass** and **remove-direct-subclass**.

class-direct-superclasses   *Generic Function*

   class

Returns a list of the direct superclasses of *class*. The elements of this list are class metaobjects. The empty list is returned if *class* has no direct superclasses. This is the defaulted value of the **:direct-superclasses** initialization argument that was associated with the class during initialization or reinitialization.

class-finalized-p   *Generic Function*

   class

Returns true if *class* has been finalized. Returns false otherwise. Also returns false if the class has not been initialized.

class-name   *Generic Function*

   class

Returns the name of *class*. This value can be any Lisp object, but is usually a symbol, or **nil** if the class has no name. This is the defaulted value of the **:name** initialization argument that was associated with the class during initialization or reinitialization. (Also see **(setf class-name)**.)

class-precedence-list   *Generic Function*
    class

Returns the class precedence list of *class*. The elements of this list are class metaobjects.

During class finalization **finalize-inheritance** calls **compute-class-precedence-list** to compute the class precedence list of the class. That value is associated with the class metaobject and is returned by **class-precedence-list**.

This generic function signals an error if *class* has not been finalized.

class-prototype   *Generic Function*
    class

Returns a prototype instance of *class*. Whether the instance is initialized is not specified. The results are undefined if a portable program modifies the binding of any slot of prototype instance.

This generic function signals an error if *class* has not been finalized.

class-slots   *Generic Function*
    class

Returns a possibly empty set of the slots accessible in instances of *class*. The elements of this set are effective slot definition metaobjects.

During class finalization **finalize-inheritance** calls **compute-slots** to compute the slots of the class. That value is associated with the class metaobject and is returned by **class-slots**.

This generic function signals an error if *class* has not been finalized.

METHODS

The specified methods for the class metaobject reader generic functions are presented below.

Each entry in the table indicates a method on one of the reader generic functions, specialized to a specified class. The number in each entry is a reference to the full description of the method. The full descriptions appear after the table.

	standard-class and funcallable-standard-class	forward-referenced-class	built-in-class
class-default-initargs	2	3	4
class-direct-default-initargs	1	4	4
class-direct-slots	1	4	4
class-direct-subclasses	9	9	7
class-direct-superclasses	1	4	7
class-finalized-p	2	6	5
class-name	1	1	8
class-precedence-list	2	3	7
class-prototype	10	10	10
class-slots	2	3	4

1. This method returns the value which was associated with the class metaobject during initialization or reinitialization.

2. This method returns the value associated with the class metaobject by **finalize-inheritance (standard-class)** or **finalize-inheritance (funcallable-standard-class)**.

3. This method signals an error.

4. This method returns the empty list.

5. This method returns true.

6. This method returns false.

7. This method returns a value derived from the information in Table 5.1, except that implementation-specific modifications are permitted as described in section "Implementation and User Specialization."

8. This method returns the name of the built-in class.

9. This methods returns a value which is maintained by **add-direct-subclass (class class)** and **remove-direct-subclass (class class)**. This method can be overridden only if those methods are overridden as well.

10. No behavior is specified for this method beyond that specified for the generic function.

Readers for Generic Function Metaobjects

The reader generic functions which simply return information associated with generic function metaobjects are presented together in this section.

Each of the reader generic functions for generic function metaobjects has the same syntax, accepting one required argument called *generic-function*, which must be a generic function metaobject; otherwise, an error is signaled. An error is also signaled if the generic function metaobject has not been initialized.

These generic functions can be called by the user or the implementation.

The list returned by this generic function will not be mutated by the implementation. The results are undefined if a portable program mutates the list returned by this generic function.

generic-function-argument-precedence-order   *Generic Function*
    generic-function

Returns the argument precedence order of the generic function. This value is a list of symbols, a permutation of the required parameters in the lambda list of the generic function. This is the defaulted value of the **:argument-precedence-order** initialization argument that was associated with the generic function metaobject during initialization or reinitialization.

generic-function-declarations   *Generic Function*
    generic-function

Returns a possibly empty list of the declarations of the generic function. The elements of this list are declarations. This list is the defaulted value of the **:declarations** initialization argument that was associated with the generic function metaobject during initialization or reinitialization.

generic-function-lambda-list   *Generic Function*
    generic-function

Returns the lambda list of the generic function. This is the defaulted value of the **:lambda-list** initialization argument that was associated with the generic function metaobject during initialization or reinitialization. An error is signaled if the lambda list has yet to be supplied.

generic-function-method-class   *Generic Function*
    generic-function

Returns the default method class of the generic function. This class must be a subclass
of the class **method**. This is the defaulted value of the **:method-class** initialization
argument that was associated with the generic function metaobject during initialization
or reinitialization.

generic-function-method-combination   *Generic Function*
    generic-function

Returns the method combination of the generic function. This is a method combination
metaobject. This is the defaulted value of the **:method-combination** initialization
argument that was associated with the generic function metaobject during initialization
or reinitialization.

generic-function-methods   *Generic Function*
    generic-function

Returns the set of methods currently connected to the generic function. This is a set of
method metaobjects. This value is maintained by the generic functions **add-method**
and **remove-method**.

generic-function-name   *Generic Function*
    generic-function

Returns the name of the generic function, or **nil** if the generic function has no name.
This is the defaulted value of the **:name** initialization argument that was associated
with the generic function metaobject during initialization or reinitialization. (Also see
(setf generic-function-name).)

METHODS
The specified methods for the generic function metaobject reader generic functions are
presented below.

generic-function-argument-precedence-order   *Primary Method*
   (*generic-function* `standard-generic-function`)

generic-function-declarations   *Primary Method*
   (*generic-function* `standard-generic-function`)

generic-function-lambda-list   *Primary Method*
   (*generic-function* `standard-generic-function`)

generic-function-method-class   *Primary Method*
   (*generic-function* `standard-generic-function`)

generic-function-method-combination   *Primary Method*
   (*generic-function* `standard-generic-function`)

generic-function-name   *Primary Method*
   (*generic-function* `standard-generic-function`)

No behavior is specified for these methods beyond that which is specified for their respective generic functions.

generic-function-methods   *Primary Method*
   (*generic-function* `standard-generic-function`)

No behavior is specified for this method beyond that which is specified for their respective generic functions.

The value returned by this method is maintained by **add-method (standard-generic-function standard-method)** and **remove-method (standard-generic-function standard-method)**.

Readers for Method Metaobjects

The reader generic functions which simply return information associated with method metaobjects are presented together here in the format described under "Readers for Class Metaobjects."

Each of these reader generic functions have the same syntax, accepting one required argument called *method*, which must be a method metaobject; otherwise, an error is signaled. An error is also signaled if the method metaobject has not been initialized.

These generic functions can be called by the user or the implementation.

For any of these generic functions which returns a list, such lists will not be mutated by the implementation. The results are undefined if a portable program allows such a list to be mutated.

method-function   *Generic Function*
   method

Returns the method function of *method*. This is the defaulted value of the **:function** initialization argument that was associated with the method during initialization.

method-generic-function   *Generic Function*
   method

Returns the generic function that *method* is currently connected to, or **nil** if it is not currently connected to any generic function. This value is either a generic function metaobject or **nil**. When a method is first created it is not connected to any generic function. This connection is maintained by the generic functions **add-method** and **remove-method**.

method-lambda-list   *Generic Function*
   method

Returns the (unspecialized) lambda list of *method*. This value is a Common Lisp lambda list. This is the defaulted value of the **:lambda-list** initialization argument that was associated with the method during initialization.

method-specializers   *Generic Function*
   method

Returns a list of the specializers of *method*. This value is a list of specializer metaobjects. This is the defaulted value of the **:specializers** initialization argument that was associated with the method during initialization.

method-qualifiers   *Generic Function*
   method

Returns a (possibly empty) list of the qualifiers of *method*. This value is a list of non-**nil** atoms. This is the defaulted value of the **:qualifiers** initialization argument that was associated with the method during initialization.

accessor-method-slot-definition   *Generic Function*
    method

This accessor can only be called on accessor methods. It returns the direct slot definition metaobject that defined this method. This is the value of the **:slot-definition** initialization argument associated with the method during initialization.

METHODS
The specified methods for the method metaobject readers are presented below.

method-function   *Primary Method*
    (*method* standard-method)

method-lambda-list   *Primary Method*
    (*method* standard-method)

method-specializers   *Primary Method*
    (*method* standard-method)

method-qualifiers   *Primary Method*
    (*method* standard-method)

No behavior is specified for these methods beyond that which is specified for their respective generic functions.

method-generic-function   *Primary Method*
    (*method* standard-method)

No behavior is specified for this method beyond that which is specified for its generic function.

The value returned by this method is maintained by **add-method (standard-generic-function standard-method)** and **remove-method (standard-generic-function standard-method)**.

accessor-method-slot-definition   *Primary Method*
    (*method* standard-accessor-method)

No behavior is specified for this method beyond that which is specified for its generic function.

Readers for Slot Definition Metaobjects

The reader generic functions which simply return information associated with slot definition metaobjects are presented together here in the format described under "Readers for Class Metaobjects."

Each of the reader generic functions for slot definition metaobjects has the same syntax, accepting one required argument called *slot*, which must be a slot definition metaobject; otherwise, an error is signaled. An error is also signaled if the slot definition metaobject has not been initialized.

These generic functions can be called by the user or the implementation.

For any of these generic functions which returns a list, such lists will not be mutated by the implementation. The results are undefined if a portable program allows such a list to be mutated.

GENERIC FUNCTIONS

slot-definition-allocation   *Generic Function*

   slot

Returns the allocation of *slot*. This is a symbol. This is the defaulted value of the **:allocation** initialization argument that was associated with the slot definition metaobject during initialization.

slot-definition-initargs   *Generic Function*

   slot

Returns the set of initialization argument keywords for *slot*. This is the defaulted value of the **:initargs** initialization argument that was associated with the slot definition metaobject during initialization.

slot-definition-initform   *Generic Function*

   slot

Returns the initialization form of *slot*. This can be any form. This is the defaulted value of the **:initform** initialization argument that was associated with the slot definition metaobject during initialization. When *slot* has no initialization form, the value returned is unspecified (however, **slot-definition-initfunction** is guaranteed to return **nil**).

slot-definition-initfunction   *Generic Function*

> *slot*

Returns the initialization function of *slot*. This value is either a function of no arguments, or **nil**, indicating that the slot has no initialization function. This is the defaulted value of the **:initfunction** initialization argument that was associated with the slot definition metaobject during initialization.

slot-definition-name   *Generic Function*

> *slot*

Returns the name of *slot*. This value is a symbol that can be used as a variable name. This is the value of the **:name** initialization argument that was associated with the slot definition metaobject during initialization.

slot-definition-type   *Generic Function*

> *slot*

Returns the allocation of *slot*. This is a type specifier name. This is the defaulted value of the **:name** initialization argument that was associated with the slot definition metaobject during initialization.

METHODS

The specified methods for the slot definition metaobject readers are presented below.

slot-definition-allocation   *Primary Method*
    (*slot-definition* `standard-slot-definition`)

slot-definition-initargs   *Primary Method*
    (*slot-definition* `standard-slot-definition`)

slot-definition-initform   *Primary Method*
    (*slot-definition* `standard-slot-definition`)

slot-definition-initfunction   *Primary Method*
    (*slot-definition* `standard-slot-definition`)

slot-definition-name   *Primary Method*
    (*slot-definition* `standard-slot-definition`)

slot-definition-type   *Primary Method*
    (*slot-definition* `standard-slot-definition`)

No behavior is specified for these methods beyond that which is specified for their respective generic functions.

DIRECT SLOT DEFINITION METAOBJECTS
The following additional reader generic functions are defined for direct slot definition metaobjects.

slot-definition-readers   *Generic Function*
    direct-slot

Returns a (possibly empty) set of readers of the *direct slot*. This value is a list of function names. This is the defaulted value of the **:readers** initialization argument that was associated with the direct slot definition metaobject during initialization.

slot-definition-writers   *Generic Function*
    direct-slot

Returns a (possibly empty) set of writers of the *direct slot*. This value is a list of function names. This is the defaulted value of the **:writers** initialization argument that was associated with the direct slot definition metaobject during initialization.

slot-definition-readers   *Primary Method*
    (*direct-slot-definition* `standard-direct-slot-definition`)

slot-definition-writers   *Primary Method*
    (*direct-slot-definition* `standard-direct-slot-definition`)

No behavior is specified for these methods beyond what is specified for their generic functions.

EFFECTIVE SLOT DEFINITION METAOBJECTS
The following reader generic function is defined for effective slot definition metaobjects.

slot-definition-location   *Generic Function*
    effective-slot-definition

Returns the location of *effective-slot-definition*. The meaning and interpretation of this value is described in the section called "Instance Structure Protocol."

slot-definition-location   *Primary Method*
    (*effective-slot-definition* `standard-effective-slot-definition`)

This method returns the value stored by **compute-slots :around (standard-class)** and **compute-slots :around (funcallable-standard-class)**.

---

reader-method-class   *Generic Function*

SYNTAX
reader-method-class
    class direct-slot **&rest** *initargs*

ARGUMENTS
The *class* argument is a class metaobject.
    The *direct-slot* argument is a direct slot definition metaobject.
    The *initargs* argument consists of alternating initialization argument names and values.

VALUES
The value returned is a class metaobject.

PURPOSE

This generic function is called to determine the class of reader methods created during class initialization and reinitialization. The result must be a subclass of **standard-reader-method**.

The *initargs* argument must be the same as will be passed to **make-instance** to create the reader method. The *initargs* must include **:slot-definition** with *slot-definition* as its value.

METHODS

reader-method-class   *Primary Method*

    (*class* `standard-class`)

    (*direct-slot* `standard-direct-slot-definition`)

    &rest *initargs*

reader-method-class   *Primary Method*

    (*class* `funcallable-standard-class`)

    (*direct-slot* `standard-direct-slot-definition`)

    &rest *initargs*

These methods return the class **standard-reader-method**. These methods can be overridden.

---

remove-dependent   *Generic Function*

SYNTAX

remove-dependent

    metaobject dependent

ARGUMENTS

The *metaobject* argument is a class or generic function metaobject.

The *dependent* argument is an object.

VALUES

The value returned by this generic function is unspecified.

PURPOSE

This generic function removes *dependent* from the dependents of *metaobject*. If *dependent* is not one of the dependents of *metaobject*, no error is signaled.

The generic function **map-dependents** can be called to access the set of dependents of a class or generic function. The generic function **add-dependent** can be called to add an object from the set of dependents of a class or generic function. The effect of calling **add-dependent** or **remove-dependent** while a call to **map-dependents** on the same class or generic function is in progress is unspecified.

The situations in which **remove-dependent** is called are not specified.

METHODS

remove-dependent   *Primary Method*
    (*class* standard-class) *dependent*

No behavior is specified for this method beyond that which is specified for the generic function.

This method cannot be overridden unless the following methods are overridden as well:

    add-dependent (standard-class t)
    map-dependents (standard-class t)

remove-dependent   *Primary Method*
    (*class* funcallable-standard-class) *dependent*

No behavior is specified for this method beyond that which is specified for the generic function.

This method cannot be overridden unless the following methods are overridden as well:

    add-dependent (funcallable-standard-class t)
    map-dependents (funcallable-standard-class t)

remove-dependent   *Primary Method*
    (*generic-function* standard-generic-function) *dependent*

No behavior is specified for this method beyond that which is specified for the generic function.

This method cannot be overridden unless the following methods are overridden as well:

    add-dependent (standard-generic-function t)
    map-dependents (standard-generic-function t)

REMARKS

See the "Dependent Maintenance Protocol" section for remarks about the use of this facility.

remove-direct-method   *Generic Function*

SYNTAX

remove-direct-method
  specializer method

ARGUMENTS

The *specializer* argument is a specializer metaobject.

The *method* argument is a method metaobject.

VALUES

The value returned by **remove-direct-method** is unspecified.

PURPOSE

This generic function is called to maintain a set of backpointers from a specializer to the set of methods specialized to it. If *method* is in the set it is removed. If it is not, no error is signaled.

This set can be accessed as a list by calling the generic function **specializer-direct-methods**. Methods are added to the set by **add-direct-method**.

The generic function **remove-direct-method** is called by **remove-method** whenever a method is removed from a generic function. It is called once for each of the specializers of the method. Note that in cases where a specializer appears more than once in the specializers of a method, this generic function will be called more than once with the same specializer as argument.

The results are undefined if the *specializer* argument is not one of the specializers of the *method* argument.

METHODS

remove-direct-method   *Primary Method*
  (*specializer* **class**)
  (*method* **method**)

This method implements the behavior of the generic function for class specializers. No behavior is specified for this method beyond that which is specified for the generic function.

This method cannot be overridden unless the following methods are overridden as well:

  add-direct-method (class method)
  specializer-direct-generic-functions (class)
  specializer-direct-methods (class)

remove-direct-method   *Primary Method*
   (*specializer* `eql-specializer`)
   (*method* `method`)

This method implements the behavior of the generic function for **eql** specializers. No behavior is specified for this method beyond that which is specified for the generic function.

---

remove-direct-subclass   *Generic Function*

SYNTAX

remove-direct-subclass
   superclass subclass

ARGUMENTS

The *superclass* argument is a class metaobject.

   The *subclass* argument is a class metaobject.

VALUES

The value returned by this generic function is unspecified.

PURPOSE

This generic function is called to maintain a set of backpointers from a class to its direct subclasses. It removes *subclass* from the set of direct subclasses of *superclass*. No error is signaled if *subclass* is not in this set.

   Whenever a class is reinitialized, this generic function is called once with each deleted direct superclass of the class.

METHODS

remove-direct-subclass   *Primary Method*
   (*superclass* `class`)
   (*subclass* `class`)

No behavior is specified for this method beyond that which is specified for the generic function.

   This method cannot be overridden unless the following methods are overridden as well:

     add-direct-subclass (class class)
     class-direct-subclasses (class)

---

remove-method   *Generic Function*

SYNTAX

remove-method
  generic-function method

ARGUMENTS

The *generic-function* argument is a generic function metaobject.

  The *method* argument is a method metaobject.

VALUES

The *generic-function* argument is returned.

PURPOSE

This generic function breaks the association between a generic function and one of its methods.

  No error is signaled if the method is not among the methods of the generic function.

  Breaking the association between the method and the generic function proceeds in four steps: (i) remove *method* from the set returned by **generic-function-methods** and arrange for **method-generic-function** to return **nil**; (ii) call **remove-direct-method** for each of the method's specializers; (iii) call **compute-discriminating-function** and install its result with **set-funcallable-instance-function**; and (iv) update the dependents of the generic function.

  The generic function **remove-method** can be called by the user or the implementation.

METHODS

remove-method   *Primary Method*
  (*generic-function* `standard-generic-function`)
  (*method* `standard-method`)

No behavior is specified for this method beyond that which is specified for the generic function.

---

set-funcallable-instance-function   *Function*

SYNTAX

set-funcallable-instance-function
  funcallable-instance function

ARGUMENTS

The *funcallable-instance* argument is a funcallable instance (it must have been returned by **allocate-instance (funcallable-standard-class)**).

  The *function* argument is a function.

VALUES

The value returned by this function is unspecified.

PURPOSE

This function is called to set or to change the function of a funcallable instance. After **set-funcallable-instance-function** is called, any subsequent calls to *funcallable-instance* will run the new function.

(setf class-name)   *Function*

SYNTAX

(setf class-name)   *Generic Function*
  new-name class

ARGUMENTS

The *class* argument is a class metaobject.

  The *new-name* argument is any Lisp object.

RESULTS

This function returns its *new-name* argument.

PURPOSE

This function changes the name of *class* to *new-name*. This value is usually a symbol, or **nil** if the class has no name.

  This function works by calling **reinitialize-instance** with *class* as its first argument, the symbol **:name** as its second argument and *new-name* as its third argument.

(setf generic-function-name) *Function*

SYNTAX

(setf generic-function-name) *Generic Function*
   new-name generic-function

ARGUMENTS

The *generic-function* argument is a generic function metaobject.

  The *new-name* argument is a function name or **nil**.

RESULTS

This function returns its *new-name* argument.

PURPOSE

This function changes the name of *generic-function* to *new-name*. This value is usually a function name (i.e., a symbol or a list of the form **(setf** *symbol*)) or **nil**, if the generic function is to have no name.

  This function works by calling **reinitialize-instance** with *generic-function* as its first argument, the symbol **:name** as its second argument and *new-name* as its third argument.

(setf slot-value-using-class) *Generic Function*

SYNTAX

(setf slot-value-using-class)
   new-value class object slot

ARGUMENTS

The *new-value* argument is an object.

  The *class* argument is a class metaobject. It is the class of the *object* argument.

  The *object* argument is an object.

  The *slot* argument is an effective slot definition metaobject.

VALUES

This generic function returns the *new-value* argument.

PURPOSE

The generic function **(setf slot-value-using-class)** implements the behavior of the **(setf slot-value)** function. It is called by **(setf slot-value)** with the class of *object* as its second argument and the pertinent effective slot definition metaobject as its fourth argument.

The generic function **(setf slot-value-using-class)** sets the value contained in the given slot of the given object to the given new value; any previous value is lost.

The results are undefined if the *class* argument is not the class of the *object* argument, or if the *slot* argument does not appear among the set of effective slots associated with the *class* argument.

METHODS

(setf slot-value-using-class)   *Primary Method*
    new-value
    (*class* `standard-class`)
    object
    (*slot* `standard-effective-slot-definition`)

(setf slot-value-using-class)   *Primary Method*
    new-value
    (*class* `funcallable-standard-class`)
    object
    (*slot* `standard-effective-slot-definition`)

These methods implement the full behavior of this generic function for slots with allocation **:instance** and **:class**. If the supplied slot has an allocation other than **:instance** or **:class** an error is signaled.

Overriding these methods is permitted, but may require overriding other methods in the standard implementation of the slot access protocol.

(setf slot-value-using-class)   *Primary Method*
    new-value
    (*class* `built-in-class`)
    object
    slot

This method signals an error.

slot-boundp-using-class   *Generic Function*

SYNTAX

slot-boundp-using-class
   class object slot

ARGUMENTS

The *class* argument is a class metaobject. It is the class of the *object* argument.

   The *object* argument is an object.

   The *slot* argument is an effective slot definition metaobject.

VALUES

This generic function returns true or false.

PURPOSE

This generic function implements the behavior of the **slot-boundp** function. It is called by **slot-boundp** with the class of *object* as its first argument and the pertinent effective slot definition metaobject as its third argument.

   The generic function **slot-boundp-using-class** tests whether a specific slot in an instance is bound.

   The results are undefined if the *class* argument is not the class of the *object* argument, or if the *slot* argument does not appear among the set of effective slots associated with the *class* argument.

METHODS

slot-boundp-using-class   *Primary Method*
   (*class* `standard-class`)
   object
   (*slot* `standard-effective-slot-definition`)

slot-boundp-using-class   *Primary Method*
   (*class* `funcallable-standard-class`)
   object
   (*slot* `standard-effective-slot-definition`)

These methods implement the full behavior of this generic function for slots with allocation **:instance** and **:class**. If the supplied slot has an allocation other than **:instance** or **:class** an error is signaled.

   Overriding these methods is permitted, but may require overriding other methods in the standard implementation of the slot access protocol.

slot-boundp-using-class   *Primary Method*
   (*class* built-in-class)
   object
   slot

  This method signals an error.

REMARKS
In cases where the class metaobject class does not distinguish unbound slots, true should
be returned.

---

slot-definition-...   *Generic Function*

The following generic functions are described together under "Readers for Slot
Definition Metaobjects" (page 221): **slot-definition-allocation**, **slot-definition-
initargs**, **slot-definition-initform**, **slot-definition-initfunction**, **slot-definition-
location**, **slot-definition-name**, **slot-definition-readers**, **slot-definition-writers**
and **slot-definition-type**.

---

slot-makunbound-using-class   *Generic Function*

SYNTAX
slot-makunbound-using-class
  class object slot

ARGUMENTS
The *class* argument is a class metaobject. It is the class of the *object* argument.
  The *object* argument is an object.
  The *slot* argument is an effective slot definition metaobject.

VALUES
This generic function returns its *object* argument.

PURPOSE
This generic function implements the behavior of the **slot-makunbound** function. It
is called by **slot-makunbound** with the class of *object* as its first argument and the
pertinent effective slot definition metaobject as its third argument.
  The generic function **slot-makunbound-using-class** restores a slot in an object to
its unbound state. The interpretation of "restoring a slot to its unbound state" depends
on the class metaobject class.

The results are undefined if the *class* argument is not the class of the *object* argument, or if the *slot* argument does not appear among the set of effective slots associated with the *class* argument.

METHODS

slot-makunbound-using-class   *Primary Method*
  (*class* `standard-class`)
  object
  (*slot* `standard-effective-slot-definition`)

slot-makunbound-using-class   *Primary Method*
  (*class* `funcallable-standard-class`)
  object
  (*slot* `standard-effective-slot-definition`)

These methods implement the full behavior of this generic function for slots with allocation **:instance** and **:class**. If the supplied slot has an allocation other than **:instance** or **:class** an error is signaled.

Overriding these methods is permitted, but may require overriding other methods in the standard implementation of the slot access protocol.

slot-makunbound-using-class   *Primary Method*
  (*class* `built-in-class`)
  object
  slot

This method signals an error.

---

slot-value-using-class   *Generic Function*

SYNTAX

slot-value-using-class
  class object slot

ARGUMENTS

The *class* argument is a class metaobject. It is the class of the *object* argument.

The *object* argument is an object.

The *slot* argument is an effective slot definition metaobject.

VALUES

The value returned by this generic function is an object.

PURPOSE

This generic function implements the behavior of the **slot-value** function. It is called by **slot-value** with the class of *object* as its first argument and the pertinent effective slot definition metaobject as its third argument.

The generic function **slot-value-using-class** returns the value contained in the given slot of the given object. If the slot is unbound **slot-unbound** is called.

The results are undefined if the *class* argument is not the class of the *object* argument, or if the *slot* argument does not appear among the set of effective slots associated with the *class* argument.

METHODS

slot-value-using-class   *Primary Method*
    (*class* standard-class)
    object
    (*slot* standard-effective-slot-definition)

slot-value-using-class   *Primary Method*
    (*class* funcallable-standard-class)
    object
    (*slot* standard-effective-slot-definition)

These methods implement the full behavior of this generic function for slots with allocation **:instance** and **:class**. If the supplied slot has an allocation other than **:instance** or **:class** an error is signaled.

Overriding these methods is permitted, but may require overriding other methods in the standard implementation of the slot access protocol.

slot-value-using-class   *Primary Method*
    (*class* built-in-class)
    object
    slot

This method signals an error.

---

specializer-direct-generic-functions   *Generic Function*

SYNTAX

specializer-direct-generic-functions
   specializer

ARGUMENTS

The *specializer* argument is a specializer metaobject.

VALUES

The result of this generic function is a possibly empty list of generic function metaobjects.

PURPOSE

This generic function returns the possibly empty set of those generic functions which have a method with *specializer* as a specializer. The elements of this set are generic function metaobjects. This value is maintained by the generic functions **add-direct-method** and **remove-direct-method**.

METHODS

specializer-direct-generic-functions   *Primary Method*
   (*specializer* class)

No behavior is specified for this method beyond that which is specified for the generic function.

This method cannot be overridden unless the following methods are overridden as well:

   add-direct-method (class method)
   remove-direct-method (class method)
   specializer-direct-methods (class)

specializer-direct-generic-functions   *Primary Method*
   (*specializer* eql-specializer)

No behavior is specified for this method beyond that which is specified for the generic function.

---

specializer-direct-methods   *Generic Function*

SYNTAX

specializer-direct-methods
  specializer

ARGUMENTS

The *specializer* argument is a specializer metaobject.

VALUES

The result of this generic function is a possibly empty list of method metaobjects.

PURPOSE

This generic function returns the possibly empty set of those methods, connected to generic functions, which have *specializer* as a specializer. The elements of this set are method metaobjects. This value is maintained by the generic functions **add-direct-method** and **remove-direct-method**.

METHODS

specializer-direct-methods   *Primary Method*
  (*specializer* `class`)

  No behavior is specified for this method beyond that which is specified for the generic function.

  This method cannot be overridden unless the following methods are overridden as well:

> **add-direct-method (class method)**
> **remove-direct-method (class method)**
> **specializer-direct-generic-functions (class)**

specializer-direct-methods   *Primary Method*
  (*specializer* `eql-specializer`)

  No behavior is specified for this method beyond that which is specified for the generic function.

---

standard-instance-access   *Function*

SYNTAX

standard-instance-access
  instance location

ARGUMENTS

The *instance* argument is an object.

  The *location* argument is a slot location.

VALUES

The result of this function is an object.

PURPOSE

This function is called to provide direct access to a slot in an instance. By usurping the normal slot lookup protocol, this function is intended to provide highly optimized access to the slots associated with an instance.

  The following restrictions apply to the use of this function:

- The *instance* argument must be a standard instance (it must have been returned by **allocate-instance (standard-class)**).
- The *instance* argument cannot be an non-updated obsolete instance.
- The *location* argument must be a location of one of the directly accessible slots of the instance's class.
- The slot must be bound.

  The results are undefined if any of these restrictions are not met.

---

update-dependent   *Generic Function*

SYNTAX

update-dependent
  metaobject dependent **&rest** *initargs*

ARGUMENTS

The *metaobject* argument is a class or generic function metaobject. It is the metaobject being reinitialized or otherwise modified.

  The *dependent* argument is an object. It is the dependent being updated.

  The *initargs* argument is a list of the initialization arguments for the metaobject redefinition.

VALUES
The value returned by **update-dependent** is unspecified.

PURPOSE
This generic function is called to update a dependent of *metaobject*.

When a class or a generic function is reinitialized each of its dependents is updated. The *initargs* argument to **update-dependent** is the set of initialization arguments received by **reinitialize-instance**.

When a method is added to a generic function, each of the generic function's dependents is updated. The *initargs* argument is a list of two elements: the symbol **add-method**, and the method that was added.

When a method is removed from a generic function, each of the generic function's dependents is updated. The *initargs* argument is a list of two elements: the symbol **remove-method**, and the method that was removed.

In each case, **map-dependents** is used to call **update-dependent** on each of the dependents. So, for example, the update of a generic function's dependents when a method is added could be performed by the following code:

```
(map-dependents generic-function
                #'(lambda (dep)
                    (update-dependent generic-function
                                      dep
                                      'add-method
                                      new-method)))
```

METHODS
There are no specified methods on this generic function.

REMARKS
See the "Dependent Maintenance Protocol" section for remarks about the use of this facility.

---

validate-superclass   *Generic Function*

SYNTAX
validate-superclass
    class superclass

ARGUMENTS
The *class* argument is a class metaobject.

The *superclass* argument is a class metaobject.

VALUES

This generic function returns true or false.

PURPOSE

This generic function is called to determine whether the class *superclass* is suitable for use as a superclass of *class*.

This generic function can be be called by the implementation or user code. It is called during class metaobject initialization and reinitialization, before the direct superclasses are stored. If this generic function returns false, the initialization or reinitialization will signal an error.

METHODS

validate-superclass   *Primary Method*

    (*class* class)

    (*superclass* class)

This method returns true in three situations:

    (i) If the *superclass* argument is the class named **t**,

    (ii) if the class of the *class* argument is the same as the class of the *superclass* argument or

    (iii) if the classes one of the arguments is **standard-class** and the class of the other is **funcallable-standard-class**.

In all other cases, this method returns false.

    This method can be overridden.

REMARKS

Defining a method on **validate-superclass** requires detailed knowledge of of the internal protocol followed by each of the two class metaobject classes. A method on **validate-superclass** which returns true for two different class metaobject classes declares that they are compatible.

writer-method-class

Generic Function

SYNTAX

writer-method-class

    class direct-slot **&rest** *initargs*

ARGUMENTS

The *class* argument is a class metaobject.

    The *direct-slot* argument is a direct slot definition metaobject.

    The *initargs* argument is a list of initialization arguments and values.

VALUES

The value returned is a class metaobject.

PURPOSE

This generic function is called to determine the class of writer methods created during class initialization and reinitialization. The result must be a subclass of **standard-writer-method**.

    The *initargs* argument must be the same as will be passed to **make-instance** to create the reader method. The *initargs* must include **:slot-definition** with *slot-definition* as its value.

METHODS

writer-method-class　　　　　　　　　　　　　　　*Primary Method*

    (*class* `standard-class`)

    (*direct-slot* `standard-direct-slot-definition`)

    &rest *initargs*

writer-method-class　　　　　　　　　　　　　　　*Primary Method*

    (*class* `funcallable-standard-class`)

    (*direct-slot* `standard-direct-slot-definition`)

    &rest *initargs*

These methods returns the class **standard-writer-method**. These methods can be overridden.

A An Introduction to the Common Lisp Object System

In this appendix, we provide a brief introduction to the basic concepts and syntax of the Common Lisp Object System (CLOS) for people who already have some familiarity with object-oriented programming. On a topic by topic basis, we compare the concepts and vocabulary of CLOS with those of two other popular object-oriented languages, Smalltalk[Goldberg&Robson 83] and C++[Ellis&Stroustrup 90]. For each topic there is an overview, language specific terminology, a description of the relevant features of CLOS, followed by brief contrasting descriptions of Smalltalk and C++. A summary chart comparing terminology and features of CLOS, Smalltalk, and C++ can be found on page 253.

A.1   Classes and Instances

Object-oriented programs are organized around *classes* that reflect the domain they are about; during execution of a program, *instances* of these classes are created, initialized, and then manipulated. Classes must be defined before instances can be created. A class *definition* specifies instance structure: that is, the named *slots* each instance must contain. Class definitions may also contain other information related to these slots; for example, it may specify the types of values that are allowed to fill them, or expressions for computing initial values when instances are created. In Smalltalk, slots are called *instance variables*. In C++, instances are called *objects of a class* and slots are called *member data elements*.

CLOS class definitions can specify, for each slot, as little as just the name, or can include a number of *slot options*. For example, here is a CLOS definition for a class named `rectangle`:

```
(defclass rectangle ()
    ((height :initarg :start-height
             :initform 5
             :accessor rectangle-height)
     (width :initarg :start-width
            :initform 8
            :accessor rectangle-width)))
```

This definition specifies that each instance of `rectangle` will contain two slots named `height` and `width`. Each slot is specified by a list starting with its slot name, followed by a number of slot options. A slot option is a keyword (a reserved symbol starting with a colon) followed by the option value. For example, the slot named `height` is followed by three options, with keywords `:initarg`, `:initform`, and `:accessor`. The first two are used to specify information for instance initialization, described below. The value associated with slot option keyword :**accessor** is the name of an automatically generated generic function. This generic function provides access to this slot for instances of this class. For example, **rectangle-height** fetches the value of the **height** slot of instances of **rectangle**.

New instances of CLOS classes are created by calling the function **make-instance** with the class name as first argument:

```
(setq r1 (make-instance 'rectangle :start-height 50 :start-width 100))
```

The result of evaluating this expression is to set the variable **r1** to a newly created instance of **rectangle**. Because of the :**initarg** options in the definition above, :**start-height** and :**start-width** in this form can serve as keywords to initialize the slots **height** and **width** to 50 and 100, respectively. If an initial value is not provided on a call to **make-instance**, the :**initform** slot option in the class definition supplies a form used to compute a default initial value for the slot; for a **rectangle**, the default values for **height** and **width** would be 5 and 8 respectively.

In Smalltalk, only the names of the instance variables are specified in class definitions. Instances are created by sending the special message **new** to the class; default initialization can be included in that method. It is more typical to provide a creation message which includes initial values to be sent to the class; this allows, for example, a **Rectangle** to be created and initialized with 50 and 100 by sending a message like:

```
Rectangle startHeight: 50 startWidth: 100
```

In C++, both the name and type of member data elements must be specified in the class definition. Default initialization expressions can be supplied for each member data element. Objects of a class are created by calling an automatically defined constructor function for the class. C++ has mechanisms for defining initial value arguments for the constructor function; if no value is provided to the constructor, the default initialization expression in the class definition is used to determine the initial value for a new instance's member data element.

A.2   Structure Inheritance

Object-oriented programming languages support the specification of a new class as an incremental modification of other previously defined classes. A new class is said to *inherit* from these other classes, which means that its effective definition is a combination of what is explicit in its own definition and what is in those of classes that it inherits from.

In CLOS and Smalltalk, the terminology used is that a new *subclass* is defined as a specialization of a previously existing *superclass*. In C++, the terminology used is that a new *derived class* is defined in terms of a previously existing *base class*.

When classes are defined in terms of other classes in this way, if the same slot name is used in the definition of more than one class, the question arises as to how many slots associated with that name will appear in any instance. In CLOS, a single slot is created in each instance for each unique slot name that appears in its class or in any of its superclasses. If there is more than one definition with the same slot name, the descriptions of like-named slots are combined. For example, consider this definition of color-rectangle as a subclass of rectangle:

```
(defclass color-rectangle (rectangle)
     ((color :initform 'red
                :initarg :color
                :accessor color)
      (clearp :initform nil
                :initarg :clearp
                :accessor clearp)
      (height :initform 10)))
```

Given the earlier definition of **rectangle**, this definition causes instances of **color-rectangle** to have four slots: the newly-defined slots **color** and **clearp**, and the slots **height** and **width** inherited from **rectangle**. The last line of the **color-rectangle** class definition does not define a new **height** slot, but provides a new default initial value for the slot of that name inherited from **rectangle**. Furthermore, this example illustrates one way descriptions for like-named slots are combined: the more specific :**initform** overrides the inherited one. For the options :**accessor** and :**initarg**, on the other hand, CLOS constructs the union of the specified option values. For the option :**type**, not illustrated here, type intersection is used.

In Smalltalk, it is illegal to specify the same name (e.g., **height**) as an instance variable in a subclass when it is also specified in a superclass. Given that restriction, and since Smalltalk class definitions only contain names of instance variables,[1] the subclass contains the simple union of instance variables named in the class definition and in its superclasses.

C++ scoping rules make each class definition be an independent name scope. Hence, in C++, declaring a like-named member data element in a derived class causes a new member data element of that name to be part of any object of that class, even if another

---

[1]In this simplified description, we omit Smalltalk class variables which are accessible to all members of a class. We also omit the corresponding class variables of CLOS, and static data elements of C++ classes.

declaration with the same name appears in a base class. Each declaration carries its own type specification and its own initialization.

Some of the most complex issues having to do with inheritance only arise when multiple inheritance is allowed; that is, when a new class can be made to inherit from more than one superclass. Both CLOS and C++ support use of multiple inheritance. Some versions of Smalltalk have experimented with multiple inheritance; however, it is not a generally supported feature.

One typical way multiple inheritance is used is to define *mixin classes* that capture useful independent fragments of structure and behavior. Such mixins are usually not designed to be instantiated on their own. Instantiable classes are then defined in terms of one principal class and one or more these mixins. For example, a `color-mixin` class might capture the behavior and structure peculiar to colored objects, and be used in the following alternative definition of `color-rectangle`:

```
(defclass color-mixin ()
    ((color :initform 'red
            :initarg :color
            :accessor color)))

(defclass color-rectangle (color-mixin rectangle)
    ((clearp :initform nil
             :initarg :clearp
             :accessor clearp)
     (height :initform 10)))
```

This definition of `color-mixin` incorporates a description of the slot `color`; behavior associated with colored objects (for example, changing the color) would also be associated with this mixin.

When mixins are not independent, rules for combinations must be used. In CLOS, the combination rules depend on use of a linearization of the set of superclasses which will not be described here. In C++, users are forced to explicitly resolve clashes from multiple base classes.

A.3   Classes and Operations

In object-oriented programming languages, operations are composed of independently defined implementations specific to particular classes. In CLOS and Smalltalk, the independently defined implementations are called *methods*. In C++, they are called *virtual member functions.* When an operation is invoked, a runtime dispatch selects the appropriate implementation. In CLOS, the terminology for invoking an operation is *calling a generic function*; in Smalltalk, *sending a message*; in C++, *calling a member function.* Object-oriented programming languages differ on how methods are associated with a class and how the dispatch is implemented.

If a method for a particular operation is defined on both a subclass and one of its superclasses, the first is said to *shadow* the second, meaning that only the more specific one will automatically be executed. All object-oriented programming languages provide some way for the more specific method to invoke the shadowed method explicitly. If the shadowed method is executed, the more specific method is said to *extend* the shadowed method; if the shadowed method is not executed, then the more specific method is said to *override* the shadowed method.

CLOS, Smalltalk and C++ use significantly different ways of associating a method with a class, syntax for invoking a generic operation, mechanisms for dispatch to the appropriate implementation, and syntax for invoking a shadowed method.

In CLOS, methods are associated as much with generic functions as with classes. Separately defined methods implement the generic function's behavior for different classes. A generic function definition specifies the interface common to all methods, namely, the generic function name and argument list:

```
(defgeneric paint (shape medium))
```

A method is associated with a class if a parameter of the method is *specialized* to that class. Semantically, what this means is that an argument bound to that parameter must be an instance of that class (or any of its subclasses). Here are two methods for **paint**, one specialized to **rectangle** and another to **circle** (the definition of the class **circle** is not shown):

```
(defmethod paint ((shape rectangle) medium)          ; method 1
  (vertical-stroke (rectangle-height shape)
                   (rectangle-width shape)
                   medium))

(defmethod paint ((shape circle) medium)             ; method 2
  (draw-circle (radius shape)
               medium))
```

In this notation, the argument list to the method indicates how the method is specialized. Each element of the argument list is either a parameter name (e.g., **medium**), or a pair consisting of a parameter name and the name of a class (e.g., **shape** and **rectangle**). For *method 1* to be *applicable*, that is used on a call to the generic function, the parameter bound to **shape** must be an instance of the class **rectangle** (or any of its subclasses). In this use, the class name **rectangle** is called a *specializer*.

A call to a generic function looks exactly like a call to an ordinary function:

```
(paint r1 *standard-display*)
```

If **r1** is bound to an instance of a **rectangle**, this call to the generic function would dispatch to *method 1* specialized for **rectangle**. If it were an instance of **circle**, dispatch would be to *method 2*. Object-oriented runtime dispatch is supported by code in the generic function that automatically selects and invokes the applicable method.

To invoke a shadowed method in CLOS, the function **call-next-method** is used within the body of a method. For example, in CLOS we might have:

```
(defmethod paint ((shape color-rectangle) medium)          ; method 3
  (unless (clearp shape)
    (call-next-method)))
```

This method, specialized on **color-rectangle**, shadows the method on **rectangle**. Unless **(clearp shape)** is true, the shadowed method is called, passing the same arguments.

In Smalltalk, a method is usually associated with a class through a visual browser, since Smalltalk is almost always used in a residential environment.[2] The operation associated with the method is identified by a symbol called the method *selector*. When behavior is invoked by sending a message to an instance, the message will consist of the selector and other arguments for the operation. The method to be run is located using the selector as a key in a method table associated with the class of the object. If the selector is not found in that table, the corresponding search is made in the superclass of the class.

The Smalltalk syntax for sending a message emphasizes the receiver of the message, putting the object first, followed by the selector, and then any other arguments; e.g.

```
r1 paint: standardDisplay
```

Within a method, to send a different message to the same object, a message is sent to the pseudo-variable **self**. To invoke a shadowed method, a message is sent to the pseudo-variable **super**:

```
super paint: standardDisplay
```

---

[2] A Smalltalk file-based syntax is defined but is almost never used by programmers; it is generated by the system when saving definitions for reloading.

The only difference between sending a message to **self** and **super** is that the search for the appropriate method associated with the selector skips the class of the object itself when the message is sent to **super**.

C++ is a language based on static scoping rules. Specific virtual member functions are associated with a class by appearing within the name scope of that class definition. Virtual member functions support run-time lookup. Because C++ is a compile/link language, a linear index can be created for each class at link time which specifies the appropriate implementation to call; invocation thus involves only an indexed lookup before dispatch to the specific code. Not all member functions in a C++ are declared virtual. For polymorphic non-virtual functions, choice of implementation is made at compile time based on declarations. Because of this compile-time choice, these non-virtual member functions do not support object-oriented specialization.

The C++ syntax emphasizes the selection of the function based on the object, with other arguments being in standard position. To invoke **paint** on **r1**, for example, C++ uses:

```
r1.paint(standard_display)
```

This is the same syntax used to invoke other kinds of member functions. If another virtual member function is to be invoked on the same object, the pseudo-variable **this** can be used. To invoke a shadowed virtual member function, a qualified name involving the base class must be used (e.g., if **rectangle** is the base class in which there is a shadowed virtual member function for **paint**, then the qualified name **rectangle::paint** can be used to refer to that virtual member function). If there is more than one base class for a derived class, shadowed methods in any or all base classes can be invoked using the appropriately qualified name.

A.4 Multiple argument dispatch

For some operations, it is often natural for the implementation to depend on the class of more than one argument. In our example for **paint**, the code should depend on both the shape and the medium. Code for painting a **circle** on a bitmap is clearly different from that for drawing a **circle** in a page-description language, and is different from that for painting a **rectangle** on either.

In CLOS, method definitions can directly specify the required classes of more than one argument. Methods where more than one argument has an explicit specializer are called *multi-methods*. As an example, consider the following code sketch:

```
(defmethod paint ((shape  rectangle) (medium vector-display))   ; method 4
    ... draw vectors on display ...)
```

```
(defmethod paint ((shape rectangle) (medium bitmap-display))    ; method 5
    ... paint pixels on display ...)
(defmethod paint ((shape rectangle) (medium pdl-stream))        ; method 6
    ... create PS lines...)
(defmethod paint ((shape circle) (medium pdl-stream))           ; method 7
    ... create PS circle ...)
```

Both arguments to **paint** are specialized; for a multi-method to be applicable, each parameter must be bound to an instance of the associated specializer class. For example, for *method 4* to be applicable, the first argument must be an instance of **rectangle**, and the second, an instance of **vector-display**.

Multi-methods are a useful extension of the notion of object-oriented programming, but are the primary place where CLOS breaks the intuition that a method belongs to exactly one class. Multi-method dispatch for generic functions allows a finer breakdown of the operation into appropriate pieces.

In Smalltalk, selection of an implementation based on the types of more than one argument to a method can be accomplished with a "chained dispatch"[Ingalls 86]. In this example, each method for **paint:** would be specialized to a shape; all shape-specialized methods send a secondary message whose selector incorporates the shape name; so the **paint:** method on **circle** sends a **paint-circle:** message to the **medium** with **self** as the argument.

```
medium paint-circle: self
```

The code for **paint-circle:** is then specialized for the medium; the selector implies the shape is to be painted.

The corresponding pair of virtual member functions would be used to achieve this run-time multi-argument selection in C++.

A.5   Structure Encapsulation

In object-oriented programming languages, the structure of an object is intended to be opaque outside of certain restricted scopes. Access to the structure is provided by operations associated with the class of the object. Of course, each language provides loopholes that allow access from outside that scope.

In CLOS, the intended public access to a slot is provided by the automatically generated access functions that can be specified in a class definition using the slot option

:accessor. For example, in the definition for rectangle, the :accessor rectangle-height slot option causes automatic definition of two generic functions: rectangle-height, to read the value of the slot height, and (setf rectangle-height),[3] to set the value of that slot. Examples of the use of these functions are:

```
(rectangle-height r1)           ;fetches the value of the height slot
(setf (rectangle-height r1) 75) ;sets the value of height slot to 75
```

Direct access to named slots is provided by slot-value. Accessor generic functions are defined in terms of slot-value. Here are examples of the use of slot-value:

```
(slot-value r1 'height)
(setf (slot-value r1 'height) 75)
```

Direct access using slot-value can be used in any context. The only requirement is that the slot name be known. However, it is better practice to use the accessors since they provide the intended public access. In addition, this allows these generic functions to be specialized, for example, replacing direct access by a computation, without requiring any change to client code.

In Smalltalk, instance variables specified in a class C or any superclass of C are accessible by name in methods defined on the class C. Outside of such methods only user-defined methods and low-level implementation loopholes can access instance variables.

Because C++ classes define a name scope, virtual member functions defined within that name scope have access to the member data elements by name. By default, virtual member functions in derived classes do not have access to member data elements declared in base classes. To extend this private naming scope to derived classes, C++ provides a protected specifier for member data elements; to extend the named access to all scopes, a corresponding public specifier is available. C++ has many different loopholes to break encapsulation. However, the preferred style for public access is through user-defined virtual member functions for the same reason that accessor functions are preferred in CLOS.

A.6   Methods in combination

Sometimes, in order to support flexibility in specializations, it is useful to design a set of interacting operations. For example, in painting it might be useful to allow specializations

---

[3]This list is indeed the name of a generic function, an example of a composite name now used in Common Lisp for functions that set values of fields.

to define an independent method that sets up initial conditions for painting, or does some cleanup afterwards.

In any language, one might write the general method for paint so that it calls prepaint and postpaint around a call to primary-paint. One could then define default methods for the former two. This would allow specializations to just add preparation operations, for example. In a language with multiple inheritance, mixins could be used to add such incremental behavior.

This pattern of coding was used frequently in earlier Lisp multiple inheritance object-oriented programming languages. Language support for this idiom is provided by CLOS. In addition to primary methods such as those we have seen, CLOS allows the definition of before-methods and after-methods that play specialized roles in the invocation of a generic function. For example, in CLOS we can define a before-method specialized on color-mixin that will set the brush color before painting by writing:

```
(defmethod paint :before ((shape color-mixin))
  (set-brush-color (color shape)))
```

In general, when a generic function is invoked, all the applicable before-methods are called, then the most specific primary method, followed by all the after-methods. Because of the order in which they are run, before-methods are usually used to do error checking and/or preprocessing, and after-methods are used for cleanup and/or auxiliary processing. The automatic invocation of before-methods, after-methods, and primary methods in the pattern described is called *standard method combination*.

Neither Smalltalk nor C++ provide any facilities for automatic method combination.

A.7 Summary

	CLOS	**Smalltalk**	**C++**
Class	class	class	class
Instance	instance	instance	object of class
Instance structure	slots	instance variables	member data elements
Inheritance	subclass direct superclasses	subclass superclass	derived class base classes
Slot descriptions	name initial value forms accessor function initializer keywords	name	name type initial value forms
Slot inheritance	one per name (combine duplicates)	one per name (no duplicates)	one per declaration
Invoking an operation	calling a generic function	sending a message	calling a virtual member function
Implementation for instances of a class	method	method	virtual member function
Linking operation to class	specializers in parameter list	through browser	defined in class scope
Multi-argument dispatch	multi-methods	chained dispatch	chained dispatch
Whole object reference	name in parameter list	`self`	`this`
Invocation of shadowed method	`call-next-method`	message to **super**	call virtual member function with qualified name
Public access to instance state	accessor functions user methods	user methods	user methods public declaration
Direct access to instance state	`slot-value`	by name within method scope	by name within class scope
Automatic method combination	yes	no	no

B Solutions to Selected Exercises

Exercise 1.1 (p. 45) The computation performed by `compute-applicable-methods-using-classes` depends only on the generic function and the list of classes. This means it can be memoized using these two values as keys. The memoization is done in two parts: (i) associated with each generic function is a table which, (ii) maps from a list of classes to a list of applicable methods. For simplicity, the table is just a Common Lisp hash table.

The definition of `standard-generic-function` is updated to include a slot for the table.

```
(defclass standard-generic-function ()
    ((name :initarg :name :accessor generic-function-name)
     (lambda-list :initarg :lambda-list
                  :accessor generic-function-lambda-list)
     (methods :initform ()
              :accessor generic-function-methods)
     (table :initform (make-hash-table :test #'equal)
            :accessor classes-to-applicable-methods-table)))
```

`apply-generic-function` is then rewritten as follows:

```
(defun apply-generic-function (gf args)
  (let* ((required-classes
           (mapcar #'class-of (required-portion gf args)))
         (applicable-methods
           (or (gethash required-classes
                        (classes-to-applicable-methods-table gf)
                        nil)
               (setf (gethash required-classes
                              (classes-to-applicable-methods-table gf))
                     (compute-applicable-methods-using-classes
                       gf
                       required-classes)))))
    (if (null applicable-methods)
        (error "No matching method for the~@
                generic function ~S,~@
                when called with arguments ~:S." gf args)
        (apply-methods gf args applicable-methods))))
```

The memoized values may become invalid when a new method is added to the generic function. In the subset of CLOS we are working with, no other events can invalidate these entries.[1] This means that `add-method` must be modified to clear the table.

```
(defun add-method (gf method)
  (setf (method-generic-function method) gf)
  (push method (generic-function-methods gf))
  (dolist (specializer (method-specializers method))
    (pushnew method (class-direct-methods specializer)))
  (clrhash (classes-to-applicable-methods-table gf))
  method)
```

Note that these modifications cannot be made to the complete Closette in Appendix D because the code there reflects revisions made in the course of Chapter 4. One effect of those revisions is to introduce this optimization.

Exercise 2.1 (p. 51)   A list of all classes in the system is kept in some global variable, call it `*all-classes*`. The after-method on `initialize-instance` for class metaobjects (page 23) is modified to push classes onto this list rather than create the direct subclass links. This is done by replacing these two lines of that method

```
  (dolist (superclass (class-direct-superclasses class))
    (push class (class-direct-subclasses superclass)))
```

with

```
  (push class *all-classes*)
```

Then `class-direct-subclasses` can be computed from the global list as follows:

```
(defun class-direct-subclasses (class)
  (remove-if-not #'(lambda (c)
                     (member class (class-direct-superclasses c)))
                 *all-classes*))
```

This strategy depends on the freedom provided by the second rule since each call to `class-direct-subclasses` constructs and returns a fresh list structure.

Exercise 2.2 (p. 58)   A class is at the apex of a diamond if it has two distinct direct subclasses which themselves have a common subclass:

---

[1]In full CLOS, where both classes and generic functions can be redefined, there are many more situations which would cause these memoized values to become invalid. As a result, the memoization scheme used in a real CLOS implementation, while similar in concept, is usually much more complex.

```
(defun has-diamond-p (class)
  (some #'(lambda (pair)
            (not (null (common-subclasses* (car pair)
                                           (cadr pair)))))
        (all-distinct-pairs (class-direct-subclasses class))))

(defun common-subclasses* (class-1 class-2)
  (intersection (subclasses* class-1) (subclasses* class-2)))
```

The helping function `all-distinct-pairs` returns the set of all distinct two-element subsets of a given set.

```
(defun all-distinct-pairs (set)
  (if (null set)
      ()
      (append (mapcar #'(lambda (rest)
                          (list (car set) rest))
                      (cdr set))
              (all-distinct-pairs (cdr set)))))
```

Exercise 2.3 (p. 64). Essentially, the exercise is to produce a form which describes the actions which `apply-generic-function` and `apply-methods` would actually take. The solution is a straightforward adaptation of those functions. Free use is made of several internal functions from Closette, all of which could have been defined using the documented metaobject accessors.

```
(defun display-effective-method (gf args)
  (let ((applicable-methods
          (compute-applicable-methods-using-classes
            gf (mapcar #'class-of (required-portion gf args)))))
    (pprint
      (if (null applicable-methods)
          '(error "No applicable methods.")
          (generate-effective-method gf applicable-methods)))))
```

```
(defun generate-effective-method (gf methods)
  (declare (ignore gf))
  (labels ((generate-method (method)
               '(method ,@(cdr (generate-defmethod
                                  method :show-body t))))
           (generate-call-method (method next-methods)
             '(call-method
                ,(generate-method method)
                ,(mapcar #'generate-method next-methods))))
     (let ((primaries (remove-if-not #'primary-method-p methods))
           (befores (remove-if-not #'before-method-p methods))
           (afters (remove-if-not #'after-method-p methods)))
       (if (null primaries)
           '(error "No primary method")
           '(progn
              ,@(mapcar
                  #'(lambda (method)
                      (generate-call-method method ()))
                  befores)
              (multiple-value-prog1
                ,(generate-call-method (car primaries)
                                       (cdr primaries))
                ,@(mapcar
                    #'(lambda (method)
                        (generate-call-method method ()))
                    (reverse afters)))))))))
```

Exercise 2.4 (p. 66)   The first approach can be implemented by adding a single new slot to method metaobjects. When its value is **reader**, the method is a reader; when its value is **writer**, the method is a writer; and when its value is **nil**, the method is neither a reader nor a writer.

```
(defclass standard-method ()
    (...
    (reader/writer :initform nil
                   :initarg :reader/writer)
    ...))
```

To properly initialize this slot, the functions `add-reader-method` and `add-writer-method` (p. 39) must be updated to supply the `:reader/writer` initialization argument. The predicates can then be implemented as:

```
(defun reader-method-p (x)
  (and (eq (class-of x) (find-class 'standard-method))
       (eq (slot-value x 'reader/writer) 'reader)))

(defun writer-method-p (x)
  (and (eq (class-of x) (find-class 'standard-method))
       (eq (slot-value x 'reader/writer) 'writer)))
```

The second approach requires two new class definitions, `standard-reader-method` and `standard-writer-method`. Each is defined as a subclass of `standard-method`. In this case, `add-reader-method` and `add-writer-method` must be modified to create instances of these new classes rather than `standard-method`. This is done by merging the previous code for these functions with the code for `ensure-method` (p. 38). (Only `add-reader-method` is shown, the definition of `add-writer-method` is analogous.)

```
(defun add-reader-method (class fn-name slot-name)
  (add-method
    (ensure-generic-function fn-name :lambda-list '(object))
    (make-instance 'standard-reader-method
                   :lambda-list '(object)
                   :qualifiers ()
                   :specializers (list class)
                   :body '(slot-value object ',slot-name)
                   :environment (top-level-environment)))
  (values))
```

Each strategy is effective at capturing a difference between objects. In the first case, the difference is captured in the value of a slot. In the second, it is captured in the class of the object. Each strategy is appropriate in certain situations, and often the choice of which to use is simply a matter of taste. But, in general, using the class of the object will make the implementation more extensible. Notice, for example, that the `eq` test on the class of the object in the first solution effectively prohibits subclassing of `standard-method`. In the full MOP, the latter solution is taken; there are special classes for reader and writer methods.

Exercise 3.1 (p. 83)   As suggested in the exercise, an around-method is used to default the `:direct-superclasses` initialization argument. When the supplied value is the empty list, a list of just `vanilla-flavor` is used instead. The class `vanilla-flavor` is itself defined as a subclass of `standard-object`, so the class precedence list of any pure flavors class will end in (... `vanilla-flavor` `standard-object` `t`). To avoid circularity problems, the class `vanilla-flavor` itself is defined as an instance of `standard-class`.[2]

```
(defclass vanilla-flavor () ())

(defmethod initialize-instance :around ((class flavors-class)
                                        &rest all-keys
                                        &key direct-superclasses)
  (apply #'call-next-method
         class
         :direct-superclasses (or direct-superclasses
                                  (list (find-class 'vanilla-flavor)))
         all-keys))
```

Exercise 3.2 (p. 89)   The solution is based on two important properties of the desired behavior. First, that slots in encapsulated classes are effectively named by a *pair* of values: the slot and class names from the `defclass` macro. Second, there is no combination of like-named slots in the inheritance process; i.e., the class `c2` has two slots "named" `foo`, one named (`foo`, `c1`) and one named (`foo`, `c2`).

This suggests a way to use the existing slot inheritance mechanism to get the desired behavior. First, each direct slot is assigned a *unique name*, which replaces the *pretty name* specified in the `defclass` form. A mapping is maintained from pairs of (`pretty-name`, `class`) to the unique names. Because each direct slot has a unique name, no combination of (what would otherwise be) like-named slots is done. Given a pretty name and a class, the unique name can be determined, and access can then be done in the normal way.

The earliest convenient point to assign unique names is during initialization of the class metaobject. A specialized around-method edits the slot property lists before calling `call-next-method`.[3]

```
(defclass encapsulated-class (standard-class) ())
```

---

[2]Full CLOS supports default initialization arguments a powerful mechanism for handling this sort of situation. When using the full MOP, where full CLOS is available, it would be appropriate for this code to use them. (Default initialization arguments are discussed at greater length in Section 3.6.)

[3]In the full MOP, the solution is somewhat more complicated because, when a class is redefined, arrangements need to be made to preserve the previous unique name of a slot.

```
(defmethod initialize-instance :around ((class encapsulated-class)
                                        &rest all-keys
                                        &key direct-slots)
  (let ((revised-direct-slots
          (mapcar
            #'(lambda (slot-properties)
                (let ((pretty-name (getf slot-properties ':name))
                      (new-properties (copy-list slot-properties)))⁴
                  (setf (getf* new-properties ':name) (gensym))
                  (setf (getf* new-properties ':pretty-name) pretty-name)
                  new-properties))
            direct-slots)))
    (apply #'call-next-method class
           :direct-slots revised-direct-slots
           all-keys)))
```

The pretty name is hung on the :pretty-name property, with the assumption that it will be stored with the direct slot definition metaobject where it can later be retrieved with the function slot-definition-pretty-name. These accessors could be defined in the same way as slot-definition-initform *(290)*.

The function private-slot-value and its allies are all defined in terms of private-slot-name which searches a class's list of direct slots looking for one with a given pretty name, returning the unique name of the slot if it finds one and reporting an error if it doesn't.

```
(defun private-slot-value (instance slot-name class)
  (slot-value instance (private-slot-name slot-name class)))

(defun private-slot-name (slot-name class)
  (let ((slot (find slot-name (class-direct-slots class)
                    :key #'slot-definition-pretty-name)))
    (if slot
        (slot-definition-name slot)
        (error "The class ~S has no private slot named ~S."
               class slot-name)))))
```

Notice that by renaming the slots before initialization, any automatically generated accessor methods will be defined with the unique names, and so have the desired behavior.

---

[4]The :name property needs to be changed. But, the restrictions outlined in Chapter 2 prohibit destructive modifications of the arguments, so a copy must be made and used instead.

Exercise 3.3 (p. 94)   The specialized method handles the :default-initargs option, expanding it according to the rules described earlier. If the option is not :default-
initargs, call-next-method is invoked which will cause the standard method to signal
the appropriate error.

```
(defmethod canonicalize-defclass-option
           ((sample-class default-initargs-class) option)
  (case (car option)
    (:default-initargs
      '(:direct-default-initargs
        (list ,@(apply #'append
                       (mapplist⁵ #'(lambda (key value)
                                      '(',key ,value))
                         (cdr option))))))
    (t (call-next-method)))))
```

Note that bootstrapping concerns mean that the Closette source code in Appendix D
cannot simply be edited to include this version of defclass. One simple way to add it
however is to define it after Closette is already loaded, perhaps by adding it to the end
of the file.

Exercise 3.4 (p. 104)   The solution simply assumes the existence of an :allocation
option, which defaults to :instance. Given this, the previous specialized method on
compute-effective-slot-definition is no longer needed since the standard inheritance allocation is what is desired.

The key difference of the change is that some slots of the class will have :dynamic allocation while others have :instance allocation. This means that the previous specialized
method definitions need to be revised to check the allocation of slots rather than simply
assuming they are all dynamic. allocate-instance is modified to only allocate a table
entry when one or more slots are dynamically allocated.

```
(defmethod allocate-instance ((class dynamic-slot-class))
  (let ((instance (call-next-method)))
    (when (some #'dynamic-slot-p (class-slots class))
      (allocate-table-entry instance))
    instance))
```

The specialized methods on the slot access generic functions are revised so that they
do not interfere with access to non-dynamic slots. Notice that by invoking call-next-
method not only when the slot is not dynamic, but also when there is no slot with the

---

⁵The non-standard mapping mapplist *(281)* maps over property lists.

given name, we allow the standard method to handle the missing slot error. (Only `slot-value-using-class` is shown, the others are similar.)

```
(defmethod slot-value-using-class ((class dynamic-slot-class)
                                   instance slot-name)
  (let ((slot (find slot-name (class-slots class)
                    :key #'slot-definition-name)))
    (if (and slot (dynamic-slot-p slot))
        (read-dynamic-slot-value instance slot-name)
        (call-next-method))))
```

Exercise 3.5 (p. 105)   This solution is similar to the implementation of dynamic slots except that instead of using a separate table for the class slots, they are stored in the class metaobject. Furthermore, as defined in CLOS, the initialization forms for class slots are evaluated at the time the class is defined.

```
(defclass class-slot-class (standard-class)
    ((class-allocated-slots
        :initform ()
        :accessor class-allocated-slots)))

(defun class-slot-p (slot)
  (eq (slot-definition-allocation slot) ':class))
```

Evaluation of the initialization forms and allocation of the class slot storage is handled by a specialized method on `initialize-instance`. A special value is used to record that a class slot is unbound.

```
(defparameter unbound-class-slot (list "unbound class slot"))
```

```
(defmethod initialize-instance :after
           ((class class-slot-class) &key)
  (setf (class-allocated-slots class)
        (mapcar
          #'(lambda (slot)
              (let ((initfunction
                      (slot-definition-initfunction slot)))
                (cons (slot-definition-name slot)
                      (if (not (null initfunction))
                          (funcall initfunction)
                          unbound-class-slot))))
          (remove-if-not #'class-slot-p
                         (class-direct-slots class)))))
```

Specialized methods on the slot access generic functions first check whether the slot is a class slot, and if it is they access the class slot storage. (Only slot-value-using-class is shown, the others are similar.)

```
(defmethod slot-value-using-class ((class class-slot-class)
                                    instance
                                    slot-name)
  (let ((slot (find slot-name (class-slots class)
                    :key #'slot-definition-name)))
    (if (and slot (class-slot-p slot))
        (class-slot-value class slot-name)
        (call-next-method))))
```

The class slot storage is found by searching, in order, the direct slots of each class in the class precedence list.

```
(defun class-slot-value (class slot-name)
  (dolist (super (class-precedence-list class))
    (let ((slot (find slot-name
                      (class-direct-slots super)
                      :key #'slot-definition-name)))
      (when slot
        (let ((value (cdr (assoc slot-name
                                 (class-allocated-slots super)))))
          (when (eq value unbound-class-slot)
            (error "The class slot ~S is unbound in the class ~S."
                   slot-name class))
          (return-from class-slot-value value))))))
```

In full CLOS, change-class and update-instance-for-different-class handle
class slots in a special way which this solution does not support. In particular, they
provide reasonable behavior for what happens when the allocation of a slot changes.
How would you modify the existing protocol so that these operations could be extended
to handle class slots?

Exercise 4.1 (p. 110)   A flag stored with the generic function metaobject keeps track
of whether tracing is currently on or off. A method on apply-generic-function checks
the flag, and when it is set, prints out appropriate information.

```
(defclass traceable-gf (standard-generic-function)
    ((tracing :initform nil :accessor tracing-enabled-p)))

(defun trace-generic-function (gf-name new-value)
  (let ((gf (fdefinition gf-name)))
    (setf (tracing-enabled-p gf) new-value)))
```

```
(defmethod apply-generic-function ((gf traceable-gf) args)
  (if (not (tracing-enabled-p gf))
      (call-next-method)
      (progn
        (format *trace-output*
                "Entering generic function ~S~@
                 with arguments ~:S.~%" gf args)
        (let ((results (multiple-value-list (call-next-method))))
          (format *trace-output*
                  "Leaving generic function ~S~@
                   value(s) being returned are: ~:S.~%" gf results)
          (values-list results)))))
```

Note that this solution cannot be added directly to the version of Closette that appears in Appendix D because the code there reflects the revised version of the generic function invocation protocol developed late in Chapter 4. (Also see the remarks at the beginning of Appendix D concerning fdefinition.)

Exercise 4.2 (p. 124)   The solution is to store the argument precedence order in the generic function metaobject, and then specialize method-more-specific-p so that it consults the stored value when ordering methods.

```
(defclass apo-gf (standard-generic-function)
     ((argument-precedence-order
        :initarg :argument-precedence-order
        :accessor argument-precedence-order)))
```

The argument precedence order is initialized from the :argument-precedence-order option to defgeneric; the value is a permuted list of the required argument names. The logical default value is the required portion of the generic function's lambda list, which means that any defaulting must be done after the lambda list has been initialized.

```
(defmethod initialize-instance :after ((gf apo-gf) &key)
  (unless (slot-boundp gf 'argument-precedence-order)
    (setf (argument-precedence-order gf)
          (gf-required-arglist gf))))
```

The specialized method on method-more-specific-p operates as before; the difference is that the order of the comparison now comes from the argument precedence order.

```
(defmethod method-more-specific-p
             ((gf apo-gf) method1 method2 required-classes)
    (flet ((apo-permute (list)
              (mapcar #'(lambda (arg-name)
                            (nth (position arg-name
                                           (gf-required-arglist gf))
                                 list))
                      (argument-precedence-order gf))))
      (mapc #'(lambda (spec1 spec2 arg-class)
                  (unless (eq spec1 spec2)
                    (return-from method-more-specific-p
                      (sub-specializer-p spec1 spec2 arg-class))))
            (apo-permute (method-specializers method1))
            (apo-permute (method-specializers method2))
            (apo-permute required-classes))
      nil))
```

Exercise 4.3 (p. 124)   Beta invokes primary methods in the opposite order of CLOS; that is, in least-specific-first order. This effect can be achieved simply by reversing the sense of method-more-specific-p, which will cause compute-applicable-methods-using-classes to sort the list of methods in least-specific-first order.

```
(defclass beta-gf (standard-generic-function) ())
(defclass beta-method (standard-method) ())

(defmethod method-more-specific-p ((gf beta-gf) method1 method2 classes)
    (if (equal (method-specializers method1)
               (method-specializers method2))
        nil
        (not (call-next-method))))
```

Alternatively, apply-methods can be specialized to pull methods off the opposite end of the list:

```
(defmethod apply-methods ((gf beta-gf) args methods)
    (when (null methods)
      (error "No primary methods for the~@
              generic function ~S." gf))
    (apply-method (car (last methods)) args (butlast methods)))
```

Either way, `inner` is implemented just like `call-next-method`. A specialized method on `extra-function-bindings` returns an entry for `inner`.

```
(defmethod extra-function-bindings ((method beta-method)
                                    args next-methods)
  (list
    (list 'inner
          #'(lambda ()
              (if (null next-methods)
                  nil
                  (apply-methods (method-generic-function method)
                                 args
                                 next-methods))))))
```

Note that neither of these solutions can be added directly to the version of Closette that appears in Appendix D because the code there reflects the revised version of the generic function invocation protocol developed late in Chapter 4.

C Living with Circularity

In contrast to normal metacircular interpreters, the program developed in the body of Part I would not work if simply typed in to a running CLOS implementation (even if the names were changed to avoid clashes with existing symbols). This program contains several kinds of *vicious* circularities; e.g., objects that must exist before they can be created, and recursions without base cases.

For example, consider what would be involved in executing the **defclass** form on page 1.3, which is intended to create the class metaobject for the class **standard-class**. This new class metaobject is itself supposed to be an instance of **standard-class**; in effect, we are asking the system to evaluate something like

```
(make-instance 'standard-class :name 'standard-class ...)
```

This is a classic chicken-and-egg problem: an object cannot be created until its class exists, but this class metaobject needs to be an instance of itself. Clearly, it will take further thought to see how to get an actual implementation off the ground.

As a second example, consider what is involved in accessing the **width** slot of a color-rectangle such as the **door** object (page 16). The function **slot-value** calls **slot-value-using-class**, which in turn calls **slot-location** to ascertain the location of the slot within the instance. Then **slot-location** calls **class-slots** on the class metaobject **color-rectangle** to get the class's list of effective slot definition metaobjects so that it can locate the slot named **width**:

```
(defun slot-value (instance slot-name)
  (slot-value-using-class (class-of instance) instance slot-name))

(defun slot-value-using-class ((class standard-class) instance slot-name)
  ... (slot-location class slot-name) ...))

(defun slot-location (class slot-name)
  ... (class-slots class) ...)
```

In this case, the applicable method on **class-slots** is a reader method specialized to standard-class, whose body consists of a single call to **slot-value** to access the class metaobject's slot named **effective-slots**:

```
(defmethod class-slots ((class standard-class))
  (slot-value class 'effective-slots))
```

But now we are back to **slot-value**, which will be evaluated in the same manner as the original. What we have is a non-well-founded recursion path, which would cause the implementation to loop indefinitely.

Although, for reasons of this sort, the program presented in the main text of Part I cannot be run as given, something very close to it can be run on a bare Common Lisp system (i.e., *sans* object system), and that something is presented in Appendix D. In this appendix we discuss the origins of the problematic circularities, and explain how to get around them.

The heart of the matter is that the introduction of metaobject protocols makes CLOS into a *procedurally reflective language* [Smith 84] and the code presented in the main text is a *reflective processor program* for CLOS, rather than a conventional metacircular processor program. The examples given above illustrate two general categories of circularity that arise in procedurally reflective systems:

Bootstrapping issues which are involved with how to get the system up and running in the first place, and

Metastability issues which have to do with how the system manages to run, and to stay running even while fundamental aspects of the implementation are being changed.

The issue of how the class metaobject for **standard-class** comes into existence is a bootstrapping issue; once this class metaobject exists, the problem evaporates. How **slot-value** will manage to avoid the apparent infinite regress is a metastability issue that does not go away even after the system has been bootstrapped. Another metastability issue has to do with **compute-discriminating-function**. When a method is added to this generic function, its discriminating function becomes invalid and so much be recomputed, which requires calling **compute-discriminating-function**.

Developing a correct implementation involves finding and breaking all vicious circles, but the techniques differ for the two kinds of cases. Because they occur before any user code has to be run, bootstrapping issues can often be dispatched by quick and dirty means. Addressing the metastability issues, on the other hand, requires taking care to ensure the (necessary) shortcuts do not invalidate the correctness of any user code. In spite of these differences, however, approaches that address one kind of issue sometimes provide solutions to the other kind; fortunately, that is the case for Closette, as the rest of this appendix will explain. A more thorough discussion of the problems associated with implementing procedurally reflective languages can be found in [des Rivières&Smith 84].

C.1   Bootstrapping Issues

Bootstrapping Closette involves two general initialization tasks: creating the initial class hierarchy and defining the standard generic functions, along with their standard methods. The insight underlying our bootstrapping technique is that there are only a finite number of initial metaobjects, and the values of their slots can all be figured out in advance (by us, the implementors). This means that these metaobjects can all be created by special hand-coded mechanisms. The only real challenge, in fact, is to find a way to create these initial metaobjects without having to write too much code that serves no other purpose.

The first circularity in the class hierarchy that must be dissolved is the fact that the class `standard-class` must exist before any metaobjects can be created with `allocate-instance`, which expects a class metaobject as an argument. The solution is to create `standard-class` entirely by other means; it can then be used in the creation of the other class metaobjects.

A second, more general, problem stems from the fact that classes and generic functions are thoroughly entangled: the creation of classes requires the prior existence of certain generic functions; conversely, the creation of generic functions and methods requires the prior existence of certain classes. These circularities need to be broken.

To see how we can do this, note that the reasons metaobject protocols are based on generic functions is that the method lookup mechanism provides both flexibility and extensibility. Neither property, however, is needed during initialization, since the initial metaobjects are always instances of the standard metaobject classes. Extensibility, that is to say, will not be needed until the user's code is read. It follows, therefore, that although we want to call generic functions during startup, there is no need to use the fully general method lookup mechanism. This can save us from the problem that the method lookup mechanism cannot work until most of the system is created. And thus we arrive at a simple solution: carry out calls to generic functions without using the method lookup mechanism until all classes, generic functions, and methods have been created.

There are a variety of ways in which this strategy is achieved. We need to be able to execute a `defclass` form for one of the initial classes while steering clear of the method lookup mechanism (the same story applies to `defgenerics` and `defmethods`). The documented execution of a `defclass` involves a call to `ensure-class`, which in turn calls the generic function `make-instance`. This last is in fact the principle generic function call; all other interesting generic function calls (e.g., to `allocate-instance` and `compute-slots`) are in service of this one call to `make-instance`. Notice, however, that when `ensure-class` calls `make-instance`, passing the class metaobject class as the first argument, the only one that can arise, during this startup phase, is `standard-class`. Because `standard-class` is a known quantity, we can predict exactly which methods of which generic functions will be invoked. This allows us to modify `ensure-class` to catch this case and call a normal function `make-instance-standard-class` with exactly the same net behavior as that call to `make-instance`. In other words, the definition

```
(defun ensure-class (...)
   ... (apply #'make-instance metaclass ...) ...)
```

can be changed to

```
(defun ensure-class (...)
   ... (apply (if (eq metaclass (find-class 'standard-class))
                  #'make-instance-standard-class
                  #'make-instance)
              metaclass ...) ...)
```

Mostly, what `make-instance-standard-class` does is to initialize slots from initialization arguments; this can be accomplished with inline calls to the metaobject slot accessors. Other initialization is performed by a class-specific after-method on `initialize-instance` and by `finalize-inheritance`. We can avoid unnecessary code duplication by moving most of the code from the standard methods into independently callable functions. E.g., the standard method for `finalize-inheritance`:

```
(defmethod finalize-inheritance ((class standard-class))
   ⟨body⟩)
```

can be split into a minimal method that calls a normal function named `std-finalize-inheritance` that does all the actual work:

```
(defmethod finalize-inheritance ((class standard-class))
   (std-finalize-inheritance class))
(defun std-finalize-inheritance (class)
   ⟨body⟩)
```

This allows the callers of the generic function the option of directly invoking the standard method in cases when it is known that only the standard method would be applicable. For example, the call

```
(finalize-inheritance class)
```

can be rewritten as

```
(funcall (if (eq (class-of class) (find-class 'standard-class))
             #'std-finalize-inheritance
             #'finalize-inheritance)
         class)
```

because it is a sure bet that instances of `standard-class` will be finalized in the regular way.

Since all classes during startup are instances of **standard-class**, the full method lookup mechanism is bypassed during startup. But when an instance of a specialized subclass of **standard-class** comes along later, the real method lookup mechanism for **finalize-inheritance** will be properly activated.

The bulk of the generic function calls are to the metaobject slot accessors (e.g., **class-slots**). There is no particular reason in Closette why these accessors need to be generic functions at all, so we have rewritten them as regular functions. This leaves only about a dozen generic functions calls that need to be special-cased in the way described above.

C.2   Metastability Issues

Once the implementation is up and running, it is still a trick to keep it running. In a normal, closed implementation, this is not a problem; in a system with metaobject protocols that allow the implementation to be extended, there is the potential for spectacular failure modes if certain situations are not properly anticipated.

In one of the examples we looked at above, one step in accessing a slot in a standard instance involves finding the relevant effective slot definition metaobject. The list of effective slot definition metaobjects to look through is stored in the class metaobject, which, unfortunately, requires another slot access to retrieve. Thus the nested chain of calls looks as follows:

```
(slot-value door 'width)
  (slot-value-using-class (class-of door) door 'width)
    (slot-location (class-of door) 'width)
      (class-slots (class-of door))
        (slot-value (class-of door) 'effective-slots)
          (slot-value-using-class (class-of (class-of door))
                                  (class-of door)
                                  'effective-slots)
            (slot-location (class-of (class-of door))
                           'effective-slots)
              (class-slots (class-of (class-of door)))
                (slot-value (class-of (class-of door)) 'effective-slots)
                  ...
```

This loop can be broken in **slot-location** *(282)* by special-casing the slot named **effective-slots** of the class metaobject for **standard-class**. That is, by ensuring that

```
(slot-location (find-class 'standard-class) 'effective-slots)
```

returns the known and fixed location of this particular slot of this particular class meta-object without recourse to further slot accesses. Catching this one special case breaks the circularity because `standard-class` is always guaranteed to turn up eventually in the sequence

```
(class-of ⟨x⟩)
(class-of (class-of ⟨x⟩))
(class-of (class-of (class-of ⟨x⟩)))
...
```

The fact that the class `standard-class` sits at the top of all `class-of` chains is a crucial property of the MOP—without it, there would not be any obvious base cases.

What is going on here is actually perfectly standard. Like any well-founded recursion, the implementation must bottom out on some known base cases. Furthermore, the technique applies to most other issues of metastability as well: the base cases are calls to system-defined generic functions with standard metaobjects as arguments—for example, computing the class precedence list of an instance of `standard-class`, computing the discriminating function of an instance of `standard-generic-function`, and computing the method function of an instance of `standard-method`. The implementation must somehow guarantee that all these base cases can be handled no matter what specializations the user may later introduce. This is one of the reasons why users cannot be allowed to add new methods that would be applicable to standard metaobjects; without such a restriction, there would be no base cases.

To see how this all matters, consider what is supposed to happen when a specialized method is added to `compute-discriminating-function`. Suppose we were to start, for example, with the following call:

```
(add-method #'compute-discriminating-function ⟨new-method⟩)
```

The function `add-method` will cause the discriminating function for the generic function metaobject (`compute-discriminating-function` in this case) to be recomputed because adding a new method constitutes a change in the context upon which the generic function's discriminating function may legitimately depend. The generic function `compute-discriminating-function` must be *called* to compute this discriminating function. In other words, we find the implementation needing to make the following self-referential call:

```
(compute-discriminating-function #'compute-discriminating-function)
```

If the implementation really tried to call `compute-discriminating-function` in order to come up with the discriminating function for `compute-discriminating-function`, the game would of course be over. On the other hand, since `compute-discriminating-function` is an instance of **standard-generic-function**, this is a base case, which can be handled by the function `std-compute-discriminating-function`. As long as `std-compute-discriminating-function` is called in this case, therefore, and assuming that it is guaranteed to return a value, this metastability issue has been resolved. Thus we see how the calls, already recast in the form

```
(funcall (if (eq (class-of gf) (find-class 'standard-generic-function))
             #'std-compute-discriminating-function
             #'compute-discriminating-function)
         gf)
```

for bootstrapping reasons, also solve Closette's issues of metastability.

D A Working Closette Implementation

This appendix contains the complete source code for Closette, as presented in Part I. It should run in any standard Common Lisp [CLtLII], including ones without built-in support for CLOS.[1] Except for some differences dealing with (setf *foo*) as a function name, the code here is also completely in line with the older version of Common Lisp [CLtL].

Besides the features of basic CLOS, this implementation includes almost all of the metaobject protocols developed in Chapters 2 and 3 of Part I. The streamlined metaobject protocols for generic function invocation that were presented in Section 4.4.4 are included in lieu of the apply-... versions from the early part of Chapter 4 (the latter are retained as normal functions which are defined in terms of the fast ones). Discriminating functions are precomputed and stored with the generic function metaobject. Effective method functions are computed on the critical path and memoized as shown in the text; however, the tables themselves are stored with the generic function metaobject (as opposed to being stored in lexical variables visible only to the regular discriminating function). Method functions are precomputed and stored with the method metaobject. Regular method functions have been reformulated so that they don't need eval and run-time environments; unfortunately, this change necessitates omitting the extra-method-bindings protocol.

This implementation also handles around-methods, method redefinition, and describe-object.

The only other noticeable difference from the code for Closette in Part I has to do with generic functions. Common Lisp only allows true function to be stored as the function value of a symbol. Since our generic function metaobjects are not true functions (technically, they are a kind of structure), Common Lisp refuses to store them there. We work around this by storing the discriminating function as the symbol's function value, and putting the generic function metaobject into an auxiliary table where it can be retrieved by name with a function called find-generic-function (exactly analogous to find-class). This solution does not support anonymous generic functions, and trouble can arise if a named generic function is passed as a functional argument. You must write (fdefinition 'paint) or #'paint when you need something that can be funcalled or apply'd, but you must use (find-generic-function 'paint) when you really need the generic function metaobject.

The remaining differences between this code and that presented in Part I happen truly backstage, and have to do with the issues of circularity discussed in Appendix C.

---

[1]It has been tested in Macintosh Allegro Common Lisp Version 1.2.2, Lucid/Sun Common Lisp 3.0.1 (Sun-4 Version for SunOS 4.0), Franz Allegro Common Lisp 3.1.13.1 (Sun 4), and Symbolics Genera Version 8.0.

There are two files: closette.lisp, which contains all of the code for Closette; and
newcl.lisp (page 313), which contains some definitions that allow the first file to run
in older versions of Common Lisp.

```
;;;-*-Mode:LISP; Package: (CLOSETTE :USE LISP); Base:10; Syntax:Common-lisp -*-
;;;
;;; Closette Version 1.0 (February 10, 1991)
;;;
;;; Copyright (c) 1990, 1991 Xerox Corporation.
;;; All rights reserved.
;;;
;;; Use and copying of this software and preparation of derivative works
;;; based upon this software are permitted.  Any distribution of this
;;; software or derivative works must comply with all applicable United
;;; States export control laws.
;;;
;;; This software is made available AS IS, and Xerox Corporation makes no
;;; warranty about the software, its performance or its conformity to any
;;; specification.
;;;
;;;
;;; Closette is an implementation of a subset of CLOS with a metaobject
;;; protocol as described in "The Art of The Metaobject Protocol",
;;; MIT Press, 1991.
;;;
;;; This program is available by anonymous FTP, from the /pcl/mop
;;; directory on arisia.xerox.com.

;;; This is the file closette.lisp

(in-package 'closette :use '(lisp))

;;; When running in a Common Lisp that doesn't yet support function names like
;;; (setf foo), you should first load the file newcl.lisp.  This next little
;;; bit imports stuff from there as needed.

#-Genera
(import '(newcl:print-unreadable-object))

#-Genera
(shadowing-import '(newcl:defun newcl:fboundp newcl:fmakunbound
                    newcl:fdefinition))

#-Genera
(export '(newcl:defun newcl:fboundp newcl:fmakunbound newcl:fdefinition))
```

```
#+Genera
(shadowing-import '(future-common-lisp:setf
                    future-common-lisp:fboundp
                    future-common-lisp:fmakunbound
                    future-common-lisp:fdefinition
                    future-common-lisp:print-unreadable-object))

#+Genera
(export '(future-common-lisp:setf
          future-common-lisp:fboundp
          future-common-lisp:fmakunbound
          future-common-lisp:fdefinition
          future-common-lisp:print-unreadable-object))

(defvar exports
        '(defclass defgeneric defmethod
          find-class class-of
          call-next-method next-method-p
          slot-value slot-boundp slot-exists-p slot-makunbound
          make-instance change-class
          initialize-instance reinitialize-instance shared-initialize
          update-instance-for-different-class
          print-object

          standard-object
          standard-class standard-generic-function standard-method
          class-name

          class-direct-superclasses class-direct-slots
          class-precedence-list class-slots class-direct-subclasses
          class-direct-methods
          generic-function-name generic-function-lambda-list
          generic-function-methods generic-function-discriminating-function
          generic-function-method-class
          method-lambda-list method-qualifiers method-specializers method-body
          method-environment method-generic-function method-function
          slot-definition-name slot-definition-initfunction
          slot-definition-initform slot-definition-initargs
          slot-definition-readers slot-definition-writers
          slot-definition-allocation
          ;;
          ;; Class-related metaobject protocol
          ;;
          compute-class-precedence-list compute-slots
          compute-effective-slot-definition
```

```
            finalize-inheritance allocate-instance
            slot-value-using-class slot-boundp-using-class
            slot-exists-p-using-class slot-makunbound-using-class
            ;;
            ;; Generic function related metaobject protocol
            ;;
            compute-discriminating-function
            compute-applicable-methods-using-classes method-more-specific-p
            compute-effective-method-function compute-method-function
            apply-methods apply-method
            find-generic-function  ; Necessary artifact of this implementation
            ))

(export exports)

;;;
;;; Utilities
;;;

;;; push-on-end is like push except it uses the other end:

(defmacro push-on-end (value location)
  '(setf ,location (nconc ,location (list ,value))))

;;; (setf getf*) is like (setf getf) except that it always changes the list,
;;;              which must be non-nil.

(defun (setf getf*) (new-value plist key)
  (block body
    (do ((x plist (cddr x)))
        ((null x))
      (when (eq (car x) key)
        (setf (car (cdr x)) new-value)
        (return-from body new-value)))
    (push-on-end key plist)
    (push-on-end new-value plist)
    new-value))

;;; mapappend is like mapcar except that the results are appended together:

(defun mapappend (fun &rest args)
  (if (some #'null args)
      ()
      (append (apply fun (mapcar #'car args))
              (apply #'mapappend fun (mapcar #'cdr args)))))
```

```
;;; mapplist is mapcar for property lists:

(defun mapplist (fun x)
  (if (null x)
      ()
      (cons (funcall fun (car x) (cadr x))
            (mapplist fun (cddr x)))))

;;;
;;; Standard instances
;;;

;;; This implementation uses structures for instances, because they're the only
;;; kind of Lisp object that can be easily made to print whatever way we want.

(defstruct (std-instance (:constructor allocate-std-instance (class slots))
                         (:predicate std-instance-p)
                         (:print-function print-std-instance))
  class
  slots)

(defun print-std-instance (instance stream depth)
  (declare (ignore depth))
  (print-object instance stream))

;;; Standard instance allocation

(defparameter secret-unbound-value (list "slot unbound"))

(defun instance-slot-p (slot)
  (eq (slot-definition-allocation slot) ':instance))

(defun std-allocate-instance (class)
  (allocate-std-instance
    class
    (allocate-slot-storage (count-if #'instance-slot-p (class-slots class))
                           secret-unbound-value)))

;;; Simple vectors are used for slot storage.

(defun allocate-slot-storage (size initial-value)
  (make-array size :initial-element initial-value))

;;; Standard instance slot access

;;; N.B. The location of the effective-slots slots in the class metaobject for
;;; standard-class must be determined without making any further slot
```

```lisp
;;; references.

(defvar the-slots-of-standard-class) ;standard-class's class-slots
(defvar the-class-standard-class)    ;standard-class's class metaobject

(defun slot-location (class slot-name)
  (if (and (eq slot-name 'effective-slots)
           (eq class the-class-standard-class))
      (position 'effective-slots the-slots-of-standard-class
                :key #'slot-definition-name)
      (let ((slot (find slot-name
                        (class-slots class)
                        :key #'slot-definition-name)))
        (if (null slot)
            (error "The slot ~S is missing from the class ~S."
                   slot-name class)
            (let ((pos (position slot
                                 (remove-if-not #'instance-slot-p
                                                (class-slots class)))))
              (if (null pos)
                  (error "The slot ~S is not an instance~@
                          slot in the class ~S."
                         slot-name class)
                  pos))))))

(defun slot-contents (slots location)
  (svref slots location))

(defun (setf slot-contents) (new-value slots location)
  (setf (svref slots location) new-value))

(defun std-slot-value (instance slot-name)
  (let* ((location (slot-location (class-of instance) slot-name))
         (slots (std-instance-slots instance))
         (val (slot-contents slots location)))
    (if (eq secret-unbound-value val)
        (error "The slot ~S is unbound in the object ~S."
               slot-name instance)
        val)))
(defun slot-value (object slot-name)
  (if (eq (class-of (class-of object)) the-class-standard-class)
      (std-slot-value object slot-name)
      (slot-value-using-class (class-of object) object slot-name)))

(defun (setf std-slot-value) (new-value instance slot-name)
  (let ((location (slot-location (class-of instance) slot-name))
```

```
        (slots (std-instance-slots instance))))
    (setf (slot-contents slots location) new-value)))
(defun (setf slot-value) (new-value object slot-name)
  (if (eq (class-of (class-of object)) the-class-standard-class)
      (setf (std-slot-value object slot-name) new-value)
      (setf-slot-value-using-class
        new-value (class-of object) object slot-name)))

(defun std-slot-boundp (instance slot-name)
  (let ((location (slot-location (class-of instance) slot-name))
        (slots (std-instance-slots instance)))
    (not (eq secret-unbound-value (slot-contents slots location)))))
(defun slot-boundp (object slot-name)
  (if (eq (class-of (class-of object)) the-class-standard-class)
      (std-slot-boundp object slot-name)
      (slot-boundp-using-class (class-of object) object slot-name)))

(defun std-slot-makunbound (instance slot-name)
  (let ((location (slot-location (class-of instance) slot-name))
        (slots (std-instance-slots instance)))
    (setf (slot-contents slots location) secret-unbound-value))
  instance)
(defun slot-makunbound (object slot-name)
  (if (eq (class-of (class-of object)) the-class-standard-class)
      (std-slot-makunbound object slot-name)
      (slot-makunbound-using-class (class-of object) object slot-name)))

(defun std-slot-exists-p (instance slot-name)
  (not (null (find slot-name (class-slots (class-of instance))
                   :key #'slot-definition-name))))
(defun slot-exists-p (object slot-name)
  (if (eq (class-of (class-of object)) the-class-standard-class)
      (std-slot-exists-p object slot-name)
      (slot-exists-p-using-class (class-of object) object slot-name)))

;;; class-of

(defun class-of (x)
  (if (std-instance-p x)
      (std-instance-class x)
      (built-in-class-of x)))

;;; N.B. This version of built-in-class-of is straightforward but very slow.

(defun built-in-class-of (x)
  (typecase x
```

```
    (null                                        (find-class 'null))
    ((and symbol (not null))                     (find-class 'symbol))
    ((complex *)                                 (find-class 'complex))
    ((integer * *)                               (find-class 'integer))
    ((float * *)                                 (find-class 'float))
    (cons                                        (find-class 'cons))
    (character                                   (find-class 'character))
    (hash-table                                  (find-class 'hash-table))
    (package                                     (find-class 'package))
    (pathname                                    (find-class 'pathname))
    (readtable                                   (find-class 'readtable))
    (stream                                      (find-class 'stream))
    ((and number (not (or integer complex float))) (find-class 'number))
    ((string *)                                  (find-class 'string))
    ((bit-vector *)                              (find-class 'bit-vector))
    ((and (vector * *) (not (or string vector)))  (find-class 'vector))
    ((and (array * *) (not vector))              (find-class 'array))
    ((and sequence (not (or vector list)))       (find-class 'sequence))
    (function                                    (find-class 'function))
    (t                                           (find-class 't))))

;;; subclassp and sub-specializer-p

(defun subclassp (c1 c2)
  (not (null (find c2 (class-precedence-list c1)))))

(defun sub-specializer-p (c1 c2 c-arg)
  (let ((cpl (class-precedence-list c-arg)))
    (not (null (find c2 (cdr (member c1 cpl)))))))

;;;
;;; Class metaobjects and standard-class
;;;

(defparameter the-defclass-standard-class  ;standard-class's defclass form
  '(defclass standard-class ()
       ((name :initarg :name)              ; :accessor class-name
        (direct-superclasses               ; :accessor class-direct-superclasses
         :initarg :direct-superclasses)
        (direct-slots)                     ; :accessor class-direct-slots
        (class-precedence-list)            ; :accessor class-precedence-list
        (effective-slots)                  ; :accessor class-slots
        (direct-subclasses :initform ())   ; :accessor class-direct-subclasses
        (direct-methods :initform ()))))   ; :accessor class-direct-methods

;;; Defining the metaobject slot accessor function as regular functions
```

```
;;; greatly simplifies the implementation without removing functionality.

(defun class-name (class) (std-slot-value class 'name))
(defun (setf class-name) (new-value class)
  (setf (slot-value class 'name) new-value))

(defun class-direct-superclasses (class)
  (slot-value class 'direct-superclasses))
(defun (setf class-direct-superclasses) (new-value class)
  (setf (slot-value class 'direct-superclasses) new-value))

(defun class-direct-slots (class)
  (slot-value class 'direct-slots))
(defun (setf class-direct-slots) (new-value class)
  (setf (slot-value class 'direct-slots) new-value))

(defun class-precedence-list (class)
  (slot-value class 'class-precedence-list))
(defun (setf class-precedence-list) (new-value class)
  (setf (slot-value class 'class-precedence-list) new-value))

(defun class-slots (class)
  (slot-value class 'effective-slots))
(defun (setf class-slots) (new-value class)
  (setf (slot-value class 'effective-slots) new-value))

(defun class-direct-subclasses (class)
  (slot-value class 'direct-subclasses))
(defun (setf class-direct-subclasses) (new-value class)
  (setf (slot-value class 'direct-subclasses) new-value))

(defun class-direct-methods (class)
  (slot-value class 'direct-methods))
(defun (setf class-direct-methods) (new-value class)
  (setf (slot-value class 'direct-methods) new-value))

;;; defclass

(defmacro defclass (name direct-superclasses direct-slots
                    &rest options)
  `(ensure-class ',name
     :direct-superclasses
       ,(canonicalize-direct-superclasses direct-superclasses)
     :direct-slots
       ,(canonicalize-direct-slots direct-slots)
     ,@(canonicalize-defclass-options options)))
```

```lisp
(defun canonicalize-direct-slots (direct-slots)
  '(list ,@(mapcar #'canonicalize-direct-slot direct-slots)))

(defun canonicalize-direct-slot (spec)
  (if (symbolp spec)
      '(list :name ',spec)
      (let ((name (car spec))
            (initfunction nil)
            (initform nil)
            (initargs ())
            (readers ())
            (writers ())
            (other-options ()))
        (do ((olist (cdr spec) (cddr olist)))
            ((null olist))
          (case (car olist)
            (:initform
             (setq initfunction
                   '(function (lambda () ,(cadr olist))))
             (setq initform '',(cadr olist)))
            (:initarg
             (push-on-end (cadr olist) initargs))
            (:reader
             (push-on-end (cadr olist) readers))
            (:writer
             (push-on-end (cadr olist) writers))
            (:accessor
             (push-on-end (cadr olist) readers)
             (push-on-end '(setf ,(cadr olist)) writers))
            (otherwise
             (push-on-end '',(car olist) other-options)
             (push-on-end '',(cadr olist) other-options))))
        '(list
          :name ',name
          ,@(when initfunction
              '(:initform ,initform
                :initfunction ,initfunction))
          ,@(when initargs '(:initargs ',initargs))
          ,@(when readers '(:readers ',readers))
          ,@(when writers '(:writers ',writers))
          ,@other-options))))

(defun canonicalize-direct-superclasses (direct-superclasses)
  '(list ,@(mapcar #'canonicalize-direct-superclass direct-superclasses)))
```

```
(defun canonicalize-direct-superclass (class-name)
  '(find-class ',class-name))

(defun canonicalize-defclass-options (options)
  (mapappend #'canonicalize-defclass-option options))

(defun canonicalize-defclass-option (option)
  (case (car option)
    (:metaclass
      (list ':metaclass
       '(find-class ',(cadr option))))
    (:default-initargs
      (list
       ':direct-default-initargs
       '(list ,@(mapappend
                  #'(lambda (x) x)
                  (mapplist
                    #'(lambda (key value)
                        '(',key ,value))
                  (cdr option)))))))
    (t (list '',(car option) '',(cadr option)))))

;;; find-class

(let ((class-table (make-hash-table :test #'eq)))

  (defun find-class (symbol &optional (errorp t))
    (let ((class (gethash symbol class-table nil)))
      (if (and (null class) errorp)
          (error "No class named ~S." symbol)
          class)))

  (defun (setf find-class) (new-value symbol)
    (setf (gethash symbol class-table) new-value))

  (defun forget-all-classes ()
    (clrhash class-table)
    (values))
 ) ;end let class-table

;;; Ensure class

(defun ensure-class (name &rest all-keys
                          &key (metaclass the-class-standard-class)
                          &allow-other-keys)
  (if (find-class name nil)
```

```lisp
          (error "Can't redefine the class named ~S." name)
          (let ((class (apply (if (eq metaclass the-class-standard-class)
                                  #'make-instance-standard-class
                                  #'make-instance)
                              metaclass :name name all-keys)))
            (setf (find-class name) class)
            class)))

;;; make-instance-standard-class creates and initializes an instance of
;;; standard-class without falling into method lookup.  However, it cannot be
;;; called until standard-class itself exists.

(defun make-instance-standard-class
        (metaclass &key name direct-superclasses direct-slots
                   &allow-other-keys)
  (declare (ignore metaclass))
  (let ((class (std-allocate-instance the-class-standard-class)))
    (setf (class-name class) name)
    (setf (class-direct-subclasses class) ())
    (setf (class-direct-methods class) ())
    (std-after-initialization-for-classes class
        :direct-slots direct-slots
        :direct-superclasses direct-superclasses)
    class))

(defun std-after-initialization-for-classes
        (class &key direct-superclasses direct-slots &allow-other-keys)
  (let ((supers
          (or direct-superclasses
              (list (find-class 'standard-object)))))
    (setf (class-direct-superclasses class) supers)
    (dolist (superclass supers)
      (push class (class-direct-subclasses superclass))))
  (let ((slots
          (mapcar #'(lambda (slot-properties)
                      (apply #'make-direct-slot-definition
                             slot-properties))
                  direct-slots)))
    (setf (class-direct-slots class) slots)
    (dolist (direct-slot slots)
      (dolist (reader (slot-definition-readers direct-slot))
        (add-reader-method
          class reader (slot-definition-name direct-slot)))
      (dolist (writer (slot-definition-writers direct-slot))
        (add-writer-method
```

```
            class writer (slot-definition-name direct-slot)))))
  (funcall (if (eq (class-of class) the-class-standard-class)
             #'std-finalize-inheritance
             #'finalize-inheritance)
           class)
  (values))

;;; Slot definition metaobjects

;;; N.B. Quietly retain all unknown slot options (rather than signaling an
;;; error), so that it's easy to add new ones.

(defun make-direct-slot-definition
       (&rest properties
        &key name (initargs ()) (initform nil) (initfunction nil)
             (readers ()) (writers ()) (allocation :instance)
        &allow-other-keys)
  (let ((slot (copy-list properties))) ; Don't want to side effect &rest list
    (setf (getf* slot ':name) name)
    (setf (getf* slot ':initargs) initargs)
    (setf (getf* slot ':initform) initform)
    (setf (getf* slot ':initfunction) initfunction)
    (setf (getf* slot ':readers) readers)
    (setf (getf* slot ':writers) writers)
    (setf (getf* slot ':allocation) allocation)
    slot))

(defun make-effective-slot-definition
       (&rest properties
        &key name (initargs ()) (initform nil) (initfunction nil)
             (allocation :instance)
        &allow-other-keys)
  (let ((slot (copy-list properties)))  ; Don't want to side effect &rest list
    (setf (getf* slot ':name) name)
    (setf (getf* slot ':initargs) initargs)
    (setf (getf* slot ':initform) initform)
    (setf (getf* slot ':initfunction) initfunction)
    (setf (getf* slot ':allocation) allocation)
    slot))

(defun slot-definition-name (slot)
  (getf slot ':name))
(defun (setf slot-definition-name) (new-value slot)
  (setf (getf* slot ':name) new-value))

(defun slot-definition-initfunction (slot)
```

```
  (getf slot ':initfunction))
(defun (setf slot-definition-initfunction) (new-value slot)
  (setf (getf* slot ':initfunction) new-value))

(defun slot-definition-initform (slot)
  (getf slot ':initform))
(defun (setf slot-definition-initform) (new-value slot)
  (setf (getf* slot ':initform) new-value))

(defun slot-definition-initargs (slot)
  (getf slot ':initargs))
(defun (setf slot-definition-initargs) (new-value slot)
  (setf (getf* slot ':initargs) new-value))

(defun slot-definition-readers (slot)
  (getf slot ':readers))
(defun (setf slot-definition-readers) (new-value slot)
  (setf (getf* slot ':readers) new-value))

(defun slot-definition-writers (slot)
  (getf slot ':writers))
(defun (setf slot-definition-writers) (new-value slot)
  (setf (getf* slot ':writers) new-value))

(defun slot-definition-allocation (slot)
  (getf slot ':allocation))
(defun (setf slot-definition-allocation) (new-value slot)
  (setf (getf* slot ':allocation) new-value))

;;; finalize-inheritance

(defun std-finalize-inheritance (class)
  (setf (class-precedence-list class)
        (funcall (if (eq (class-of class) the-class-standard-class)
                     #'std-compute-class-precedence-list
                     #'compute-class-precedence-list)
                 class))
  (setf (class-slots class)
        (funcall (if (eq (class-of class) the-class-standard-class)
                     #'std-compute-slots
                     #'compute-slots)
                 class))
  (values))

;;; Class precedence lists
```

```
(defun std-compute-class-precedence-list (class)
  (let ((classes-to-order (collect-superclasses* class)))
    (topological-sort classes-to-order
                      (remove-duplicates
                        (mapappend #'local-precedence-ordering
                                   classes-to-order))
                      #'std-tie-breaker-rule)))
```

```
;;; topological-sort implements the standard algorithm for topologically
;;; sorting an arbitrary set of elements while honoring the precedence
;;; constraints given by a set of (X,Y) pairs that indicate that element
;;; X must precede element Y.  The tie-breaker procedure is called when it
;;; is necessary to choose from multiple minimal elements; both a list of
;;; candidates and the ordering so far are provided as arguments.
```

```
(defun topological-sort (elements constraints tie-breaker)
  (let ((remaining-constraints constraints)
        (remaining-elements elements)
        (result ()))
    (loop
     (let ((minimal-elements
            (remove-if
             #'(lambda (class)
                 (member class remaining-constraints
                         :key #'cadr))
             remaining-elements)))
       (when (null minimal-elements)
         (if (null remaining-elements)
             (return-from topological-sort result)
             (error "Inconsistent precedence graph.")))
       (let ((choice (if (null (cdr minimal-elements))
                         (car minimal-elements)
                         (funcall tie-breaker
                                  minimal-elements
                                  result))))
         (setq result (append result (list choice)))
         (setq remaining-elements
               (remove choice remaining-elements))
         (setq remaining-constraints
               (remove choice
                       remaining-constraints
                       :test #'member)))))))
```

```
;;; In the event of a tie while topologically sorting class precedence lists,
;;; the CLOS Specification says to "select the one that has a direct subclass
```

```
;;; rightmost in the class precedence list computed so far."  The same result
;;; is obtained by inspecting the partially constructed class precedence list
;;; from right to left, looking for the first minimal element to show up among
;;; the direct superclasses of the class precedence list constituent.
;;; (There's a lemma that shows that this rule yields a unique result.)

(defun std-tie-breaker-rule (minimal-elements cpl-so-far)
  (dolist (cpl-constituent (reverse cpl-so-far))
    (let* ((supers (class-direct-superclasses cpl-constituent))
           (common (intersection minimal-elements supers)))
      (when (not (null common))
        (return-from std-tie-breaker-rule (car common))))))

;;; This version of collect-superclasses* isn't bothered by cycles in the class
;;; hierarchy, which sometimes happen by accident.

(defun collect-superclasses* (class)
  (labels ((all-superclasses-loop (seen superclasses)
              (let ((to-be-processed
                      (set-difference superclasses seen)))
                (if (null to-be-processed)
                    superclasses
                    (let ((class-to-process
                            (car to-be-processed)))
                      (all-superclasses-loop
                        (cons class-to-process seen)
                        (union (class-direct-superclasses
                                  class-to-process)
                               superclasses)))))))
    (all-superclasses-loop () (list class))))

;;; The local precedence ordering of a class C with direct superclasses C_1,
;;; C_2, ..., C_n is the set ((C C_1) (C_1 C_2) ...(C_n-1 C_n)).

(defun local-precedence-ordering (class)
  (mapcar #'list
          (cons class
                (butlast (class-direct-superclasses class)))
          (class-direct-superclasses class)))

;;; Slot inheritance

(defun std-compute-slots (class)
  (let* ((all-slots (mapappend #'class-direct-slots
                               (class-precedence-list class)))
         (all-names (remove-duplicates
```

```
                        (mapcar #'slot-definition-name all-slots))))
     (mapcar #'(lambda (name)
                 (funcall
                   (if (eq (class-of class) the-class-standard-class)
                       #'std-compute-effective-slot-definition
                       #'compute-effective-slot-definition)
                   class
                   (remove name all-slots
                           :key #'slot-definition-name
                           :test-not #'eq)))
             all-names)))

(defun std-compute-effective-slot-definition (class direct-slots)
  (declare (ignore class))
  (let ((initer (find-if-not #'null direct-slots
                             :key #'slot-definition-initfunction)))
    (make-effective-slot-definition
      :name (slot-definition-name (car direct-slots))
      :initform (if initer
                    (slot-definition-initform initer)
                    nil)
      :initfunction (if initer
                        (slot-definition-initfunction initer)
                        nil)
      :initargs (remove-duplicates
                  (mapappend #'slot-definition-initargs
                             direct-slots))
      :allocation (slot-definition-allocation (car direct-slots)))))

;;;
;;; Generic function metaobjects and standard-generic-function
;;;

(defparameter the-defclass-standard-generic-function
  '(defclass standard-generic-function ()
       ((name :initarg :name)        ; :accessor generic-function-name
        (lambda-list                 ; :accessor generic-function-lambda-list
           :initarg :lambda-list)
        (methods :initform ())       ; :accessor generic-function-methods
        (method-class                ; :accessor generic-function-method-class
           :initarg :method-class)
        (discriminating-function)    ; :accessor generic-function-
                                     ;    -discriminating-function
        (classes-to-emf-table        ; :accessor classes-to-emf-table
           :initform (make-hash-table :test #'equal)))))
```

```lisp
(defvar the-class-standard-gf) ;standard-generic-function's class metaobject

(defun generic-function-name (gf)
  (slot-value gf 'name))
(defun (setf generic-function-name) (new-value gf)
  (setf (slot-value gf 'name) new-value))

(defun generic-function-lambda-list (gf)
  (slot-value gf 'lambda-list))
(defun (setf generic-function-lambda-list) (new-value gf)
  (setf (slot-value gf 'lambda-list) new-value))

(defun generic-function-methods (gf)
  (slot-value gf 'methods))
(defun (setf generic-function-methods) (new-value gf)
  (setf (slot-value gf 'methods) new-value))

(defun generic-function-discriminating-function (gf)
  (slot-value gf 'discriminating-function))
(defun (setf generic-function-discriminating-function) (new-value gf)
  (setf (slot-value gf 'discriminating-function) new-value))

(defun generic-function-method-class (gf)
  (slot-value gf 'method-class))
(defun (setf generic-function-method-class) (new-value gf)
  (setf (slot-value gf 'method-class) new-value))

;;; Internal accessor for effective method function table

(defun classes-to-emf-table (gf)
  (slot-value gf 'classes-to-emf-table))
(defun (setf classes-to-emf-table) (new-value gf)
  (setf (slot-value gf 'classes-to-emf-table) new-value))

;;;
;;; Method metaobjects and standard-method
;;;

(defparameter the-defclass-standard-method
  '(defclass standard-method ()
    ((lambda-list :initarg :lambda-list)      ; :accessor method-lambda-list
     (qualifiers :initarg :qualifiers)        ; :accessor method-qualifiers
     (specializers :initarg :specializers)    ; :accessor method-specializers
     (body :initarg :body)                    ; :accessor method-body
     (environment :initarg :environment)      ; :accessor method-environment
     (generic-function :initform nil)         ; :accessor method-generic-function
```

```
    (function))))                              ; :accessor method-function

(defvar the-class-standard-method)     ;standard-method's class metaobject

(defun method-lambda-list (method) (slot-value method 'lambda-list))
(defun (setf method-lambda-list) (new-value method)
  (setf (slot-value method 'lambda-list) new-value))

(defun method-qualifiers (method) (slot-value method 'qualifiers))
(defun (setf method-qualifiers) (new-value method)
  (setf (slot-value method 'qualifiers) new-value))

(defun method-specializers (method) (slot-value method 'specializers))
(defun (setf method-specializers) (new-value method)
  (setf (slot-value method 'specializers) new-value))

(defun method-body (method) (slot-value method 'body))
(defun (setf method-body) (new-value method)
  (setf (slot-value method 'body) new-value))

(defun method-environment (method) (slot-value method 'environment))
(defun (setf method-environment) (new-value method)
  (setf (slot-value method 'environment) new-value))

(defun method-generic-function (method)
  (slot-value method 'generic-function))
(defun (setf method-generic-function) (new-value method)
  (setf (slot-value method 'generic-function) new-value))

(defun method-function (method) (slot-value method 'function))
(defun (setf method-function) (new-value method)
  (setf (slot-value method 'function) new-value))

;;; defgeneric

(defmacro defgeneric (function-name lambda-list &rest options)
  '(ensure-generic-function
     ',function-name
     :lambda-list ',lambda-list
     ,@(canonicalize-defgeneric-options options)))

(defun canonicalize-defgeneric-options (options)
  (mapappend #'canonicalize-defgeneric-option options))

(defun canonicalize-defgeneric-option (option)
  (case (car option)
    (:generic-function-class
```

```
         (list ':generic-function-class
               '(find-class ',(cadr option))))
       (:method-class
         (list ':method-class
               '(find-class ',(cadr option))))
       (t (list '',(car option) '',(cadr option)))))))

;;; find-generic-function looks up a generic function by name.  It's an
;;; artifact of the fact that our generic function metaobjects can't legally
;;; be stored a symbol's function value.

(let ((generic-function-table (make-hash-table :test #'equal)))

  (defun find-generic-function (symbol &optional (errorp t))
    (let ((gf (gethash symbol generic-function-table nil)))
      (if (and (null gf) errorp)
          (error "No generic function named ~S." symbol)
          gf)))

  (defun (setf find-generic-function) (new-value symbol)
    (setf (gethash symbol generic-function-table) new-value))

  (defun forget-all-generic-functions ()
    (clrhash generic-function-table)
    (values))
  ) ;end let generic-function-table

;;; ensure-generic-function

(defun ensure-generic-function
       (function-name
        &rest all-keys
        &key (generic-function-class the-class-standard-gf)
             (method-class the-class-standard-method)
        &allow-other-keys)
  (if (find-generic-function function-name nil)
      (find-generic-function function-name)
      (let ((gf (apply (if (eq generic-function-class the-class-standard-gf)
                           #'make-instance-standard-generic-function
                           #'make-instance)
                       generic-function-class
                       :name function-name
                       :method-class method-class
                       all-keys)))
        (setf (find-generic-function function-name) gf)
        gf)))
```

```
;;; finalize-generic-function

;;; N.B. Same basic idea as finalize-inheritance.  Takes care of recomputing
;;; and storing the discriminating function, and clearing the effective method
;;; function table.

(defun finalize-generic-function (gf)
  (setf (generic-function-discriminating-function gf)
        (funcall (if (eq (class-of gf) the-class-standard-gf)
                     #'std-compute-discriminating-function
                     #'compute-discriminating-function)
                 gf))
  (setf (fdefinition (generic-function-name gf))
        (generic-function-discriminating-function gf))
  (clrhash (classes-to-emf-table gf))
  (values))

;;; make-instance-standard-generic-function creates and initializes an
;;; instance of standard-generic-function without falling into method lookup.
;;; However, it cannot be called until standard-generic-function exists.

(defun make-instance-standard-generic-function
       (generic-function-class &key name lambda-list method-class)
  (declare (ignore generic-function-class))
  (let ((gf (std-allocate-instance the-class-standard-gf)))
    (setf (generic-function-name gf) name)
    (setf (generic-function-lambda-list gf) lambda-list)
    (setf (generic-function-methods gf) ())
    (setf (generic-function-method-class gf) method-class)
    (setf (classes-to-emf-table gf) (make-hash-table :test #'equal))
    (finalize-generic-function gf)
    gf))

;;; defmethod

(defmacro defmethod (&rest args)
  (multiple-value-bind (function-name qualifiers
                        lambda-list specializers body)
      (parse-defmethod args)
    `(ensure-method (find-generic-function ',function-name)
       :lambda-list ',lambda-list
       :qualifiers ',qualifiers
       :specializers ,(canonicalize-specializers specializers)
       :body ',body
       :environment (top-level-environment))))
```

```
(defun canonicalize-specializers (specializers)
  '(list ,@(mapcar #'canonicalize-specializer specializers)))

(defun canonicalize-specializer (specializer)
  '(find-class ',specializer))

(defun parse-defmethod (args)
  (let ((fn-spec (car args))
        (qualifiers ())
        (specialized-lambda-list nil)
        (body ())
        (parse-state :qualifiers))
    (dolist (arg (cdr args))
      (ecase parse-state
        (:qualifiers
          (if (and (atom arg) (not (null arg)))
              (push-on-end arg qualifiers)
              (progn (setq specialized-lambda-list arg)
                     (setq parse-state :body))))
        (:body (push-on-end arg body))))
    (values fn-spec
            qualifiers
            (extract-lambda-list specialized-lambda-list)
            (extract-specializers specialized-lambda-list)
            (list* 'block
                   (if (consp fn-spec)
                       (cadr fn-spec)
                       fn-spec)
                   body))))

;;; Several tedious functions for analyzing lambda lists

(defun required-portion (gf args)
  (let ((number-required (length (gf-required-arglist gf))))
    (when (< (length args) number-required)
      (error "Too few arguments to generic function ~S." gf))
    (subseq args 0 number-required)))

(defun gf-required-arglist (gf)
  (let ((plist
          (analyze-lambda-list
            (generic-function-lambda-list gf))))
    (getf plist ':required-args)))

(defun extract-lambda-list (specialized-lambda-list)
  (let* ((plist (analyze-lambda-list specialized-lambda-list))
```

```
          (requireds (getf plist ':required-names))
          (rv (getf plist ':rest-var))
          (ks (getf plist ':key-args))
          (aok (getf plist ':allow-other-keys))
          (opts (getf plist ':optional-args))
          (auxs (getf plist ':auxiliary-args)))
     '(,@requireds
       ,@(if rv '(&rest ,rv) ())
       ,@(if (or ks aok) '(&key ,@ks) ())
       ,@(if aok '(&allow-other-keys) ())
       ,@(if opts '(&optional ,@opts) ())
       ,@(if auxs '(&aux ,@auxs) ()))))

(defun extract-specializers (specialized-lambda-list)
  (let ((plist (analyze-lambda-list specialized-lambda-list)))
    (getf plist ':specializers)))

(defun analyze-lambda-list (lambda-list)
  (labels ((make-keyword (symbol)
             (intern (symbol-name symbol)
                     (find-package 'keyword)))
           (get-keyword-from-arg (arg)
             (if (listp arg)
                 (if (listp (car arg))
                     (caar arg)
                     (make-keyword (car arg)))
                 (make-keyword arg))))
    (let ((keys ())              ; Just the keywords
          (key-args ())          ; Keywords argument specs
          (required-names ())    ; Just the variable names
          (required-args ())     ; Variable names & specializers
          (specializers ())      ; Just the specializers
          (rest-var nil)
          (optionals ())
          (auxs ())
          (allow-other-keys nil)
          (state :parsing-required))
      (dolist (arg lambda-list)
        (if (member arg lambda-list-keywords)
            (ecase arg
              (&optional
                (setq state :parsing-optional))
              (&rest
                (setq state :parsing-rest))
              (&key
```

```
              (setq state :parsing-key))
            (&allow-other-keys
              (setq allow-other-keys 't))
            (&aux
              (setq state :parsing-aux)))
          (case state
            (:parsing-required
             (push-on-end arg required-args)
             (if (listp arg)
                 (progn (push-on-end (car arg) required-names)
                        (push-on-end (cadr arg) specializers))
                 (progn (push-on-end arg required-names)
                        (push-on-end 't specializers))))
            (:parsing-optional (push-on-end arg optionals))
            (:parsing-rest (setq rest-var arg))
            (:parsing-key
             (push-on-end (get-keyword-from-arg arg) keys)
             (push-on-end arg key-args))
            (:parsing-aux (push-on-end arg auxs)))))
      (list  :required-names required-names
             :required-args required-args
             :specializers specializers
             :rest-var rest-var
             :keywords keys
             :key-args key-args
             :auxiliary-args auxs
             :optional-args optionals
             :allow-other-keys allow-other-keys))))

;;; ensure method

(defun ensure-method (gf &rest all-keys)
  (let ((new-method
          (apply
            (if (eq (generic-function-method-class gf)
                    the-class-standard-method)
                #'make-instance-standard-method
                #'make-instance)
            (generic-function-method-class gf)
            all-keys)))
    (add-method gf new-method)
    new-method))

;;; make-instance-standard-method creates and initializes an instance of
;;; standard-method without falling into method lookup.  However, it cannot
```

```
;;; be called until standard-method exists.

(defun make-instance-standard-method (method-class
                                       &key lambda-list qualifiers
                                            specializers body environment)
  (declare (ignore method-class))
  (let ((method (std-allocate-instance the-class-standard-method)))
    (setf (method-lambda-list method) lambda-list)
    (setf (method-qualifiers method) qualifiers)
    (setf (method-specializers method) specializers)
    (setf (method-body method) body)
    (setf (method-environment method) environment)
    (setf (method-generic-function method) nil)
    (setf (method-function method)
          (std-compute-method-function method))
    method))

;;; add-method

;;; N.B. This version first removes any existing method on the generic function
;;; with the same qualifiers and specializers.  It's a pain to develop
;;; programs without this feature of full CLOS.

(defun add-method (gf method)
  (let ((old-method
          (find-method gf (method-qualifiers method)
                          (method-specializers method) nil)))
    (when old-method (remove-method gf old-method)))
  (setf (method-generic-function method) gf)
  (push method (generic-function-methods gf))
  (dolist (specializer (method-specializers method))
    (pushnew method (class-direct-methods specializer)))
  (finalize-generic-function gf)
  method)

(defun remove-method (gf method)
  (setf (generic-function-methods gf)
        (remove method (generic-function-methods gf)))
  (setf (method-generic-function method) nil)
  (dolist (class (method-specializers method))
    (setf (class-direct-methods class)
          (remove method (class-direct-methods class))))
  (finalize-generic-function gf)
  method)

(defun find-method (gf qualifiers specializers
```

```
                              &optional (errorp t))
      (let ((method
             (find-if #'(lambda (method)
                          (and (equal qualifiers
                                      (method-qualifiers method))
                               (equal specializers
                                      (method-specializers method))))
                      (generic-function-methods gf))))
        (if (and (null method) errorp)
            (error "No such method for ~S." (generic-function-name gf))
            method)))

;;; Reader and write methods

(defun add-reader-method (class fn-name slot-name)
  (ensure-method
    (ensure-generic-function fn-name :lambda-list '(object))
    :lambda-list '(object)
    :qualifiers ()
    :specializers (list class)
    :body '(slot-value object ',slot-name)
    :environment (top-level-environment))
  (values))

(defun add-writer-method (class fn-name slot-name)
  (ensure-method
    (ensure-generic-function
      fn-name :lambda-list '(new-value object))
    :lambda-list '(new-value object)
    :qualifiers ()
    :specializers (list (find-class 't) class)
    :body '(setf (slot-value object ',slot-name)
                 new-value)
    :environment (top-level-environment))
  (values))

;;;
;;; Generic function invocation
;;;

;;; apply-generic-function

(defun apply-generic-function (gf args)
  (apply (generic-function-discriminating-function gf) args))

;;; compute-discriminating-function
```

```
(defun std-compute-discriminating-function (gf)
  #'(lambda (&rest args)
      (let* ((classes (mapcar #'class-of
                               (required-portion gf args)))
             (emfun (gethash classes (classes-to-emf-table gf) nil)))
        (if emfun
            (funcall emfun args)
            (slow-method-lookup gf args classes)))))

(defun slow-method-lookup (gf args classes)
  (let* ((applicable-methods
           (compute-applicable-methods-using-classes gf classes))
         (emfun
           (funcall
             (if (eq (class-of gf) the-class-standard-gf)
                 #'std-compute-effective-method-function
                 #'compute-effective-method-function)
             gf applicable-methods)))
    (setf (gethash classes (classes-to-emf-table gf)) emfun)
    (funcall emfun args)))

;;; compute-applicable-methods-using-classes

(defun compute-applicable-methods-using-classes
       (gf required-classes)
  (sort
    (copy-list
      (remove-if-not #'(lambda (method)
                         (every #'subclassp
                                required-classes
                                (method-specializers method)))
                     (generic-function-methods gf)))
    #'(lambda (m1 m2)
        (funcall
          (if (eq (class-of gf) the-class-standard-gf)
              #'std-method-more-specific-p
              #'method-more-specific-p)
          gf m1 m2 required-classes)))))

;;; method-more-specific-p

(defun std-method-more-specific-p (gf method1 method2 required-classes)
  (declare (ignore gf))
  (mapc #'(lambda (spec1 spec2 arg-class)
            (unless (eq spec1 spec2)
              (return-from std-method-more-specific-p
```

```
                    (sub-specializer-p spec1 spec2 arg-class))))
        (method-specializers method1)
        (method-specializers method2)
        required-classes)
  nil)

;;; apply-methods and compute-effective-method-function

(defun apply-methods (gf args methods)
  (funcall (compute-effective-method-function gf methods)
           args))

(defun primary-method-p (method)
  (null (method-qualifiers method)))
(defun before-method-p (method)
  (equal '(:before) (method-qualifiers method)))
(defun after-method-p (method)
  (equal '(:after) (method-qualifiers method)))
(defun around-method-p (method)
  (equal '(:around) (method-qualifiers method)))

(defun std-compute-effective-method-function (gf methods)
  (let ((primaries (remove-if-not #'primary-method-p methods))
        (around (find-if #'around-method-p methods)))
    (when (null primaries)
      (error "No primary methods for the~@
              generic function ~S." gf))
    (if around
        (let ((next-emfun
                (funcall
                  (if (eq (class-of gf) the-class-standard-gf)
                      #'std-compute-effective-method-function
                      #'compute-effective-method-function)
                  gf (remove around methods))))
          #'(lambda (args)
              (funcall (method-function around) args next-emfun)))
        (let ((next-emfun (compute-primary-emfun (cdr primaries)))
              (befores (remove-if-not #'before-method-p methods))
              (reverse-afters
                (reverse (remove-if-not #'after-method-p methods))))
          #'(lambda (args)
              (dolist (before befores)
                (funcall (method-function before) args nil))
              (multiple-value-prog1
                (funcall (method-function (car primaries)) args next-emfun)
```

```
                (dolist (after reverse-afters)
                  (funcall (method-function after) args nil))))))))))

;;; compute an effective method function from a list of primary methods:

(defun compute-primary-emfun (methods)
  (if (null methods)
      nil
      (let ((next-emfun (compute-primary-emfun (cdr methods))))
        #'(lambda (args)
            (funcall (method-function (car methods)) args next-emfun)))))

;;; apply-method and compute-method-function

(defun apply-method (method args next-methods)
  (funcall (method-function method)
           args
           (if (null next-methods)
               nil
               (compute-effective-method-function
                 (method-generic-function method) next-methods))))

(defun std-compute-method-function (method)
  (let ((form (method-body method))
        (lambda-list (method-lambda-list method)))
    (compile-in-lexical-environment (method-environment method)
      '(lambda (args next-emfun)
         (flet ((call-next-method (&rest cnm-args)
                  (if (null next-emfun)
                      (error "No next method for the~@
                              generic function ~S."
                             (method-generic-function ',method))
                      (funcall next-emfun (or cnm-args args))))
                (next-method-p ()
                  (not (null next-emfun))))
           (apply #'(lambda ,(kludge-arglist lambda-list)
                      ,form)
                  args))))))

;;; N.B. The function kludge-arglist is used to pave over the differences
;;; between argument keyword compatibility for regular functions versus
;;; generic functions.

(defun kludge-arglist (lambda-list)
  (if (and (member '&key lambda-list)
           (not (member '&allow-other-keys lambda-list)))
```

```
          (append lambda-list '(&allow-other-keys))
          (if (and (not (member '&rest lambda-list))
                   (not (member '&key lambda-list)))
              (append lambda-list '(&key &allow-other-keys))
              lambda-list)))

;;; Run-time environment hacking (Common Lisp ain't got 'em).

(defun top-level-environment ()
  nil) ; Bogus top level lexical environment

(defun compile-in-lexical-environment (env lambda-expr)
  (declare (ignore env))
  (compile nil lambda-expr))

;;;
;;; Bootstrap
;;;

(progn  ; Extends to end-of-file (to avoid printing intermediate results).
(format t "Beginning to bootstrap Closette...")
(forget-all-classes)
(forget-all-generic-functions)
;; How to create the class hierarchy in 10 easy steps:
;; 1. Figure out standard-class's slots.
(setq the-slots-of-standard-class
      (mapcar #'(lambda (slotd)
                  (make-effective-slot-definition
                    :name (car slotd)
                    :initargs
                      (let ((a (getf (cdr slotd) ':initarg)))
                        (if a (list a) ()))
                    :initform (getf (cdr slotd) ':initform)
                    :initfunction
                      (let ((a (getf (cdr slotd) ':initform)))
                        (if a #'(lambda () (eval a)) nil))
                    :allocation ':instance))
              (nth 3 the-defclass-standard-class)))
;; 2. Create the standard-class metaobject by hand.
(setq the-class-standard-class
      (allocate-std-instance
        'tba
        (make-array (length the-slots-of-standard-class)
                    :initial-element secret-unbound-value)))
;; 3. Install standard-class's (circular) class-of link.
(setf (std-instance-class the-class-standard-class)
```

```
        the-class-standard-class)
;; (It's now okay to use class-... accessor).
;; 4. Fill in standard-class's class-slots.
(setf (class-slots the-class-standard-class) the-slots-of-standard-class)
;; (Skeleton built; it's now okay to call make-instance-standard-class.)
;; 5. Hand build the class t so that it has no direct superclasses.
(setf (find-class 't)
  (let ((class (std-allocate-instance the-class-standard-class)))
    (setf (class-name class) 't)
    (setf (class-direct-subclasses class) ())
    (setf (class-direct-superclasses class) ())
    (setf (class-direct-methods class) ())
    (setf (class-direct-slots class) ())
    (setf (class-precedence-list class) (list class))
    (setf (class-slots class) ())
    class))
;; (It's now okay to define subclasses of t.)
;; 6. Create the other superclass of standard-class (i.e., standard-object).
(defclass standard-object (t) ())
;; 7. Define the full-blown version of standard-class.
(setq the-class-standard-class (eval the-defclass-standard-class))
;; 8. Replace all (3) existing pointers to the skeleton with real one.
(setf (std-instance-class (find-class 't))
      the-class-standard-class)
(setf (std-instance-class (find-class 'standard-object))
      the-class-standard-class)
(setf (std-instance-class the-class-standard-class)
      the-class-standard-class)
;; (Clear sailing from here on in).
;; 9. Define the other built-in classes.
(defclass symbol (t) ())
(defclass sequence (t) ())
(defclass array (t) ())
(defclass number (t) ())
(defclass character (t) ())
(defclass function (t) ())
(defclass hash-table (t) ())
(defclass package (t) ())
(defclass pathname (t) ())
(defclass readtable (t) ())
(defclass stream (t) ())
(defclass list (sequence) ())
(defclass null (symbol list) ())
(defclass cons (list) ())
(defclass vector (array sequence) ())
```

```
(defclass bit-vector (vector) ())
(defclass string (vector) ())
(defclass complex (number) ())
(defclass integer (number) ())
(defclass float (number) ())
;; 10. Define the other standard metaobject classes.
(setq the-class-standard-gf (eval the-defclass-standard-generic-function))
(setq the-class-standard-method (eval the-defclass-standard-method))
;; Voila! The class hierarchy is in place.
(format t "Class hierarchy created.")
;; (It's now okay to define generic functions and methods.)

(defgeneric print-object (instance stream))
(defmethod print-object ((instance standard-object) stream)
  (print-unreadable-object (instance stream :identity t)
    (format stream "~:(~S~)"
                    (class-name (class-of instance)))))
  instance)

;;;; Slot access

(defgeneric slot-value-using-class (class instance slot-name))
(defmethod slot-value-using-class
          ((class standard-class) instance slot-name)
  (std-slot-value instance slot-name))

(defgeneric (setf slot-value-using-class) (new-value class instance slot-name))
(defmethod (setf slot-value-using-class)
          (new-value (class standard-class) instance slot-name)
  (setf (std-slot-value instance slot-name) new-value))
;;; N.B. To avoid making a forward reference to a (setf xxx) generic function:
(defun setf-slot-value-using-class (new-value class object slot-name)
  (setf (slot-value-using-class class object slot-name) new-value))

(defgeneric slot-exists-p-using-class (class instance slot-name))
(defmethod slot-exists-p-using-class
          ((class standard-class) instance slot-name)
  (std-slot-exists-p instance slot-name))

(defgeneric slot-boundp-using-class (class instance slot-name))
(defmethod slot-boundp-using-class
          ((class standard-class) instance slot-name)
  (std-slot-boundp instance slot-name))

(defgeneric slot-makunbound-using-class (class instance slot-name))
(defmethod slot-makunbound-using-class
```

```
          ((class standard-class) instance slot-name)
  (std-slot-makunbound instance slot-name))

;;; Instance creation and initialization

(defgeneric allocate-instance (class))
(defmethod allocate-instance ((class standard-class))
  (std-allocate-instance class))

(defgeneric make-instance (class &key))
(defmethod make-instance ((class standard-class) &rest initargs)
  (let ((instance (allocate-instance class)))
    (apply #'initialize-instance instance initargs)
    instance))
(defmethod make-instance ((class symbol) &rest initargs)
  (apply #'make-instance (find-class class) initargs))

(defgeneric initialize-instance (instance &key))
(defmethod initialize-instance ((instance standard-object) &rest initargs)
  (apply #'shared-initialize instance t initargs))

(defgeneric reinitialize-instance (instance &key))
(defmethod reinitialize-instance
          ((instance standard-object) &rest initargs)
  (apply #'shared-initialize instance () initargs))

(defgeneric shared-initialize (instance slot-names &key))
(defmethod shared-initialize ((instance standard-object)
                              slot-names &rest all-keys)
  (dolist (slot (class-slots (class-of instance)))
    (let ((slot-name (slot-definition-name slot)))
      (multiple-value-bind (init-key init-value foundp)
          (get-properties
            all-keys (slot-definition-initargs slot))
        (declare (ignore init-key))
        (if foundp
            (setf (slot-value instance slot-name) init-value)
            (when (and (not (slot-boundp instance slot-name))
                       (not (null (slot-definition-initfunction slot)))
                       (or (eq slot-names t)
                           (member slot-name slot-names)))
              (setf (slot-value instance slot-name)
                    (funcall (slot-definition-initfunction slot)))))))))
  instance)

;;; change-class
```

```
(defgeneric change-class (instance new-class &key))
(defmethod change-class
           ((old-instance standard-object)
            (new-class standard-class)
            &rest initargs)
  (let ((new-instance (allocate-instance new-class)))
    (dolist (slot-name (mapcar #'slot-definition-name
                               (class-slots new-class)))
      (when (and (slot-exists-p old-instance slot-name)
                 (slot-boundp old-instance slot-name))
        (setf (slot-value new-instance slot-name)
              (slot-value old-instance slot-name))))
    (rotatef (std-instance-slots new-instance)
             (std-instance-slots old-instance))
    (rotatef (std-instance-class new-instance)
             (std-instance-class old-instance))
    (apply #'update-instance-for-different-class
           new-instance old-instance initargs)
    old-instance))

(defmethod change-class
           ((instance standard-object) (new-class symbol) &rest initargs)
  (apply #'change-class instance (find-class new-class) initargs))

(defgeneric update-instance-for-different-class (old new &key))
(defmethod update-instance-for-different-class
           ((old standard-object) (new standard-object) &rest initargs)
  (let ((added-slots
          (remove-if #'(lambda (slot-name)
                         (slot-exists-p old slot-name))
                     (mapcar #'slot-definition-name
                             (class-slots (class-of new))))))
    (apply #'shared-initialize new added-slots initargs)))

;;;
;;;  Methods having to do with class metaobjects.
;;;

(defmethod print-object ((class standard-class) stream)
  (print-unreadable-object (class stream :identity t)
    (format stream "~:(~S~) ~S"
            (class-name (class-of class))
            (class-name class)))
  class)

(defmethod initialize-instance :after ((class standard-class) &key &rest args)
```

```
  (apply #'std-after-initialization-for-classes class args))

;;; Finalize inheritance

(defgeneric finalize-inheritance (class))
(defmethod finalize-inheritance ((class standard-class))
  (std-finalize-inheritance class)
  (values))

;;; Class precedence lists

(defgeneric compute-class-precedence-list (class))
(defmethod compute-class-precedence-list ((class standard-class))
  (std-compute-class-precedence-list class))

;;; Slot inheritance

(defgeneric compute-slots (class))
(defmethod compute-slots ((class standard-class))
  (std-compute-slots class))

(defgeneric compute-effective-slot-definition (class direct-slots))
(defmethod compute-effective-slot-definition
           ((class standard-class) direct-slots)
  (std-compute-effective-slot-definition class direct-slots))

;;;
;;; Methods having to do with generic function metaobjects.
;;;

(defmethod print-object ((gf standard-generic-function) stream)
  (print-unreadable-object (gf stream :identity t)
    (format stream "~:(~S~) ~S"
            (class-name (class-of gf))
            (generic-function-name gf)))
  gf)

(defmethod initialize-instance :after ((gf standard-generic-function) &key)
  (finalize-generic-function gf))

;;;
;;; Methods having to do with method metaobjects.
;;;

(defmethod print-object ((method standard-method) stream)
  (print-unreadable-object (method stream :identity t)
    (format stream "~:(~S~) ~S~{ ~S~} ~S"
```

```
                    (class-name (class-of method))
                    (generic-function-name
                      (method-generic-function method))
                    (method-qualifiers method)
                    (mapcar #'class-name
                            (method-specializers method))))
  method)

(defmethod initialize-instance :after ((method standard-method) &key)
  (setf (method-function method) (compute-method-function method)))

;;;
;;; Methods having to do with generic function invocation.
;;;

(defgeneric compute-discriminating-function (gf))
(defmethod compute-discriminating-function ((gf standard-generic-function))
  (std-compute-discriminating-function gf))

(defgeneric method-more-specific-p (gf method1 method2 required-classes))
(defmethod method-more-specific-p
           ((gf standard-generic-function) method1 method2 required-classes)
  (std-method-more-specific-p gf method1 method2 required-classes))

(defgeneric compute-effective-method-function (gf methods))
(defmethod compute-effective-method-function
           ((gf standard-generic-function) methods)
  (std-compute-effective-method-function gf methods))

(defgeneric compute-method-function (method))
(defmethod compute-method-function ((method standard-method))
  (std-compute-method-function method))

;;; describe-object is a handy tool for enquiring minds:

(defgeneric describe-object (object stream))
(defmethod describe-object ((object standard-object) stream)
  (format t "A Closette object~
             ~%Printed representation: ~S~
             ~%Class: ~S~
             ~%Structure "
          object
          (class-of object))
  (dolist (sn (mapcar #'slot-definition-name
                      (class-slots (class-of object))))
    (format t "~%    ~S <- ~:[not bound~;~S~]"
```

```
            sn
            (slot-boundp object sn)
            (and (slot-boundp object sn)
                 (slot-value object sn)))))
  (values))
(defmethod describe-object ((object t) stream)
  (lisp:describe object)
  (values))

(format t "~%Closette is a Knights of the Lambda Calculus production.")

(values)) ;end progn

;;;-*-Mode:LISP; Package:NEWCL; Base:10; Syntax:Common-lisp -*-

;;; This is the file newcl.lisp

(in-package 'newcl :use '(lisp))
(shadow '(defun fmakunbound fboundp))
(export '(fdefinition defun fmakunbound fboundp print-unreadable-object))

;;; New macros to support function names like (setf foo).

(lisp:defun setf-function-symbol (function-specifier)
  (if (consp function-specifier)
      (let ((print-name (format nil "~A" function-specifier)))
        (intern print-name
                (symbol-package (cadr function-specifier))))
      function-specifier))

(lisp:defun fboundp (function-specifier)
  (if (consp function-specifier)
      (lisp:fboundp (setf-function-symbol function-specifier))
      (lisp:fboundp function-specifier)))

(lisp:defun fdefinition (function-specifier)
  (if (consp function-specifier)
      (lisp:symbol-function (setf-function-symbol function-specifier))
      (lisp:symbol-function function-specifier)))

(lisp:defun fmakunbound (function-specifier)
  (if (consp function-specifier)
      (lisp:fmakunbound (setf-function-symbol function-specifier))
      (lisp:fmakunbound function-specifier)))

(defsetf fdefinition (function-specifier) (new-value)
  '(set-fdefinition ,new-value ,function-specifier))
```

```
(lisp:defun set-fdefinition (new-value function-specifier)
  (if (consp function-specifier)
      (progn
        (setf (symbol-function (setf-function-symbol function-specifier))
              new-value)
        (eval '(defsetf ,(cadr function-specifier)
                        (&rest all-args)
                        (new-value)
                 '(,',(setf-function-symbol function-specifier)
                    ,new-value
                    ,@all-args))))
        (setf (symbol-function function-specifier) new-value)))

(defmacro defun (name formals &body body)
  (cond ((symbolp name)
         '(lisp:defun ,name ,formals ,@body))
        ((and (consp name) (eq (car name) 'setf))
         '(progn
            (lisp:defun ,(setf-function-symbol name) ,formals ,@body)
            (defsetf ,(cadr name) ,(cdr formals) (,(car formals))
              (list ',(setf-function-symbol name) ,@formals))))))

#| Minimal tests:
(macroexpand '(defun (setf foo) (nv x y) (+ x y)))
(defun (setf baz) (new-value arg)
  (format t "setting value of ~A to ~A" arg new-value))
(macroexpand '(setf (baz (+ 2 2)) (* 3 3)))
|#

;;;
;;; print-unreadable-object
;;;

;;; print-unreadable-object is the standard way in the new Common Lisp
;;; to generate #< > around objects that can't be read back in.  The option
;;; (:identity t) causes the inclusion of a representation of the object's
;;;  identity, typically some sort of machine-dependent storage address.

(defmacro print-unreadable-object
          ((object stream &key type identity) &body body)
  '(let ((.stream. ,stream)
         (.object. ,object))
     (format .stream. "#<")
     ,(when type
        '(format .stream. "~S" (type-of .object.)))
     ,(when (and type (or body identity))
```

```
      '(format .stream. " "))
,@body
,(when (and identity body)
   '(format .stream. " "))
,(when identity
   #+Genera '(format .stream. "~O" (si:%pointer .object.))
   #+Lucid  '(format .stream. "~O" (sys:%pointer .object.))
   #+Excl   '(format .stream. "~O" (excl::pointer-to-fixnum .object.))
   #+:coral '(format .stream. "~O" (ccl::%ptr-to-int .object.))
   )
(format .stream. ">")
nil))
```

E Full MOP Cross Reference

This appendix provides an alphabetical cross-reference from the simplified metaobject protocol developed in Part I to the full CLOS Metaobject Protocol presented in Part II. Each entry describes the counterpart in the full MOP of a class, generic function, function or macro introduced in Part I. Note that some of these things are actually in basic CLOS rather than the MOP (e.g., `class-of`). This appendix clearly identifies these cases.

(add-method ⟨*generic-function*⟩ ⟨*method*⟩)

    This generic function is actually specified in full CLOS. Its use in Part I and in the full MOP are in accordance with full CLOS.

(add-reader-method ⟨*fn-name*⟩ ⟨*slot-name*⟩ ⟨*class*⟩)

    No generic function with this name or functionality exists. But, the same effect can be achieved in two steps: (i) use **reader-method-class** to control the class of the reader method metaobject and (ii) use either **add-method** or **initialize-instance** for specialized behavior when adding or initializing the method.

(add-writer-method ⟨*fn-name*⟩ ⟨*slot-name*⟩ ⟨*class*⟩)

    No generic function with this name or functionality exists. But, the same effect can be achieved in two steps: (i) use **writer-method-class** to control the class of the writer method metaobject and (ii) use either **add-method** or **initialize-instance** for specialialized behavior when adding or initializing the method.

(allocate-instance ⟨*class*⟩)

    This generic function exists with the same name and essentially unchanged functionality. The only significant difference is that the initialization arguments passed to `make-instance` are passed along to `allocate-instance`.

(apply-generic-function ⟨*gf*⟩ ⟨*args*⟩)

    In later parts of Chapter 4, the protocol surrounding this generic function is redesigned, and a new generic function called `compute-discriminating-function` is introduced. See its entry in this appendix for more information.

(apply-method ⟨*method*⟩ ⟨*args*⟩ ⟨*next-methods*⟩)

    In later parts of Chapter 4, the protocol surrounding this generic function is redesigned, and a new generic function called `compute-method-function` is introduced. See its entry in this appendix for more information.

(apply-methods ⟨*gf*⟩ ⟨*args*⟩ ⟨*methods*⟩)

    In later parts of Chapter 4, the protocol surrounding this generic function is redesigned, and a new generic function called `compute-effective-method-function` is introduced. See its entry in this appendix for more information.

(change-class ⟨*object*⟩ ⟨*class*⟩ &key)

    This generic function is actually specified in full CLOS. Its use in Part I and in the full MOP are in accordance with full CLOS. The keyword arguments do not appear in the original CLOS Specification, but are expected to appear in the final ANSI Common Lisp standard.

(class-direct-methods ⟨*class*⟩)

The generic function `specializer-direct-methods` is the direct analog of this function. The difference in the name reflects the fact that the full Metaobject Protocol supports specializers which are not classes (i.e., `eql` specializers).

(class-direct-slots ⟨*class*⟩)

This class accessor is actually a generic function with the same name and essentially unchanged behavior. The critical difference is that the direct slot definition metaobjects returned are not property lists, but rather are instances of a subclass of `direct-slot-definition`.

(class-direct-subclasses ⟨*class*⟩)

This class accessor is actually a generic function with the same name and behavior.

(class-direct-superclasses ⟨*class*⟩)

This class accessor is actually a generic function with the same name and behavior.

(class-name ⟨*class*⟩)

This class accessor is actually specified as a generic function in full CLOS. Its use in Part I and in the full MOP are in accordance with full CLOS.

(class-of ⟨*object*⟩)

This function is actually specified in full CLOS. Its use in Part I and in the full MOP are in accordance with full CLOS.

(class-precedence-list ⟨*class*⟩)

This class accessor is actually a generic function with the same name and behavior. It can't be called until after the class has been finalized.

(class-slots ⟨*class*⟩)

This class accessor is actually a generic function with the same name and essentially unchanged behavior. The critical difference is that the effective slot definition metaobjects returned are not property lists, but rather are instances of a subclass of `effective-slot-definition`. In addition, it can't be called until after the class has been finalized.

(compute-applicable-methods-using-classes ⟨*gf*⟩ ⟨*required-classes*⟩)

This generic function exists with the same name, but in order to support `eql` and other non-class specializers, it is required to return a second value. The second value indicates whether any of the returned methods in fact contain a non-class specializer.

(compute-class-precedence-list ⟨*class*⟩)

This generic function exists with the same name and functionality.

(compute-discriminating-function ⟨*gf*⟩)

This generic function exists with the same name and functionality.

(compute-effective-method-function ⟨gf⟩ ⟨methods⟩)

The closest counterpart to this generic function is compute-effective-method. The difference is that compute-effective-method returns a form which is then converted to a function by the implementation.

(compute-effective-slot-definition ⟨class⟩ ⟨slots⟩)

This generic function exists with the same name and essentially unchanged functionality. The critical difference is that the effective slot definition metaobject returned is not a property list, but rather is an instance of a subclass of effective-slot-definition. In addition, the slot name is interposed between the two other arguments.

(compute-method-function ⟨method⟩)

The closest counterpart to this generic function in the full MOP is make-method-lambda. This allows the same capability of processing the bodies of methods, but in order to make it possible to compile method functions during file compilation, it is called during the expansion of the **defmethod** form.

(compute-slots ⟨class⟩)

This generic function exists with the same name and essentially unchanged functionality. The critical difference is that the effective slot definition metaobjects returned are not property lists, but rather are instances of a subclass of effective-slot-definition.

(defclass ⟨name⟩ ⟨supers⟩ ⟨slots⟩ &rest ⟨options⟩)

This macro is is actually specified in full CLOS. Its use in Part I and in the full MOP are in accordance with full CLOS, except that it also accepts several additional options not described in Part I. In addition, class definitions can be modified by editing and re-executing defclass forms.

(defgeneric ⟨name⟩ ⟨lambda-list⟩ &rest ⟨options⟩)

This macro is actually specified in full CLOS. Its use in Part I and in the full MOP are in accordance with full CLOS, except that it also accepts several additional options not described in Part I. In addition, generic function definitions can be modified by suitably editing and re-executing defgeneric forms.

(defmethod ⟨name⟩ ⟨lambda-list⟩ &body ⟨body⟩)

This macro is actually specified in full CLOS. Its use in Part I and in the full MOP are in accordance with full CLOS, except that it also accepts several additional options not described in Part I. In addition, method definitions can be modified by editing and re-executing defmethod forms.

(ensure-class ⟨name⟩ &key)

A function exists with this name and essentially unchanged functionality. The critical difference is that, as with defclass, a class can be redefined by calling ensure-class again with the same class name. In addition, the exact format of the arguments is different.

(ensure-generic-function ⟨*name*⟩ **&key)**

This function is actually specified in full CLOS. Its use in Part I and in the full MOP are in accordance with full CLOS. The critical difference is that, as with **defgeneric**, a generic function can be redefined by calling **ensure-generic-function** again with the same function name. In addition, the exact format of the arguments is different.

(ensure-method ⟨*name*⟩ **&key)**

No function with this name or functionality exists.

(extra-method-bindings ⟨*method*⟩ ⟨*args*⟩ ⟨*next-methods*⟩**)**

The method body processing protocol is not specified at this level. Instead, a higher level generic function **make-method-lambda** is called to process the entire body of the method. Specialized methods defined on **make-method-lambda** can add bindings by wrapping appropriate forms around the body of the method.

(finalize-inheritance ⟨*class*⟩**)**

This generic function exists with the same name and essentially unchanged functionality. To support class redefinition, **finalize-inheritance** is called again each time a class is redefined.

(find-class ⟨*symbol*⟩ **&optional** ⟨*errorp*⟩**)**

This function is actually specified in full CLOS. Its use in Part I and in the full MOP are in accordance with full CLOS.

(generic-function-lambda-list ⟨*gf*⟩**)**

This generic function accessor is actually a generic function with the same name and behavior.

(generic-function-methods ⟨*gf*⟩**)**

This generic function accessor is actually a generic function with the same name and behavior.

(generic-function-name ⟨*gf*⟩**)**

This generic function accessor is actually a generic function with the same name and behavior.

(initialize-instance ⟨*object*⟩ **&key** ⟨*initargs*⟩**)**

This generic function is actually specified in full CLOS. Its use in Part I and in the full MOP are in accordance with full CLOS.

(make-instance ⟨*class*⟩ **&key** ⟨*initargs*⟩**)**

This generic function is actually specified in full CLOS. Its use in Part I and in the full MOP are in accordance with full CLOS.

(method-body ⟨*method*⟩**)**

No function with this name exists. The source text of a method function is not normally preserved. Instead, the generic function **method-function** can be called to get a function which, when called, executes the method body in its appropriate lexical environment.

(**method-environment** ⟨*method*⟩)

No function with this name exists. See the entry for **compute-method-function**.

(**method-generic-function** ⟨*method*⟩)

This method accessor is actually a generic function with the same name and behavior.

(**method-lambda-list** ⟨*method*⟩)

This method accessor is actually a generic function with the same name and behavior.

(**method-more-specific-p** ⟨*gf*⟩ ⟨*method1*⟩ ⟨*method2*⟩ ⟨*classes*⟩)

The method lookup protocol is not specified at this level of detail.

(**method-qualifiers** ⟨*method*⟩)

This method accessor is actually a generic function with the same name and behavior.

(**method-specializers** ⟨*method*⟩)

This method accessor is actually a generic function with the same name and behavior.

(**print-object** ⟨*object*⟩ ⟨*stream*⟩)

This generic function is actually specified in full CLOS. Its use in Part I and in the full MOP are in accordance with full CLOS.

(**reinitialize-instance** ⟨*object*⟩ **&key**)

This generic function is actually specified in full CLOS. Its use in Part I and in the full MOP are in accordance with full CLOS.

(**shared-initialize** ⟨*object*⟩ ⟨*slot-names*⟩ **&key**)

This generic function is actually specified in full CLOS. Its use in Part I and in the full MOP are in accordance with full CLOS, except that in the full MOP and CLOS, class-allocated slots are handled specially.

(**slot-definition-allocation** ⟨*slot*⟩)

This slot definition accessor is actually a generic function with the same name and behavior.

(**slot-definition-initargs** ⟨*slot*⟩)

This slot definition accessor is actually a generic function with the same name and behavior.

(**slot-definition-initform** ⟨*slot*⟩)

This slot definition accessor is actually a generic function with the same name and behavior.

(**slot-definition-initfunction** ⟨*slot*⟩)

This slot definition accessor is actually a generic function with the same name and behavior.

(slot-definition-name ⟨*slot*⟩)

This slot definition accessor is actually a generic function with the same name and behavior.

(slot-definition-readers ⟨*slot*⟩)

This slot definition accessor is actually a generic function with the same name and behavior.

(slot-definition-writers ⟨*slot*⟩)

This slot definition accessor is actually a generic function with the same name and behavior.

(slot-boundp ⟨*object*⟩ ⟨*slot-name*⟩)

This function is actually specified in full CLOS. Its use in Part I and in the full MOP are in accordance with full CLOS.

(slot-boundp-using-class ⟨*class*⟩ ⟨*instance*⟩ ⟨*slot-name*⟩)

This generic function exists with the same name and essentially unchanged functionality. The critical difference is that the third argument is not a slot name, but rather the effective slot definition metaobject for that slot.

(slot-exists-p ⟨*object*⟩ ⟨*slot-name*⟩)

This function is actually specified in full CLOS. Its use in Part I and in the full MOP are in accordance with full CLOS.

(slot-makunbound ⟨*object*⟩ ⟨*slot-name*⟩)

This function is actually specified in full CLOS. Its use in Part I and in the full MOP are in accordance with full CLOS.

(slot-makunbound-using-class ⟨*class*⟩ ⟨*instance*⟩ ⟨*slot-name*⟩)

This generic function exists with the same name and essentially unchanged functionality. The critical difference is that the third argument is not a slot name, but rather the effective slot definition metaobject for that slot.

(slot-value ⟨*object*⟩ ⟨*slot-name*⟩)

This function is actually specified in full CLOS. Its use in Part I and in the full MOP are in accordance with full CLOS.

(slot-value-using-class ⟨*class*⟩ ⟨*instance*⟩ ⟨*slot-name*⟩)

This generic function exists with the same name and essentially unchanged functionality. The critical difference is that the third argument is not a slot name, but rather the effective slot definition metaobject for that slot.

((setf slot-value) ⟨*value*⟩ ⟨*object*⟩ ⟨*slot-name*⟩)

This function is actually specified in full CLOS. Its use in Part I and in the full MOP are in accordance with full CLOS.

((setf slot-value-using-class) ⟨*value*⟩ ⟨*class*⟩ ⟨*object*⟩ ⟨*slot-name*⟩)

This generic function exists with the same name and essentially unchanged functionality. The critical difference is that the fourth argument is not a slot name, but rather the effective slot definition metaobject for that slot.

standard-class

This class exists with the same name and essentially unchanged functionality.

standard-generic-function

This class exists with the same name and essentially unchanged functionality.

standard-method

This class exists with the same name and essentially unchanged functionality.

(subclassp ⟨*c1*⟩ ⟨*c2*⟩)

The Common Lisp function subtypep can be used to achieve the same behavior.

(update-instance-for-different-class ⟨*old*⟩ ⟨*new*⟩ &key)

This generic function is actually specified in full CLOS. Its use in Part I and in the full MOP are in accordance with full CLOS.

References

[Barstow et al. 84] Barstow, David, Howard Shrobe, and Eric Sandewall (eds.) *Interactive Programming Environments*, McGraw-Hill, New York, 1984.

[Bobrow et al. 87] Bobrow, Daniel G., David S. Fogelsong, and Mark S. Miller "Definition Groups: Making Sources Into First-Class Objects," in Bruce Shriver and Peter Wegner (eds.) *Research Directions in Object-Oriented Programming*, MIT Press, 1987, 129–46.

[Bobrow&Stefik 83] Bobrow, Daniel G. and Mark Stefik *The Loops Manual*, Intelligent Systems Laboratory, Xerox PARC, 1983.

[Cannon 82] Cannon, Howard I. "Flavors: A Non-Hierarchical Approach to Object-Oriented Programming," 1982.

[CLtL] Steele, Guy *Common Lisp: The Language*, Digital Press, 1984.

[CLtLII] Steele, Guy *Common Lisp: The Language*, Second Edition, Digital Press, 1990.

[des Rivières&Smith 84] des Rivières, Jim and Brian C. Smith "The Implementation of Procedurally Reflective Languages," *Proceedings 1984 ACM Symposium on LISP and Functional Programming*, Austin, Texas, August 1984, 331–347.

[Dussud 89] Dussud, Patrick "TICLOS: An Implementation of CLOS for the Explorer Family," *1989 ACM OOPSLA Conference Proceedings*, New Orleans, Louisiana, September 1989, 215–220.

[Ellis&Stroustrup 90] Ellis, Margaret A. and Bjarne Stroustrup *The Annotated C++ Reference Manual*, Addison-Wesley, 1990.

[Goldberg&Robson 83] Goldberg, Adele and David Robson *Smalltalk-80: The Language and its Implementation*, Addison-Wesley, 1983.

[Keene 89] Keene, Sonya E. *Object-Oriented Programming in Common Lisp: A Programmer's Guide to CLOS*, Addison-Wesley, 1989.

[Ingalls 86] Daniel H. H. Ingalls "A Simple Technique for Handling Multiple Polymorphism," *OOPSLA '86 Conference Proceedings*, Portland, Oregon, September 1986; appeared as a special issue of *SIGPLAN Notices* **21**, 11, November 1986, 347–9.

[Kiczales&Rodriguez 90] Kiczales, Gregor and Luis Rodriguez "Efficient Method Dispatch in PCL," *Proceedings 1990 ACM Conference on LISP and Functional Programming*, Nice, France, June 1990, 99–105.

[Kristensen et al. 87] Kristensen, Bent B. Ole L. Madsen, Birger Møller-Pedersen, and Kristen Nygaard "The BETA Programming Language," in Bruce Shriver and Peter Wegner (eds.) *Research Directions in Object Oriented Programming*, MIT Press, 1987, 7–48.

[Maes&Nardi 88] Maes, Pattie and Daniele Nardi (eds.) *Meta-Level Architectures and Reflection*, North-Holland, 1988.

[Moon 86] Moon, David A. "Object-Oriented Programming with Flavors," *OOPSLA '86 Conference Proceedings*, Portland, Oregon, September 1986; appeared as a special issue of *SIGPLAN Notices* **21**, 11, November 1986, 1–8.

[Paepcke 90] Paepcke, Andreas "PCLOS: Stress Testing CLOS," *OOPSLA/ECOOP '90 Proceedings*, Ottawa, Canada, October 1990, 194–211.

[Smith 84] Smith, Brian C. "Reflection and Semantics in LISP," *Proceedings 11th Annual ACM Symposium on Principles of Programming Languages*, Salt Lake City, Utah, January 1984, 23–35.

[Smith,Barth&Young 87] Smith, Reid G. and Paul S. Barth and Robert L. Young "A Substrate for Object-Oriented Interface Design," in Bruce Shriver and Peter Wegner (eds.) *Research Directions in Object-Oriented Programming*, MIT Press, 1987, 253–315.

[Snyder 86] Snyder, Alan "Encapsulation and Inheritance in Object-Oriented Programming," *OOPSLA '86 Conference Proceedings*, Portland, Oregon, September 1986; appeared as a special issue of *SIGPLAN Notices* **21**, 11, November 1986, 38–45.

[X3J13] Bobrow, Daniel G. Linda G. Demichiel, Richard P. Gabriel, Sonya E. Keene, Gregor Kiczales, and David A. Moon *Common Lisp Object System Specification*, X3J13 Document 88-002R, June 1988; appears in *Lisp and Symbolic Computation* **1**, 3/4, January 1989, 245–394, and as Chapter 28 of [CLtLII], 770–864.

Index

A

:accessor
  slot option, 20
accessor-method-slot-definition
  full-specification, 220
add-dependent
  full-specification, 164
add-direct-method
  full-specification, 165
add-direct-subclass
  full-specification, 166
add-function-bindings, 44
add-method, 38, 301
add-method
  full-specification, 167
add-reader-method, 39
add-variable-bindings, 43
add-writer-method, 39
after-method. *See* method combination
after-method-p, 43, 304
all-generic-functions, 62
allocate-instance, 28, 309
  method for dynamic-slot-class, 102
  method for standard-class, 101
  mini-specification, 100
allocate-instance
  full-specification, 168
allocate-slot-storage, 27
allocate-std-instance, 27
allocate-table-entry, 103
allocation. *See* instance, allocation
applicable method. *See* method, applicable
apply-generic-function, 40, 302
  before-method for counting-gf, 109
  method for standard-generic-
    function, 121
  method for trusting-gf, 113
  mini-specification, 108
apply-method, 44, 305
  before-method for counting-method, 109
  method for encapsulated-method, 116
  method for standard-method, 118
  mini-specification, 108
apply-methods, 43, 304
  method for gf-with-append, 123

method for gf-with-arounds, 123
method   for
    standard-generic-function, 122
  mini-specification, 120
around-method, 122
around-method-p, 123, 304
attributes-class, 87

B

backstage, 13, 15
  summary in Closette, 45
before-method. *See* method combination
before-method-p, 43, 304
browsers, 48
  for classes, 52
  for generic functions and methods, 58, 60
built-in-class-of, 28, 283

C

C++, 243
call-next-method, 44
canonicalization
  class options, 76, 94
  direct slots, 20
  direct superclasses, 19
canonicalize-defclass-option, 287
canonicalize-defclass-options, 287
canonicalize-direct-slots, 286
canonicalize-direct-superclasses, 286
canonicalize-specializers, 298
change-class, 310
  method for (standard-object
    standard-class), 33
  method for (standard-object
    symbol), 33
circularity, 269
  due to bootstrapping, 270
  due to metastability, 270
class-default-initargs, 94
class-default-initargs
  full-specification, 212
class-direct-default-initargs, 91–92,
    94

`class-direct-default-initargs`
full-specification, 212
`class-direct-generic-functions`, 63
`class-direct-methods`, 18, 285
mini-specification, 50
`class-direct-slots`, 18, 285
mini-specification, 50
`class-direct-slots`
full-specification, 213
`class-direct-subclasses`, 18, 285
mini-specification, 50
`class-direct-subclasses`
full-specification, 213
`class-direct-superclasses`, 18, 285
mini-specification, 50
`class-direct-superclasses`
full-specification, 213
`class-finalized-p`
full-specification, 213
`class-name`, 18, 285
mini-specification, 50
`class-name`
full-specification, 213
`class-of`, 28, 283
mini-specification, 49
`class-precedence-list`, 18, 285
mini-specification, 50
`class-precedence-list`
full-specification, 214
`class-prototype`
full-specification, 214
`class-slots`, 18, 285
mini-specification, 50
`class-slots`
full-specification, 214
classes
in object-oriented programming, 243
class metaobject, 18
accessor functions, 19
identity conditions, 50
initialization, 22
public access to, 49
representation, 18
specialization, 72
standard vs. specialized, 74

class precedence list, 24
Flavors-style, 81
Loops-style, 81
protocol for computing, 78–82
CLOS. *See* Common Lisp Object System
Closette, 13
CLOS subset implemented by, 14
removing circularities, 269–275
source code, 277–315
`collect-superclasses*`, 25
`color-mixin`
class definition, 15
`color-rectangle`
class definition, 15
class precedence list, 24
Common Lisp Object System, 2, 243
`compute-applicable-methods`
full-specification, 170
`compute-applicable-methods-using-
     classes`, 41, 121, 303
mini-specification, 120
`compute-applicable-methods-using-
     classes`
full-specification, 171
`compute-class-default-initargs`, 92
`compute-class-precedence-list`, 24, 311
method for `flavors-class`, 81
method for `loops-class`, 82
method for `standard-class`, 80
mini-specification, 80
`compute-class-precedence-list`
full-specification, 173
`compute-default-initargs`
full-specification, 174
`compute-discriminating-function`, 312
method for `counting-gf`, 129
method for `standard-generic-
     function`, 129–130
`compute-discriminating-function`
full-specification, 175
`compute-effective-method`
full-specification, 176
`compute-effective-method-function`, 312
method for `standard-generic-
     function`, 126–127

compute-effective-slot-definition, 311
    method for attributes-class, 88
    method for dynamic-slot-class, 102
    method for standard-class, 87
    mini-specification, 86
compute-effective-slot-definition
    full-specification, 177
compute-method-function, 312
    method for counting-method, 128
compute-slots, 25, 311
    method for attributes-class, 88
    method for standard-class, 86
    mini-specification, 85
compute-slots
    full-specification, 178
counting-gf, 109
counting-method, 109
currying, 125

D
default-initargs-class, 91, 94
defclass, 17–26, 285
    :metaclass option, 76
    macro definition, 19
    regenerating form, 53
defgeneric, 34–35, 295
    :generic-function-class option, 107
    :method-class option, 107
    macro definition, 35
    regenerating form, 60
defmethod, 36–39, 297
    macro definition, 38
    regenerating form, 60
demon method combination. *See* method
        combination, standard
depth-first-preorder-superclasses*, 82
describe-object, 312
design of metaobject protocols, 107–132
direct-slot-definition-class
    full-specification, 180
direct slot definition metaobject, 21
direct slots
    canonicalization, 20
direct superclasses

canonicalization, 19
discriminating functions, 128
    memoization, 129
display-defclass, 53
display-defclass*, 55
display-defgeneric, 61
display-generic-function, 61
dynamic-slot-boundp, 104
dynamic-slot-class, 102
dynamic-slot-makunbound, 104
dynamic-slot-p, 102

E
effective-slot-definition-class
    full-specification, 181
effective method functions, 125
    memoization, 130
effective slot definition metaobject, 25
encapsulation, 89, 114
    in object-oriented programming, 250
ensure-class, 21, 77, 287
ensure-class
    full-specification, 182
ensure-class-using-class
    full-specification, 183
ensure-generic-function, 35, 296
ensure-generic-function
    full-specification, 185
ensure-generic-function-using-class
    full-specification, 186
ensure-method, 38, 300
environment
    of defmethod, 38
    used by eval, 43
eql-specializer-object
    full-specification, 188
examples
    adding around-methods, 122
    alternative class precedence lists, 80
    append method combination, 123
    counting class instances, 72
    counting invocations, 108
    default initialization arguments, 90
    displaying inherited information, 55

dynamic slots, 99
encapsulated methods, 114
finding all generic functions, 62
finding all slot accessors, 64
finding relevant generic functions, 63
finding subclasses, 52
listing all class names, 48, 52
monitoring slot access, 97
multiple inheritance class order, 56
precomputed default initialization argu-
     ments, 92
programmatic class creation, 66
regenerating `defclass` form, 53
regenerating `defgeneric` form, 60
regenerating `defmethod` form, 60
slot attributes, 83–85, 87–89
trusting generic functions, 112
exercises
accessor method predicates, 66
adding `vanilla-flavor`, 83
alternative implementation of
     `class-direct-subclasses`, 51
argument precedence order, 124
Beta's `inner`, 124
class-allocated slots, 105
criteria for meta-ness, 70
`defclass` protocol, 94
dynamic slots, 104
encapsulated classes, 89
form-based protocols, 132
generic function tracing, 110
memoizing applicable methods, 45
metaobject protocols and smaller lan-
     guages, 124
multiple inheritance diamonds, 58
residential environments, 70
tools in other languages, 70
visualizing an effective method, 64
`extra-function-bindings`
method for `encapsulated-method`, 119
method for `standard-method`, 118
mini-specification, 117
`extract-lambda-list`
full-specification, 188
`extract-specializer-names`

full-specification, 189

F
fair use rules, 50
finalization
of classes, 23
`finalize-inheritance`, 24, 93, 311
after-method   for
     `default-initargs-class`, 94
mini-specification, 93
`finalize-inheritance`
full-specification, 190
`find-class`, 22, 287
mini-specification, 49
`setf` function, 22
`find-generic-function`, 296
`find-method`, 301
`find-method-combination`
full-specification, 191
`find-programmatic-class`, 68
`flavors-class`, 81
`funcallable-standard-instance-access`
full-specification, 191
functional protocols, 110

G
`generate-defclass`, 53
`generate-defclass*`, 55
`generate-defgeneric`, 60
`generate-defmethod`, 60
`generate-inherited-slot-`
     `specification`, 55
`generate-slot-specification`, 54
`generate-specialized-arglist`, 61
`generic-function-argument-`
     `precedence-order`
full-specification, 216
`:generic-function-class`
`defgeneric` option, 107
`generic-function-declarations`
full-specification, 216
`generic-function-discriminating-`
     `function`, 294

generic-function-lambda-list, 34, 294
    mini-specification, 60
generic-function-lambda-list
    full-specification, 216
generic-function-method-class, 108, 294
generic-function-method-class
    full-specification, 217
generic-function-method-combination
    full-specification, 217
generic-function-methods, 34, 294
    mini-specification, 60
generic-function-methods
    full-specification, 217
generic-function-name, 34, 294
    mini-specification, 59
generic-function-name
    full-specification, 217
generic function
    adding accessor methods to, 39
    adding methods to, 38
    invocation, 40–45
        high-performance, 129
        protocols for, 108–131
    representation, 34
generic function metaobject, 34
    accessor functions, 34
    specialization, 107
    standard vs. specialized, 74
gf-with-append, 123
gf-with-arounds, 123
glue layer, 17

I
in-order-p, 57
inheritance, 23
    in object-oriented programming, 244
    multiple, 42, 56
        detecting diamonds, 58
        in Loops and Flavors, 78
    protocol for class finalization, 93
    protocol for slots, 85–87
:initarg
    slot option, 20
    use in initialization, 32

:initargs
    slot property, 20
:initform
    slot option, 20
    slot property, 20
    use in initialization, 32
:initfunction
    slot property, 20
initialize-instance, 309
    after-method for standard-class, 23
    method for standard-object, 31
instance
    accessing slot bindings, 28
        protocols for, 96
    allocation, 27
        protocol for, 99
    changing class of, 32
    class of, 28
    creation, 30
    identity, 27
    initialization, 31
    reinitialization, 31
    representation, 26
    representation for a color-rectangle, 27
    storage for slots, 28
instance-slot-p, 102, 281
instances
    in object-oriented programming, 243
intercessory metaobject protocols, 71
intern-eql-specializer
    full-specification, 206
introspective metaobject protocols, 48

K
Knights of the Lambda Calculus, 313

L
layering. See metaobject protocol, See also
    layering
local-precedence-ordering, 292
loops-class, 81

M
make-direct-slot-definition, 21, 25, 289
make-effective-slot-definition, 289
make-instance, 30, 309
  after-method for counted-class, 73
  method for default-initargs-
    class, 92, 94
  method for standard-class, 30, 73
  method for symbol, 30
  mini-specification re: metaobject
    classes, 68
make-instance
  full-specification, 206
make-method-lambda
  full-specification, 207
make-programmatic-class, 69
make-programmatic-instance, 67
map-dependents
  full-specification, 210
mapappend, 280
mapplist, 281
memoization, 45
  and functional protocols, 111
  and procedural protocols, 111
  applicable methods, 45
  during generic function invocation, 125
  of discriminating functions, 129
  of effective method functions, 130
  of method functions, 130
  of slot locations, 80
metacircular interpreters, 269
:metaclass
  defclass option, 76
metalevel, 17
metaobject
  accessor functions
    fair use rules, 50
  accessor functions for
    class, 19
    generic function, 34
    method, 37
    slot, 21
  class, 18
  definition, 17
  direct slot definition, 21

  effective slot definition, 25
  for color-rectangle class, 18
  for paint generic function, 35
  for paint method, 36
  generic function, 34
  method, 36
metaobject protocol
  based on generic functions, 111
  class finalization, 93
  design, 107–132
    summary, 131
  fair use rules, 50
  functional, 110
  intercessory, 71
  introspective, 48
  layering, 119
  non-specializable, 120
  procedural, 111
  slot binding access, 96
  slot inheritance, 85
metaobjects
  standard vs. specialized, 75
metastability, 270
method
  accessor, 39
  applicable, 41
    next methods, 44
    ordering, 41
    sequencing, 42
  combination, 43
  invocation, 43
  representation, 36
  specificity, 41
method-body, 37, 295
  mini-specification, 60
:method-class
  defgeneric option, 107
method-environment, 37, 295
  mini-specification, 60
method-function, 295
method-function
  full-specification, 219
method-generic-function, 37, 295
  mini-specification, 60
method-generic-function

full-specification, 219
`method-lambda-list`, 37, 295
    mini-specification, 60
`method-lambda-list`
    full-specification, 219
`method-more-specific-p`, 42, 312
    method for `standard-generic-
        function`, 122
    mini-specification, 120
`method-qualifiers`, 37, 295
    mini-specification, 60
`method-qualifiers`
    full-specification, 219
`method-specializers`, 37, 295
    mini-specification, 60
`method-specializers`
    full-specification, 219
method combination, 122, 251
    standard, 43
method dispatch. *See* generic function,
        invocation
method functions, 127
    memoization, 130
method lookup. *See* generic function,
        invocation
method metaobject, 36
    accessor functions, 37
    specialization, 107
    standard vs. specialized, 74
methods
    in object-oriented programming, 246
`monitored-class`, 97
multi-methods, 124, 249
multiple argument dispatch. *See* multi-
        methods

N
`:name`
    slot property, 20
`next-method-p`, 44
`note-operation`, 98

O
on-backstage, 70
on-stage, 13
    summary, 47
optimization. *See* performance
overriding of methods, 112

P
`paint`
    generic function definition, 15
    method definition, 15
`parse-defmethod`, 298
performance, 45
    and memoization, 45, 125
    of generic function invocation, 125–131
`primary-method-p`, 43, 304
primary method. *See* method combination
`print-object`, 26, 308
    method for `standard-class`, 50, 77
    method for `standard-generic-
        function`, 59
    method for `standard-method`, 59
    method for `standard-object`, 26
`print-unreadable-object`, 314
printing of objects. *See* `print-object`
procedural protocols, 111
procedural reflection, 270
producers, 13
program analysis tools, 48
protocol. *See* metaobject protocol

R
`read-dynamic-slot-value`, 103
`:reader`
    slot option, 20
`reader-method-class`
    full-specification, 224
`reader-method-p`, 65
`:readers`
    slot property, 20
`rectangle`
    class definition, 15
reflection, 7, 270

reinitialize-instance, 309
    method for standard-object, 31
relevant-generic-functions, 63, 65
remove-dependent
    full-specification, 225
remove-direct-method
    full-specification, 227
remove-direct-subclass
    full-specification, 228
remove-method, 301
remove-method
    full-specification, 229
required-portion, 298
reset-slot-access-history, 98

S
set-funcallable-instance-function
    full-specification, 230
(setf class-name)
    full-specification, 230
(setf find-class), 22
(setf generic-function-name)
    full-specification, 231
(setf slot-attribute), 89
(setf slot-value), 29, 97
(setf slot-value-using-class)
    before-method for monitored-class, 97
    full-specification, 231
    method for standard-class, 97
shared-initialize, 309
    method for standard-object, 31
slot-access-history, 98
slot-attribute, 88
    setf function, 89
slot-attribute-bucket, 89
slot-boundp, 29, 97, 283
slot-boundp-using-class, 308
    before-method for monitored-class, 97
    method for standard-class, 97
slot-boundp-using-class
    full-specification, 233
slot-contents, 27
slot-definition-allocation, 290
    mini-specification, 101

slot-definition-allocation
    full-specification, 221
slot-definition-initargs, 21, 290
    mini-specification, 53
slot-definition-initargs
    full-specification, 221
slot-definition-initform, 21, 290
    mini-specification, 53
slot-definition-initform
    full-specification, 221
slot-definition-initfunction, 21, 289
    mini-specification, 53
slot-definition-initfunction
    full-specification, 222
slot-definition-location
    full-specification, 224
slot-definition-name, 21, 289
    mini-specification, 53
slot-definition-name
    full-specification, 222
slot-definition-readers, 21, 290
    mini-specification, 54
slot-definition-readers
    full-specification, 223
slot-definition-type
    full-specification, 222
slot-definition-writers, 21, 290
    mini-specification, 54
slot-definition-writers
    full-specification, 223
slot-exists-p, 30, 283
slot-exists-p-using-class, 308
slot-location, 29, 101, 282
slot-makunbound, 30, 97, 283
slot-makunbound-using-class, 308
    before-method for monitored-class, 97
    method for standard-class, 97
slot-makunbound-using-class
    full-specification, 234
slot-value, 29, 96, 282
    setf function, 29
slot-value-using-class, 308
    before-method for monitored-class, 97
    method for dynamic-slot-class, 103
    method for standard-class, 97

mini-specification, 96
   setf function, 97
slot-value-using-class
   full-specification, 235
slot bindings
   protocol for accessing, 96
slot definition metaobject
   accessor functions, 21
slot inheritance rules, 25
slot options, 20
slot properties, 20
slots
   in object-oriented programming, 243
Smalltalk, 243
specialized metaobject classes, 74
specialized metaobjects, 74
specialized methods, 74
specializer-direct-generic-functions
   full-specification, 237
specializer-direct-methods
   full-specification, 238
specificity, class. *See* class precedence list
specificity, method. *See*
      method-more-specific-p
standard-class, 284
  accessor functions, 19
  class definition, 18
  specialization, 72
standard-generic-function, 293
  accessor functions, 34
  class definition, 34
standard-instance-access
  full-specification, 239
standard-method, 294
  accessor functions, 37
  class definition, 37
standard-object
  initialization, 30
standard metaobject classes, 74
standard metaobjects, 74
standard methods, 74
  allowing overriding, 113
  prohibiting overriding, 113
std-instance, 281
std-instance-class, 27

std-instance-p, 27
std-instance-slots, 27
std-tie-breaker-rule, 292
sub-specializer. *See* sub-specializer-p
sub-specializer-p, 42
subclasses, 52
subclasses*, 52
subclassp, 41
subprotocols. *See* metaobject protocol,
    layering

T
theatre metaphor, 13
topological-sort, 291
trusting-counting-gf, 113
trusting-gf, 112

U
update-dependent
  full-specification, 239
update-instance-for-different-
    class, 34, 310

V
validate-superclass
  full-specification, 240
veneer layer, 17

W
write-dynamic-slot-value, 103
:writer
  slot option, 20
writer-method-class
  full-specification, 242
writer-method-p, 65
:writers
  slot property, 20

The MIT Press, with Peter Denning as general consulting editor, publishes computer science books in the following series:

ACM Doctoral Dissertation Award and Distinguished Dissertation Series

Artificial Intelligence
Patrick Winston, founding editor
J. Michael Brady, Daniel G. Bobrow, and Randall Davis, editors

Charles Babbage Institute Reprint Series for the History of Computing
Martin Campbell-Kelly, editor

Computer Systems
Herb Schwetman, editor

Explorations with Logo
E. Paul Goldenberg, editor

Foundations of Computing
Michael Garey and Albert Meyer, editors

History of Computing
I. Bernard Cohen and William Aspray, editors

Information Systems
Michael Lesk, editor

Logic Programming
Ehud Shapiro, editor; Fernando Pereira, Koichi Furukawa, Jean-Louis Lassez, and David H. D. Warren, associate editors

The MIT Press Electrical Engineering and Computer Science Series

Research Monographs in Parallel and Distributed Processing
Christopher Jesshope and David Klappholz, editors

Scientific and Engineering Computation
Janusz Kowalik, editor

Technical Communication and Information Systems
Ed Barrett, editor